Informality Revisited Perspectives on Housing Markets

The *Bulletin of Latin American Research* Book Series
BLAR/SLAS

The *Bulletin of Latin American Research* publishes original research of current interest on Latin America, the Caribbean, inter-American relations and the Latin American Diaspora from all academic disciplines within the social sciences, history and cultural studies. The BLAR/SLAS book series was launched in 2008 with the aim of publishing research monographs and edited collections that compliment the wide scope of the Bulletin itself. It is published and distributed in association with Wiley-Blackwell. We aim to make the series the home of some of the most exciting, innovatory work currently being undertaken on Latin America and we welcome outlines or manuscripts of interdisciplinary, single-authored, jointly-authored or edited volumes. If you would like to discuss a possible submission to the series, please contact the editors at blar@liverpool.ac.uk

Informality Revisited: Latin American Perspectives on Housing, the State and the Market

EDITED BY CLARA SALAZAR

Contents

Preface Urban Informality in Latin America in Global Perspective

ANN VARLEY

That there is a need to decolonise knowledge could perhaps be described as a truth now universally acknowledged. Contemporary thinkers challenge the division between a global north producing scientific knowledge and theory, and a global south supplying 'unprocessed data' (Comaroff and Comaroff, 2012b: 1). Calls to theorise from the south have emerged alongside a recognition that cities now house most of the world's population, and that it is the global south which is now leading the world's urbanisation. Not surprisingly, then, urbanists have responded enthusiastically to the demand for 'new geographies' of urban theory (Roy, 2009: 819; Robinson, 2014).

What this means for scholarship on cities of the global south is a commitment to seeing them, not as defined by deficiency but as the '"new normal" of the urban world' (Oldfield and Parnell, 2014: 1). In addition, researchers are keen to ask what lessons southern cities might hold for the global north, particularly in relation to economic deregulation and experimentation or environmental concerns (Brand, 2006; Comaroff and Comaroff, 2012b). In this context, there has been an upsurge of interest in informality – both in the economy and especially in housing and the built environment – which shows no sign of abating. Informality, it is suggested, is 'a new paradigm for understanding urban culture' (AlSayyad, 2004: 9).

The result is a fruitful (if sometimes fraught) encounter between the 'critiques of neoliberalism' currently dominating urban studies, and already attuned to thinking about how neoliberal policies enter different geographical arenas, and a concern for characteristically '"Southern" urban issues, such as urban informality' (Parnell and Robinson, 2012: 594–595). That coincidence is reflected in the focus of *Informality Revisited* on neoliberal 'solutions' or alternatives to informality, particularly those (re)asserting the supremacy of private property rights in land and housing.

There is, however, a considerable irony in how a drive to theorise from the global south, a drive emphasising the significance of location and resistance to the idea of convergence, has dealt with Latin America. The literature generally emphasises cities in South Asia and Africa, and in particular the cities of former British colonies (Varley, 2013). The tendency to exclude Latin America and focus on *northern* European imperialism has also been noted (for over 25 years) with regard to broader postcolonial scholarship (Coronil, 1992; Mignolo, 1993; Thurner, 1996; Moraña et al., 2008). The particular irony here is that efforts to analyse urban informality began in Latin America. It would not have occurred to those of us starting our research on informal housing in Latin America in British universities in the 1980s to have ignored the well-established work of the region's urban theorists. In addition, the shared neo-Marxist perspective meant there was no sense of division between southern and northern contributions: the influence of French urban sociologists such as Christian Topalov was widely acknowledged and welcomed in Latin America. Two decades later, the strength of the Latin American heritage was acknowledged in one of the works marking a resurgence of interest from architects and planners in urban informality, yet the editors explicitly proposed to 'decouple' informality from Latin American scholarship (Roy and AlSayyad, 2004: vii).

It may be argued that concerns about a new intellectual imperialism miss the point: to talk about the global south is to talk about relations not regions, circulations not locations (Robinson, 2014; Roy, 2014). The reference to Africa in the Comaroffs' sub-title – 'How Euro-America is Evolving toward Africa' – is partly about personal locations and partly 'ironic' (2012a, 2012b). That said, adopting a view from anywhere and everywhere does not fully guard against the dangers of universalism; it is no less utopian than the transcendental view from nowhere (Young, 1990). Its blind-spots, moreover, are not random. They still provoke the concern that, in urban studies, 'the conditions of Latin America often elude inclusion among descriptions and propositions applied to much of Asia and Africa' (Mabin, 2014: 23–24). Language of publication offers at least part of the explanation for this pattern in Anglo-American urban scholarship (Varley, 2013; Mabin, 2014).

Insofar as attention is paid to Latin American contributions to theorising from the south, they are too often pigeonholed in terms of dependency theory, as though the region's urbanists have had little to say for the past half-century. That this is far from the case is demonstrated, to cite just one example, by the two-volume compilation on *Teorías sobre la ciudad en América Latina*, bringing together scholars from a range of countries to provide an overview of relevant literatures (Ramírez Váquez and Pradilla Cobos, eds., 2013). Given the language issue, however, such publications merit translation to increase the likelihood of their speaking to a wider audience. It is in this spirit that the Society for Latin American Studies and Wiley have undertaken the translation of *Informality Revisited*, originally published as *Irregular: suelo y mercado en América Latina* by El Colegio de México.

Editor Clara Salazar provides an overview of the chapters in context, but it is worth pinpointing a few of the ways in which this book contributes to key debates about urban informality. Julio Calderón challenges the neoliberal views of influential economist Hernando de Soto (2000) about the uses of property formalisation to provide residents with access to credit as a strategy to promote small businesses and combat poverty, on an institutional and ultimately a global scale. Calderón uses data from de Soto's own country, Peru, to show that those with formal title are no more likely than others to seek or obtain formal credit, and that formal title does not necessarily lead to formal property transactions when people come to sell. Edith Jiménez, Heriberto Cruz and Claudia Ubaldo add their voices to the growing recognition of 'the new informality' (Varley, 2010: 92): what happens in the next generation, after those who received title from a government formalisation agency die. Reluctance to identify an heir or heirs in order to avoid conflict between siblings, a desire for family continuity, legal misinformation and the wish to avoid tax on land transfers all lead to people dying intestate, resulting in legalised properties returning to a state of legal ambiguity in just a few years. In other words, formalisation does not lead to the definitive resolution of tenure often assumed by its advocates.

Dissatisfaction with neoliberal solutions to the problems of urban informality has led critics to recommend alternatives based on non-state actors, especially communal landowners such as indigenous groups. Clara Salazar shows, however, that legal changes in Mexico allowing agrarian communities to oversee the formalisation of human settlements on their land have led to residents being denied the benefits to which they should be entitled. She questions whether it is fitting to allow one group of citizens to control the property rights of others and suggests that doing so is likely to lead to new social conflicts.

Some Latin American countries, particularly Chile, Brazil and Mexico, have experimented with neoliberal alternatives to informality involving large, architecturally homogeneous, developments of small houses, with urban services, around and well beyond the urban periphery. This demand-led model of formal housing, with subsidies and mortgages for lower paid workers, has been widely criticised on the grounds of location and quality (e.g. Rolnik, 2019). But to what extent can it provide an alternative to informality? Considering the scope of eligibility for housing loans is one way of approaching this question, but Priscilla Connolly makes innovative use of digital cartography to show that urban growth around Mexico City is concentrated in particular places at any one time, and that new formal and informal housing developments go hand-in-hand in those places. The two processes are linked.

The conclusion is clear: researchers in urban studies have a great deal still to investigate, both empirically and theoretically, about the formal and the informal and the relationship between them. The task is pressing. Expansion of formal housing developments for a lower-income population enables politicians to claim that they have 'solved' their country's housing problem: so why should they tolerate any further growth of informal settlements? The original emergence of interest in urban informality in Latin America was inspired in part by opposition to demolition. The bulldozers are still waiting.

References

AlSayyad, N. (2004) 'Urban Informality as a "New" Way of Life' in A. Roy and N. AlSayyad (eds.) *Urban Informality: Transnational Perspectives from the Middle East, Latin America, and South Asia*. Lexington Books: Lanham, 7–30.

Brand, S. (2006) 'City Planet'. *Strategy and Business* **42**(Spring): 78–91.

Comaroff, J. and Comaroff, J. L. (2012a) '*Theory from the South: A Rejoinder*', *The Salon*: Volume 5. Johannesburg Workshop in Theory and Criticism. [WWW document]. URL http://jwtc.org.za/salon_volume_5/jean_and_john_comaroff.htm [accessed 10 August 2019].

Comaroff, J. and Comaroff, J. L. (2012b) *Theory from the South: Or, How Euro-America Is Evolving toward Africa*. Paradigm Publishers: Boulder and London.

Coronil, F. (1992) 'Can Postcoloniality be Decolonized? Imperial Banality and Postcolonial Power'. *Public Culture* **5**(1): 89–108.

de Soto, H. (2000) *The Mystery of Capital: Why Capitalism Triumphs in the West and Fails Everywhere Else*. Bantam Press: London.

Mabin, A. (2014) 'Grounding Southern City Theory in Time and Place' in S. Parnell and S. Oldfield (eds.) *The Routledge Handbook of Cities of the Global South*. Routledge: London and New York, 21–36.

Mignolo, W. D. (1993) 'Colonial and Postcolonial Discourse: Cultural Critique or Academic Colonialism?'. *Latin American Research Review* **28**(3): 120–134.

Moraña, M., Dussel, E. and Jáuregui, C. A. (2008) 'Colonialism and its Replicants' in M. Moraña, E. Dussel and C. A. Jáuregui (eds.) *Coloniality at Large: Latin America and the Postcolonial Debate*. Duke University Press: Durham, 1–20.

Oldfield, S. and Parnell, S. (2014) 'From the South' in S. Parnell and S. Oldfield (eds.) *The Routledge Handbook of Cities of the Global South*. Routledge: London and New York, 1–4.

Parnell, S. and Robinson, J. (2012) '(Re)Theorizing Cities from the Global South: Looking beyond Neoliberalism'. *Urban Geography* **33**(4): 593–617.

Ramírez Vázquez, B. R. and Pradilla Cobos, E. (eds.) (2013) *Teorías sobre la ciudad en América Latina*. Universidad Autónoma Metropolitana: México CDMX.

Robinson, J. (2014) 'New Geographies of Theorizing the Urban: Putting Comparison to Work for Global Urban Studies' in S. Parnell and S. Oldfield (eds.) *The Routledge Handbook of Cities of the Global South*. Routledge: London and New York, 57–70.

Rolnik, R. (2019) *Urban Warfare: Housing under the Empire of Finance*. Verso: London.

Roy, A. (2009) 'The 21st-Century Metropolis: New Geographies of Theory'. *Regional Studies* **43**(6): 819–830.

Roy, A. (2014) 'Worlding the South: Toward a Post-Colonial Urban Theory' in S. Parnell and S. Oldfield (eds.) *The Routledge Handbook of Cities of the Global South*. Routledge: London and New York, 9–20.

Roy, A. and AlSayyad, N. (2004) 'Preface' in A. Roy and N. AlSayyad (eds.) *Urban Informality: Transnational Perspectives from the Middle East, Latin America, and South Asia*. Lexington Books: Lanham, vii–viii.

Thurner, M. (1996) 'Historicizing "The Postcolonial" from Nineteenth-Century Peru'. *Journal of Historical Sociology* **9**(1): 1–18.

Varley, A. (2010) 'Modest Expectations: Gender and Property Rights in Urban Mexico'. *Law and Society Review* **44**(1): 67–100.

Varley, A. (2013) 'Postcolonialising Informality?'. *Environment and Planning D: Society and Space* **31**(1): 4–22.

Young, I. M. (1990) *Justice and the Politics of Difference*. Princeton University Press: Princeton.

Introduction

CLARA SALAZAR

El Colegio de México

Before the introducing the general context of this volume, I should like to say how lucky I am that I had the full support of the editorial team at The Bulletin of Latin American Research Book Series. Particularly, I would like to thank Lucy Taylor, BLAR editor, who has worked tirelessly with all of the authors and book editor to prepare the manuscript for publication and has supported us through the final hurdles of finishing the book. I was equally fortunate to have shared the material of this book at the outset, with Ann Varley. I wish to express sincere thanks to her for her friendship and invaluable intellectual company. I would also like to express thanks to El Colegio de México for facilitating the publication of this work in English. All of them played a pivotal role in enabling this project.

Debates on policies of formalisation urban land tenure aimed at establishing private property as the only alternative for achieving development and overcoming poverty occupy a prominent place in the academic and governmental circles of the Global South; the Latin American region is no exception. For the United Nations, the implementation of these policies means the recognition of a set of rights for slum dwellers (McAuslan, 2002).

For more than four decades, the World Bank has supported the formalisation of land policies. In the 1970s, its efforts focused on land demarcation and the provision of title deeds as part of broader rural development programmes or settlements in specific areas. In the 1980s, its focus shifted to modernising land registration institutions at the national level; since the mid-1990s, it has significantly intensified its support in several Eastern European countries, the former Soviet Union (World Bank, 2007) and Southeast Asia (Tjondrondronegoro, 2006), in a move from state ownership of land and property in controlled economies to private ownership in market economies (Sieguel and Childress, 2013; World Bank, 2014). Between 1981 and 2013, 39 projects were approved for the Latin American and Caribbean region, 22 of which (worth almost US$530 million) were dedicated exclusively to regularisation and improvement of land management systems (BID, 2014).

In Latin America, the World Bank continues to support the modernisation of national land administration systems and targets aid to areas it considers problematic, such as the formalisation of property rights in slums, informal settlements (ISs), and indigenous and community-owned lands. To this end, legal changes have been made in some of the region's countries, aimed at increasingly favouring free market institutions and private property rights. In a very few cases, such as Colombia, some legislative changes have been aimed at intervening in the land market in order to make collective and social rights effective. In both cases, the new legal order legitimises the transformation of previous institutional forms and requires that social actors adjust to new legal orders. Given that not all sectors of society have been considered beneficiaries of this new order, some resistance has arisen, as well as adjustments and demands for its implementation.

This book focuses on examining the shift that is taking place in the policies implemented in legal property known titling programmes or regularisation programmes, and the effects on society as a whole – particularly the politically and economically weakest sectors – in four Latin American countries. The book includes contributions resulting from individual research in Brazil, Peru, Colombia and Mexico, but this is no mere compilation. The work included here aims to analyse the institutional framework (norms and rules) that aims to regulate the forms of access to urban land based on the argument that the titling program makes it possible to reduce poverty and increase the quality of life for large sectors of the population who cannot afford finished housing at market prices.

In the international literature on the subject, it is common to find debates on the usual premises on which property formalisation programmes are based in the countries of the Global South, both in urban and rural areas. The debate has been aimed at defending or questioning the effectiveness and efficiency of these programmes, given that the results of the property title programmes are ambiguous. For example, Deinenger (2003: 28), in line with international organisations, argues that the individual allocation of property rights is the provision that provides the greatest incentives for the efficient use of resources. Similarly, the Peruvian economist Hernando de Soto (2000) maintains that the legal security of property protects the owners of a property against involuntary evictions, and that it can also make them creditworthy, because by establishing the rules of the transaction, the land becomes a capital asset that serves as a guarantee for loans and investments. In contrast, Bromley (1991, 2008) argues that empirical research on the formalisation of land tenure has been unable to establish a robust and reliable connection between tenure security and increased agricultural productivity. As other researchers (Sjaasted and Cousin, 2008) argue, the formalisation of land tenure does not necessarily reduce poverty and the inhabitants of ISs who have obtained property title deeds cannot take advantage of bank sector credit because they lack jobs (Durand-Lasserve and Royston, 2002). Likewise, it is argued that the lack of access to the formal market continues to sustain informality and that governments, in the absence of alternatives, tolerate and reproduce them (Abramo, 2011: 294; Durand-Lasserve et al., 2015: xxii). In the particular case of urban Mexico, Bouquet (2009) assumes that the regularisation was not fulfilled, and the agricultural GDP was not regularised, nor did it grow. Consequently, it can be concluded that these authors agree that providing certainty in the possession of land is positive but it is not a condition for reactivating the agricultural sector, and that the formalisation of property rights does not necessarily guarantee the expected results.

Among the fundamental contributions of this book are the controversies the authors establish with the ideological assumptions of neoliberalism, from different disciplinary perspectives. On the one hand, the authors of the chapters included in this text reveal the model's various paradoxes: the promotion of individual private property rights and providing assistance to free market and trade institutions has not contributed to the reduction of poverty; the individualisation of land ownership rights has not generated economic development or increased human wellbeing; guaranteeing the freedom of entrepreneurs and corporations, as a source of innovation and wealth, has not led to its redistribution; imposing a legal system that does not consider principles of equity does not imply that all people can act under the same regulatory framework, nor that such a framework protects the majority of the population. The neoliberal principles on which the policy of legal security of the land is based strengthen inequitable power relations that widen the gap in the population's living standards, destroy previous institutions, and create new forms of social relations that are neither more efficient nor more effective. The changes in law that tend to be imposed do not include criteria of equity but of competitiveness, and tend to be imposed and disciplinary; this leads to social conflicts and institutional misunderstandings. The return or reaffirmation of the land market as the force behind an unequal socio-spatial structure – albeit under different institutional forms – is thus observed.

On the other hand, in several chapters the authors discuss the ideological links between the proposal for the legal certification of property and the types of land commodification characteristic of capitalism. The texts expose the consequences, tensions and contradictions that state policies and actions have on the functioning of the formal and informal land markets, the interaction between the actors involved, and public management. To give substance to their claims, the authors develop their reasoning from very different approaches. Some of them reflect on economic rights and others on legal issues. Some focus on the explanatory factors behind the permanence of informal urbanisation and its interrelationship with the formal land market; others discuss the recitals behind the outright defence of private property rights and the arguments for the allocation of these rights through property formalisation policies; yet others unravel how these processes are woven into social practice and their associated effects. Thus, as a whole, the chapters bring together the fundamental contributions of this text: on the one hand, to reveal and to theoretically and empirically debate the validity of the assumptions supporting the various means through which civil laws and free market institutions reorient the land and housing policies of Latin American countries in the twenty-first century, and fail both in their arguments and in the fulfilment of their promises; on the other hand, to draw attention to the need to discuss the perception that 'legal security of property' is valuable in itself and is all that is needed to end poverty. As Sen (1997) points out, any utilitarian conception of public management ignores the discussion of the need to put political mechanisms in place that do not prioritise aggregative factors over redistributive ones.

Structure of the Book

The book is composed of two parts. The first part offers a discussion of: (i) the assumptions of property formalisation policies based on the privatisation of assets and their contradictions; (ii) the permanence of the informal market in the urban periphery; and (iii) the difficulties of regulating and managing land and housing even with mechanisms prescribed by law. The second part of the book is reserved for analyses concerning Mexico. This is because, in the legal heterogeneity of land tenure in this country, there is an overlap of two of the complex situations relating to property rights in the scope of this book: the informal occupation of land in the urban periphery, and the transfer of land from the communal land to the private individualised realm. Both have culminated in contradictory titling policies.

The first part of the book opens with the chapter by Pedro Abramo, which constitutes an important effort to revise the liberal concept of 'informality', as well as the effects of neoliberal ideology on urban policy and on the structure of cities. Based on the case of Brazilian cities, the author points to the market as the generator of a phenomenon: the COMP-FUSED city – compact or intensive in land use and diffuse or extensive in territory without sustainable environmental conditions. In addition to coining this concept, another of the significant contributions of his work is in developing a taxonomy of the informal land sub-markets and the elements that determine their structure.

We continue the debate by offering a broad reflection on the ideology that has prevailed in the property formalisation policies in the countries in South America. Julio Calderón Cockburn presents critical reflections on the neoliberal ideas of the Peruvian economist Hernando de Soto and their adoption as a paradigm by the World Bank. Calderón addresses conceptual aspects and practical experience through an in-depth analysis of the Plan Nacional de Formalización (PNF, National Policy for the Formalisation of Property) in that country. An examination of the results confirms their inconsistencies: titling is not an incentive for permanent investment in housing improvement by the owners; title holders continue to face difficulties in receiving credit from private banks, or do not request it; titling raises urban land prices, which perpetuates purchasing in the informal market, while not preventing the evasion of costs involved in the formalisation of property rights.

We move on to the chapter by María Mercedes Maldonado, where urban regulation is analysed. But unlike the previous chapter, which highlights the effect of regulations, Maldonado shows the resistance of economic actors to complying with a regulation based on urban legislation in Colombia, considered the most progressive and advanced in the Latin American region. The author focuses on analysing the advances, limitations and obstacles that arise when attempting to apply the standards that have applied in Colombia since the 1991 Political Charter. One of the great contributions of this work is to dismantle the belief that the increase in land prices is inevitable, by presenting innovative management instruments through which the scarcity of affordable urbanised land can be addressed for Priority Interest Housing (VIP) programmes.

Section II begins with Carlos Morales' text which introduces an explanation of how land markets operate and how public policies influence their behaviour. The author points out that the reduction of obligations to private property associated with the deficient application of public resources creates a vicious circle of informality-formalisation-informality, and that this increases the price of land and puts pressure on the income of those excluded from the formal system. In this sense, he asserts that the imbalance between the rights and obligations of landowners allows them to retain this land without providing capital or work, and at the same time, appropriate the capital gains produced by public investments.

We continue with the chapter by Clara Salazar, who presents the evolution of the property formalisation programme of the Informal Settlements (ISs) in the urban peripheries of Mexico initiated in 1973, and another property formalisation programme implemented since 1993, aimed at transforming the communal property regime into a private individualised one. The author argues that the mechanisms created to facilitate the individualisation of communal property (communal lands) and its liberalisation for the market, have had paradoxical effects in terms of consolidating property rights. On the one hand, they have made it possible for citizens (*ejidatarios* or rights holders of communal lands) who illegally sold their land to other citizens (irregular squatter inhabitants) to decide today on their property rights. On the other hand, they have given way to the transfer of the same process of formalisation of property ownership from the public to the private sector, diminishing the state's responsibility to protect the social rights of the population, and forging discrimination and conflict around the definition of property rights between members of the agrarian communities and the inhabitants of the ISs in the urban periphery.

In this context of legal transformations and institutional change, Priscilla Connolly analyses the evolution of informal urbanisation in the Metropolitan Mexico City. The author discusses the main changes in the informal production of housing and existing buildings, as well as their expression in urban growth. Considering that the concept of 'informality' is not easy to define or measure, one of her contributions is of a methodological nature. In her study she alludes to the different concepts of 'types of settlement', integrating dates of urbanisation, land ownership and socio-demographic indicators. Through the combination of spatial techniques, Geographic Information Systems (GIS) and qualitative analysis, Connolly is able to characterise the ISs and present recent overlaps with formal urban developments. Her results reveal a great weight of informal urbanisation in metropolitan expansion, through the densification of existing urbanisations, but also the contribution of new housing in the new periphery/peripheries, through housing developments.

Finally, we have the chapter by Edith Jiménez, Heriberto Cruz and Claudia Ubaldo. The authors delve into a dimension of informality that is little explored in the specialised literature and still less implemented in long-term public policies. They draw attention to the vacuum that exists in property formalisation programmes in the face of the changing needs of families. They state that after providing legal security to the inhabitants, there is a 'new informality' in property rights, which is rooted in the difficulties of legal succession; property formalisation programmes do not provide for the transfer of property; for the state, populations are no longer subject to public management.

Other Contributions to the Discussion on Informal Urbanisation and the Legal System, in the Original Version of this Work

It is important to inform the reader that this work has been updated and published from a book entitled: *Irregular. Suelo y mercado en América Latina (Land and Market in Latin America)*, which was published in Spanish by El Colegio de México in 2012. The original version consists of ten chapters, three of which were excluded from this work for editorial reasons only. In order to recognise the validity of these works and for interested readers to be able to refer to them, we would like to give you a brief overview of them.

One of the chapters mentioned is that of Samuel Jaramillo (2012), entitled 'Informal Urbanisation: Diagnoses and Policies. A Review of the Latin American Debate Reflecting on Current Lines of Action'. The author channels his theoretical discussion of informality through a new reading of the theory of marginality. Jaramillo suggests that informal land occupation persists because in the transition from a traditional to a modern society, values remain and are reproduced, anchored in groups with limited possibilities for adaptation, and thus remaining outside the process of modernisation. Thus, the precarious situation that currently exists is a functional result of the current structural process of capitalist accumulation. Jaramillo also shows the limited progress of the policies implemented by the Latin American states to confront informality and discusses the two positions formulated in this regard. On the one hand, it does not identify those responsible, and promotes state intervention to integrate the population into the legal system through property formalisation programmes. On the other hand, it proposes that the dominant groups be held responsible and that state resources be directed towards supporting social (not real estate) access to housing.

Another chapter referred to is by Edesio Fernandes (2012), entitled *'A Critical Reading of Hernando de Soto'*, which debates Hernando de Soto's proposal on the legal empowerment of the poor through titling as a determining factor in economic development and poverty reduction. It also questions government actions related to informal development in our countries, which are solely and mistakenly focused on providing tenure security and supporting the business and economic dimensions of that process. As an argument to support his analysis, Fernandes outlines the close relationship between the assumptions of Hernando de Soto's neoliberal proposal and the policy of property formalisation in Peru. As mentioned above, this proposal is discussed in detail in this volume by Julio Calderón.

The last chapter to refer to is by Vicente Ugalde (2012), entitled: *'Land Disputes in Agrarian Law'*. This author reflects on the institutions and instruments promoted by Mexican agrarian law to deal with the conflicts inherent in communal property on the periphery of cities. To this end, he presents and classifies the different legal processes through which litigation and regulatory incentives have been transforming the motivations and development of conflicts and practices associated with peri-urban land. According to his analysis, the conflicting interests that accompany the possibilities of individualised appropriation of communal land implemented since 1992 have encouraged legal and extra-legal conflicts and have generated great tensions between inhabitants and real estate companies. Thus, while the structure of ownership and the unequal distribution of land are key factors in struggles over agrarian land, their dispute and resolution are not always carried out according to the law. When the author delves deeper into the procedural role of agrarian courts, he concludes that the substantive dispute in all the processes reviewed has been the possession and ownership of land, and that in the areas of urban expansion, the land of agrarian communities is becoming increasingly evident as a causal territory for all kinds of struggles, promoted by the power that agrarian subjects have been gaining over urbanisation processes, thanks to the incentives of the 1992 reform.

References

Abramo, P. (2011) *La producción de las ciudades latinoamericanas: mercado inmobiliario y estructura urbana*. Organización Latinoamericana de Centros Históricos and Municipio del Distrito Metropolitano de Quito: Quito.

Banco Interamericano de Desarollo (2014) *Proyectos de regularización y administración de tierras*. https://www.google.com/search?client=firefox-b-d&q=iadb.Proyectos+de+Reguraizacion+y+Administracion+de+TierrasOficina+de+Evaluación+y+Supervisión,+OVE&nfpr=1&sa=X&ved=0ahUKEwjUvLji3engAhUEUKwKHSe8DfQQvgUIKygB&biw=1481&bih=1035 [accessed 4 March 2019].

Bouquet, E. (2009) 'State-Led Land Reform and Local Institutional Change: Land Titles, Land Markets and Tenure Security in Mexican Communities'. *World Development* **37**(8): 1390–1399.

Bromley, D. W. (1991) *Environment and Economy: Property Rights and Public Policy*. Blackwell: Oxford.

Bromley, D. W. (2008) 'Formalising Property Relations in the Developing World: The Wrong Prescription for the Wrong Malady'. *Land Use Policy* **26**(1): 20–27.

Deininger, K. (2003) *Land Policies for Growth and Poverty Reduction*. World Bank and Oxford University Press: Oxford.

de Soto, H. (2000) *The Mystery of Capital: Why Capitalism Triumphs in the West and Fails Everywhere Else*. Basic Books: New York.

Durand-Lasserve, A., Durand-Lasserve, M. and Selod, H. (2015) *Land Delivery Systems in West African Cities: The Example of Bamako, Mali*. World Bank and Agence Française de Développement: Washington. [WWW document. https://openknowledge.worldbank.org/handle/10986/21613. accessed 6 February 2019.

Durand-Lasserve, A. and Royston, L. (2002) *Holding their Ground: Secure Land Tenure for the Urban Poor in Developing Countries*. Earthscan Publications: London.

Fernandes, E. (2012) 'Una lectura crítica de Hernando de Soto' in C. Salazar (ed.) *Irregular. Suelo y mercado en América Latina*. El Colegio de México: Mexico FD, 213–239.

Jaramillo, S. (2012) 'Urbanización informal: diagnósticos y políticas. Una revisión al debate latinoamericano para pensar líneas de acción actuales' in C. Salazar (ed.) *Irregular. Suelo y mercado en América Latina*. El Colegio de México: Mexico FD, 33–83.

McAuslan, P. (2002) 'Tenure and the Law: the Legality of Illegality and the Illegality of Legality' in G. Payne (ed.) *Land, Rights and Innovation: Improving Tenure Security for Urban Poor*. ITDG: London.

Sen, A. (1997) *Bienestar, justicia y mercado*. Paidós Ibérica: Madrid.
Sieguel, P. and Childress, M. D. (2013) *Reflections on 20 Years of Land-Related Development Projects in Central America: 10 Things You Might Not Expect, and Future Directions*. [WWW document] URL http://documents.worldbank.org/curated/pt/129481468213001644/pdf/839760WP0Knowl0Box0382124B00 PUBLIC0.pdf [accessed 4 March 2019].
Sjaasted, E. and Cousin, B. (2008) 'Formalization and Land Rights in the South: an Overview'. *Land Use Policy* **26**(1): 1–9.
Tjondronegoro, S. M. P. (2006) *Land Policies in Indonesia*. EASRD working paper. [WWW document] URL http://documents.worldbank.org/curated/en/777651468260378738/pdf/374350IND0Land0policies1PUBLIC1.pdf [accessed 6 February 2019].
Ugalde, V. (2012) 'Controversias por el territorio en el derecho agrario' in C. Salazar (ed.) *Irregular. Suelo y mercado en América Latina*. El Colegio de México: Mexico, 307–335.
World Bank (2007) *India: Land Policies for Growth and Poverty Reduction*. Oxford University Press: New Delhi. http://documents.worldbank.org/curated/en/485171468309336484/310436360_20050007001644/additional/multi0page.pdf [accessed February 2019].
World Bank (2014) *The World Bank Annual Report* [WWW document] URL https://openknowledge.worldbank.org/handle/10986/20093 [accessed February 2019].

1

The Informal COMP-FUSED City: Market and Urban Structure in Latin American Metropolises

PEDRO ABRAMO

University of Rio de Janeiro, Rio de Janeiro, Brazil

Introduction

The crisis of urban Fordism that has appeared since the early 1980s in the most industrialised countries, and the emergence of what some authors have called the 'new urban policy', can be considered to be the formal framework for the institutionalisation of the neoliberal city (Moulaert, Rodríguez and Swyngedouw, 2003). Other processes accompany this movement, in particular the criticism of the constructivist rationalism of modern urbanism and the dissemination of the discourse of urban multiculturalism and ethnic-cultural and religious fragmentation in large cities (Taylor, 2002). In this text, we address an essential feature of the structural construction of the neoliberal city: the return of the market as a determining element of post-Fordist urban production.

The crisis of urban Fordism is manifested above all through two axes of change: on the one hand, the crisis of modernist and regulatory urbanism and the trend towards urban flexibility; on the other, the crisis of the state financing of urban housing, facilities and infrastructure and some collective urban services. In both cases, the market is re-emerging as the main mechanism for coordinating the production of urban housing, facilities and infrastructure. Thus, in contrast to the urban Fordism period, the predominance of the market as a mechanism for coordinating land use decisions is a characteristic feature of the neoliberal city. The crisis of urban Fordism therefore opens the door to the 'return of the market' as a determining element in the production of the neoliberal city.

In Latin American countries, the creation of modern cities results from the functioning of two logics of social coordination – that of the market and that of the state – but also from a third, the logic of necessity. This last one is the one that has moved, and continues to move, a set of individual and collective actions that promoted the production of 'self-built cities', with their usual cycle of occupation/self-construction/self-urbanisation and finally of consolidation of Informal Settlements (ISs). Recently, a new production variant of the self-built city has emerged that articulates the logic of the market with that of necessity and manifests itself socially as the 'informal land market' (Abramo, 2003a, 2009).

The working hypothesis we propose reaffirms that the market, as the main mechanism of hegemony in the coordination of land use decisions, produces an urban structure or form of a particular city that is characteristic of Latin America: a 'hybrid' city structure from the point of view of its morphology of land use *vis-à-vis* the traditional models of the modern city. This modern city has two paradigms of urban morphology resulting from the use of land and built space. The first is the 'Mediterranean model' or 'continental model' and its urban structure is configured as a 'compact' city, where land use is intensive. The second is the 'Anglo-Saxon model' whose spatial manifestation is the 'diffuse' city, with a strongly extensive land use and a low land (per plot) and residential (per dwelling) density. Thus, the hypothesis we will develop throughout this chapter is the following: the functioning of the land market in large Latin American cities simultaneously promotes a compact and diffuse city structure. Thus, Latin American cities have an urban structure of land use and housing, facilities and infrastructure that are compacted and spread out, or spread out and compacted simultaneously as a result of the functioning of the land market. In this sense, the production of the urban structure of these cities reconciles the compact and diffuse form of land use, and thus promotes a particular urban form: the COMP-FUSED city (one which combines both 'compact' and 'diffuse' characteristics).

We will show that the informal land and building market produces simultaneously – for specific reasons linked to its own operating logic – a COMP-FUSED city. We will illustrate that the functioning of the informal market produces a perverse feedback loop of the COMP-FUSED form where compaction feeds diffusion and diffusion feeds compaction. In other words, the return of the invisible hand of the land market produces and powers the spatial structure of a COMP-FUSED city.

The Production and Reproduction of the Informal City: The Informal Urban Land Market

The self-built or informal city in Latin America is not a recent phenomenon. Since colonial times and in practically all the countries of Portuguese and Spanish colonisation we can identify the production processes of self-built urban territories outside official rules and norms. But the accelerated urbanisation of the twentieth century had a determining role in the amplification of this process of production of informal self-built cities. The accelerated and exclusionary Fordist urbanisation in Latin America promoted an urban welfare state that in practice served only a limited portion of the urban population. The extremely stratified social structure, with great economic and social inequalities, generated the emergence of collective or individual urban actions of land occupation (organised and/or spontaneous) impelled by the logic of the need to have access to urban life (Abramo, 2005) or, in Agamben's terms, a movement of reaffirmation of life in relation to the right that did not incorporate life into law (Agamben, 2004: 130). The logic of necessity drove the process of occupation of urban land by the people at the beginning of the twentieth century, and since the rapid urbanisation of the 1950s it has become the dominant form of access to urban land for the poor in most Latin American countries. But the crisis of the 1980s and of national housing provision systems had as major urban consequences the consolidation and enhancement of an informal urban land market.

This informal market has existed in many countries since the beginning of the twentieth century, either in the form of the rental market in tenements or other unstable types of housing, or in the illegal commodification of peri-urban lands. From the 1950s onwards, we find some Latin American countries where the dominant form of access to urban land is the informal land market. The Mexican case is a concrete example of the predominance of the informal market from the individualised privatisation (sale of individual plots) of collective rural communal property (Azuela, 1989). Another known case is that of the city of Bogotá, where practically the entire self-built city has its origin in the informal sale of urban land operated by the informal land market mechanism (Jaramillo, 2001; Maldonado, 2005). In short, the informal urban land market has been growing in practically all Latin American countries since the 1980s and has become an important mechanism for providing land and housing for the poor.

The exception to this general statement is the case of Chile, where in recent years its neoliberal policy of housing provision has been substantially reducing the country's housing deficit (Sabatini, 2003). However, the relative success of the Chilean case is paradoxical, since it entailed a significant increase in the prices of urban and peri-urban land and, consequently, the displacement of the new complexes towards areas much further away from urban centres (Sabatini, 2005), as well as, in parallel, a rapid process of informalisation of the formal (Rodrígez and Sugranyes, 2004).

Thus, the growth of the informal land market is a reality in large Latin American cities, and the expectations of the adoption of neoliberal titling policies promoted by international agencies may reinforce this trend (Fernandes, 2003; Smolka, 2003). The next section will present some elements for a first approach to the functioning of the informal land market and its consequences, in terms of land use and urban structure in informal urban areas.

Towards a Framework for the Informal Land Market: What is the Informal Market? Does it Really Exist?

A sensitive issue and the subject of much discussion is the very definition of 'informality' (Azuela, 2001). We are not going to revisit this debate here, but rather make a clear choice about the notion that we are going to use to refer to urban informality or land use. The first observation is that informality is not a concept, such as exploitation, marginalisation, plunder, or others that serve to describe Latin American urban phenomena. Our perspective in this chapter is to take the term as descriptive, and therefore pre-analytical. Informality, in its descriptive and polyphonic sense, serves to describe phenomena in various disciplines (economics, sociology, linguistics, anthropology, law, etc.) and particular situations in social life. We are going to restrict ourselves to the urban dimension itself, namely the use of urban land. Our first approach to the term informality is based on the definition proposed by Bagnasco which refers us to the disciplinary field of law:

> we call the formal economy the process of production and exchange of goods and services regulated by the market and promoted and carried out by industrial and commercial companies, with the objective of profit and acting under the rules of commercial, fiscal and labour law, etc.; we can call the informal economy the entire process of production and exchange that is not subject to one of these aspects. (Bagnasco, 1999: 36, author's translation)

Thus, we can draw two interesting lessons from the above quotation from Bagnasco. The first concerns a minimalist definition of the urban informal economy, where this would be an act of commercialisation and/or rental of (built) land that would be outside the institutional framework of urban planning law, economic and commercial law, property law and other civil rights that regulate the use and ownership of urban land. That is to say, the informal market commercialises an asset (tangible or intangible) outside the regulatory framework of the legal-political sphere of the modern rule of law.

Following Bagnasco's approach, we can say that urban informality is a set of irregularities, or a-regularities, in relation to rights: urban irregularity, constructive irregularity and irregularity in relation to the right to land ownership (Alegría and Ordoñez, 2005). In the case of the informal land market, the informality of the economy of land use refers us to these three irregularities, but also to other irregularities relating to market contracts that regulate commercial transactions. Thus, the informal market would also be (ir)regular or (a)regular in relation to economic rights. So the informal land use market consists of two dimensions of informality: urban informality and economic informality.

Most economists would say that the market is regulated by strong institutions which guarantee that its regulation is within the framework of legal rights, that is, those rights which would be contemplated and guaranteed by a legal system associated with the state. For traditional institutional (neo-institutional) economists, when we find informal institutions in market relations, they would be subordinate to legal institutions and would serve to increase their institutional effectiveness, i.e. minimise transaction costs (Williamson, 1985).

Starting from this framework, we can seek to overcome the definition of traditional institutional economics and increase the possibility of the existence of a set of institutions and informal norms historically produced in self-built settlements through social practices, which in fact form a system of informal regulation of informal commercial transactions. We propose, then, a second criterion for the existence of an informal market. The informal land market must be outside the framework of rights; indeed, it must have its own institutional structure that guarantees the temporary reproduction of informal commercial practices of buying, selling and renting land and/or real estate. In other words, the informal market must have informal institutions that allow the functioning of the market and guarantee in intertemporal and inter-generational terms the contracts of an implicit nature established in informal market transactions.

In the case of the informal land market, where we have irregularities (informalities) regarding the status of the title deed, and of the urban planning and construction rules, the purchase, sale and rental contracts could not be considered contracts under the protection of the law, since their objects would be irregular in relation to regulatory rights. This means that any conflict cannot be resolved by legal mediation and enforcement. In other words, these transactions would not be subject to the regulations and sanctions that serve as a guarantee to agents involved in all contractual relations in the formal economy.

When the law does not constitute the guaranteeing element of contractual market relations, other forms of guarantee must be developed to re-establish a relationship of trust between the parties involved in the contractual market relationship. When there is no confidence that contracts will be respected and there are no enforcement mechanisms between the parties, they cease to exist.

In other words, the market is not reproduced or ceases to exist as a mechanism for coordinating individual actions (Bruni, 2006).

In the case of the informal and urban land market, other forms of guarantees must be socially constructed so that the parties can create a relationship of trust with respect to the contractual terms established between buyers and sellers in the sales market and between tenants and landlords in the rental market. Otherwise, the relationship of commercial exchange does not come into being, due to the mutual distrust of a possible unilateral breach of the informal contract. In other words, without formal institutions, the informal land market must establish its own regulatory institutions, including enforcement mechanisms in the case of unilateral breach of contract by one of the parties (Abramo, 2011). These informal market institutions allow implicit contracts established between the parties to be respected in intertemporal and inter-generational terms.

In the case of the informal urban land market, an important basis for its functioning and contractual chains are the relationships of trust and loyalty that the two contracting parties establish between themselves. Consequently, buyers and sellers, such as tenants and landlords, have a mutual relationship of trust due to the expectation of reciprocity based on a relationship of loyalty. The basis of this informal market institution is not legal but depends on the permanence in time of a particular form of social contract, based on trust and loyalty. This relationship of inter-personal reciprocity marks many social relations; however, in the case of commercial relations, it is excluded by the market characteristic of promoting a contractual encounter between anonymous people.

In the informal and consolidated settlement land market, where the reciprocal relationship of trust and loyalty is one of the founding institutions of the possibility of the existence of informal commercial exchange, we need a personalisation of contractual relations. Such personalisation may be opaque, but personalisation (someone who sells or rents and someone who bought or rented) introduces the possibility of a trust-loyalty relationship into the constitution of a contractual relationship that is by definition implicit (informal), i.e. not guaranteed by the rights governing economic contracts. Thus, in the informal land market, it is precisely the elimination of the anonymity and personalisation of the contractual relationship that guarantees the mechanisms of trust and loyalty that a contract of sale and purchase or informal rental allows (Abramo, 2011).

Figures 1 and 2 on the informational characteristics of the informal market in consolidated settlements or favelas in Brazil (Figure 1), and in particular in Rio de Janeiro (Figure 2), are very significant, as they reveal that practically all buyers and tenants had access to information on the properties or plots they bought or rented from a relative or friend. This person, who transmitted

Figure 1.   Characteristics of the Informal Market in Consolidated Settlements (Brazil, 2006)

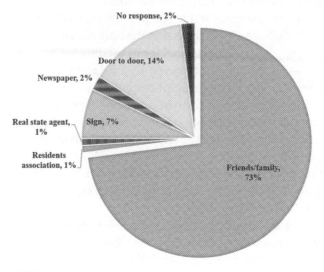

Source: Abramo, 2006

market information, is a relative or friend of the sellers and landlords and acts as 'interpersonal glue' in establishing the relationship of trust and loyalty between the two parties to the informal land market transaction. As such, the commercial deals or transactions of this informal market are not governed by civil law but are part of a web of friendship and/or kinship relationships that guarantee temporary stability to the relationships of trust and loyalty among the agents that assume a relationship of purchase and sale of land (Abramo, 2011).

However, the world of the informal land market cannot be seen as a space where there are no opportunistic and conflicting relations between the contracting parties. As poets say, the human soul is an unknown entity which reveals itself through dreams, ghosts, passions and hatred. Thus, commercial transactions are a social form of intermediation of personal relationships that are established from the changes in possession or ownership of goods or services (tangible or intangible) that involve men and women with a human soul and who are, therefore, liable to change their attitude or behaviour according to their emotions, pleasures, interests and madness. In this sense, a network of friendship and/or kinship relationships, no matter how well established, does not guarantee a lasting and perfect form of trust and loyalty in the commercial dealings of the informal land market. The possibility of a unilateral breach of implicit treatment and of the existing relationship of trust and loyalty will be a threat to the functioning of the informal market. Here

Figure 2. Characteristics of the Informal Market in some Consolidated Settlements in Rio de Janeiro

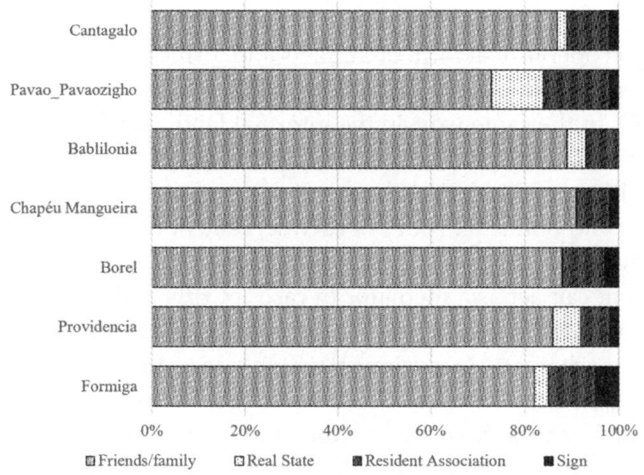

0%   20%   40%   60%   80%   100%

☑ Friends/family   ☐ Real State   ■ Resident Association   ■ Sign

Source: Abramo, 2011

the need arises for some institutional mediation that assumes the position of a third party; that is to say, a figure above the parties involved, and whose position and action are conducive to a return to the terms of the initial informal treatment or, eventually, opens a space for negotiation between the parties, to redefine the previously agreed terms.

The institutional mediation acts as the 'authority' and serves as an agreed mediator, is decisive in maintaining informal transactions and their permanence over time and guarantees the intertemporal and inter-generational condition of these informal land market deals. The hypothesis we put forward from our fieldwork on the contractual mechanisms of the informal land market (Abramo, 2005) is that in informal consolidated settlements a 'local authority' is constituted which serves as a mediator of conflicts in these communities. These local 'authorities' are the result of historical processes (of each local community), attributing authority to an infinite number of legitimising social processes. This legitimacy can be of a religious, ethnic, cultural, or even political nature, or based on violence and control by force, as we have seen in some empirical research on the informal market in Latin America (Abramo, 2009). As the economic anthropology literature tells us, in many studies, the mechanisms of community coexistence that guarantee the local social order require some kind of coercive means to restrict and control conflicting (or deviant) behaviour. These can take the form of a passive, representative and/or tax-based collective coercive force (Duty and Weber, 2007).

In the case of the informal land market, the local authority (or authorities) serves as an institution to mediate contractual conflicts and allows such deals to be respected and/or negotiated between the parties, thus ensuring their intertemporal and inter-generational maintenance. Many anthropological studies on the operational form of markets and formal organisations describe forms of coercion, which are not restricted to their legal dimension (Duty and Weber, 2007). In the same way, in the informal land market we identify very different forms and mechanisms of coercion, which serve to guarantee what we could call the 'contractual agreement' of the market.

The social and political history of each settlement builds and deconstructs these coercive mechanisms. The important fact is that there is indeed a 'local authority' that can act as a mediator in cases of rifts and conflicts in the fulfilment of commercial dealings in the informal market and, in addition, that has coercive mechanisms (punishment) in the case of an unsuccessful peaceful mediation (Abramo, 2009). As we know, there is no market without institutions that establish interpersonal mediation in commercial relations. In this sense, the informal land market in the consolidated settlements depends on the existence of relationships of trust and loyalty between the two parties to the informal contract, in general, sustained by the web of friendship and/or kinship. This network allows for an opaque or transparent personalisation of the business relationship and the establishment of implicit contracts and the figure of a 'local authority', which serves as a guarantor of these deals, in intertemporal and inter-generational terms. These two characteristics define the basic core of informal land market institutions.

Before attempting to establish a taxonomy of informal land sub-markets, we wish to return to Bagnasco's second suggestion, which emphasises the importance of not transforming the informal economy into an object of analysis in itself. This author asserts, an argument we agree with, that the best way to understand the informal economy is through its relationship of interaction with the formal economy. In a previous work, we stressed that the forms of interaction between formal and informal land markets can be complementary in nature in both concurrence and edge effects, with mutual influence on the behaviour and strategies of the agents of both markets (Abramo, 2005).

In this chapter, we will highlight the interaction between the formal and informal land market based on its aggregate results, in terms of the use of urban land; that is, in the production and reproduction of the urban structure of large Latin American cities. As we argued in the introduction, we intend to demonstrate that there is a similarity of spatial outcomes from the functioning of the formal and informal sub-markets. As we will see later, the operation of these two sub-markets simultaneously produces a compact and diffuse structure of land use. In addition, the two sub-markets also provide feedback on the production dynamics of the COMP-FUSED urban structure.

The Two Sub-Markets of Urban Informal Land

The informal land market can be classified into two major real estate sub-markets. Traditionally, the literature on land use economics uses the criterion of 'substitutability' of real estate to define these sub-markets. Using a set of criteria that we will present below, we can, in schematic terms, classify the informal urban land market as follows:

The Two Sub-Markets of Urban Informal Land

1. Sub-Market Land Plots (Pirate Housing Estates)

   a. Clandestine
   b. Irregular

2. Sub-Market in Consolidated Informal Settlements (ISs):

   a. Residential

      i. Commercialisation
      ii. Rent

   b. Commercial

      i. Commercialisation
      ii. Rent

We incorporated the definition of irreplaceability as one of the key variables for an axiomatic construction of studies on the structure of the market and we analysed other elements that we consider important to define a first cleavage of the informal market. Thus, we define the following as determining elements of the market structure:

- characteristics of land supply and demand;
- market power of economic agents (supply and demand);
- informational characteristics of the market (information asymmetries and transparencies);
- characteristics of products (homogeneous or heterogeneous);
- externalities (exogenous and endogenous);
- rationalities of agents (parametric, strategic, etc.); and
- decision-making environment (probabilistic risk or radical uncertainty).

The identification of these variables conceptually approximates our approach to the informal market to the modern treatment of the economic theory of the market, thus allowing us to conceptually identify the particularities and

Table 1.   A Comparative Framework of the Characteristics of the Informal Sub-Market in Land Plots Consolidated Settlements

Characteristic	Land plots	Consolidated settlements
Markets structure	Oligopolistic	Concurrence with 'rationed' market
Dominant actor and price determination	Owner able to sub-divide plots and generate urban mark-up	Buyer (in-coming) and vendor (exiting). Tension between supply and demand
Asymmetry of power relations in the market	Strong	Varied
Characteristic of the housing	Relatively homogeneous (plot) but varied location and land conditions	Heterogeneous
Externalities	*Exogenous* (various grades of accessibility and physical conditions)	Endogenous and exogenous
Rationale and timelines	*Strategic* based on incomplete information (playing on the timely provision of infrastructure)	Variety of rationales and objetives in advance
Information	Incomplete and imperfect (rough ground)	Asymmetries of information and unpredictability

Source: author.

similarities of the informal land market with other formal markets of the economy. Based on these variables, we sought to identify substantive differences in informal land markets in order to establish a first approximation of the definition of informal sub-markets. The result of this exercise can be seen in Table 1, which allows us to define two large sub-markets of informal land that we call: (1) sub-market of land plots, and (2) sub-market of consolidated areas (Abramo, 2003b, 2005, 2009).

The first of these sub-markets (land plots) is largely defined by an oligopolistic market structure, while the second (consolidated settlements) has a competitive structure, but with a rationed offer, i.e. the offer in the sub-market of consolidated informal self-built areas (ISs) is inelastic in relation to the increase in supply. As we will see later in the description of the perverse feedback loop of the sub-markets, this characteristic of inelasticity will play an important role in the growth of informal prices in consolidated areas, inducing some families to move to the periphery through the gateway to the informal market for land plots. In other words, the inelasticity of supply in the sub-market in consolidated areas will generate a potential demand for the informal plot sub-market.

The two informal land sub-markets can be identified in the urban structure of the city in very precise areas and with different functionalities in the process of urban structuring. In the first sub-market, there is a subdivision of land on the periphery of cities, constituting the main reason for the expansion of the urban network and the dynamics of the slum periphery, whose main characteristic in large Latin American cities is the lack (or precariousness) of infrastructure, services and urban accessibility. The logic of the operation of this plot market is oligopolistic, as is the setting of their prices, but the practices of product definition and financing refer us to pre-modern mercantile traditions, where the 'opaque personification' acquires an important role in adjusting the supply of preferences and the spending capacity of demand.

The oligopolistic structure in the price formation is one of the factors of the high commercial profitability of this activity, but the flexibility in the adjustment of products and in the familiar adaptation of the forms of informal financing is an attractive factor for low-income people. These two characteristics articulate the aspect of oligopolistic modernity and postmodern flexibility in relation to the supply of informal plots with a traditional dimension of customisation of the commercial relationship, defined as a modern-traditional nexus of a new nature in the informal market that ensures its attraction, both for 'pirate developers' and for low-income demand. The products of this sub-market of plots are relatively homogeneous and their main differentiating factors refer to physical and topographical dimensions and exogenous externalities related to the position of the land plots in the hierarchy of accessibility and urban infrastructures. In this sense, the informal production of plots can acquire a certain economy of scale, although the timing of the sale of these plots is very unstable and depends on factors external to the variables of the informal market itself.

The logic of price formation in the sub-market of informal land plots is due to a composition of factors that together define the final price of the informal plots. In our perspective of relating the functioning of the land market (formal and informal) to the production of the urban structure, what is important are the relative prices, that is, the variation of a price in a particular location-spatiality in relation to the other location prices.

Thus, we can suggest that the strategy of informal land developers will always be to look for plots in order to divide them up, minimising subdivision costs and maximising the factors that allow them to appropriate the wealth produced by the variation in the relative prices of urban land. Under these conditions, the best strategy from the spatial point of view is the search for cheap land without infrastructure in the urban land occupation area. The result in terms of production of the form of land occupation of the city is a trend towards continuous extension, producing a diffuse structure of territoriality of urban informality. In short, the functioning of the sub-market of informal land plots promotes the extension of land use and its result is the production of a diffuse form of informal territory. Examining the layout of

Figure 3.   Location of Informal Land Plots and Consolidated Settlements in the Municipality of Rio de Janeiro

Source: Rio de Janeiro, City Council http://pcrj.maps.arcgis.com/apps/webappviewer/index

the informality of the city of Rio de Janeiro (Figure 3) we can clearly see the sub-market of land plots promoting the enlargement of the urban area.

The sub-market of the consolidated settlements has very different characteristics compared with the land plots sub-market. We presented some of them in the comparative Table 1 that established the distinction between the two informal sub-markets and we will not develop these differences in this paper (see Abramo, 2005, 2009, 2011). However, we would like to stress that positive endogenous externalities in consolidated informal settlements are very important in price formation. We believe that there are two endogenous externalities highly valued in the informal market of these settlements. The first of these externalities is called the 'externality of urban and constructive freedom'. This externality allows the buyer of an informal property to exercise a right to use the land (subdivision and/or created land) that is not regulated by the urban and property rights of the current legal-political system of the state.

The possibility of making more intensive use of the land, without the mediation of the state, can be seen as a freedom for those who have the possession or informal ownership, either of a plot or of a building. This externality (urban freedom) will be incorporated in the final prices of the informal market in consolidated areas and will also be an attraction for the demand of that market (Abramo, 2005, 2011). To use traditional terminology, we can say that urban planning and construction freedom is an important comparative advantage in relation to the formal land market and, when exercised, promotes a process of compaction in consolidated settlements.

A second positive endogenous externality in consolidated informal set-tlements is what we call 'community externality'. This second positive externality is the result of an economy of reciprocity, where families have access to goods and services on the basis of gift and counter-gift relationships, where they do not pay monetary values to access certain goods and services (Caille, 2000). Community externality is sustained by social networks and illustrates the dynamics of organised proximity (Rallet and Torre, 2007) that allow inter-family interactions that are temporarily rendered with the ties of gift and counter-gift giving. These ties establish a dynamic of exchanges based on relationships of trust and loyalty (Pelligia, 2007).

The condition for entering into this economy of reciprocity (which, as we indicate, guarantees access to goods and services without compromising a part of the family's monetary resources) is to live in an informal settlement and have reciprocal relations in that neighbourhood. Thus, this community externality tends to be capitalised on in land prices and is captured by sub-market sellers in consolidated ISs (Abramo, 2009). For the discussion on the form of informal territoriality, we insist that the proximity factor is an element valued by the informal land market. The demand in this market seeks the externalities of urban and constructive freedom, together with the community externalities.

The concrete result of the practice (usufruct) of this externality is the com-paction of the informal territory of the settlements with the subdivision of the plots, the increase of the property and family densification and the ten-dency towards informal verticalisation. In the same way, the existence and maintenance of community externalities depends on the dynamics of territo-rial agglomeration and the social ties (networks) formed from this agglomera-tion. Thus, the two most important positive externalities of the informal land sub-market in consolidated areas promote and feed off spatial compaction. Therefore, we can hypothesise that the functioning of the informal sub-market in the consolidated ISs is stimulated by a search for compaction agglomera-tion effects, whose result in terms of land use is an intensification of land use and, therefore, a compaction of the consolidated informal territory.

A third factor affecting the process of compacting informal consolidated areas is the growth in transport costs over the last two decades, which is reflected in the greater weight of this item in the family budget of the lower-income sectors. The phenomenon of the 'super-peripheries' reveals its perverse and socially inequitable aspect, such as growing family expenditure in relation to the costs of relocation. A response from these social groups may lead to the decision to move to more accessible areas. Census data in many countries reveal what we might call the 'return' of the poor to the centre and, in most cases, their mode of return is indeed via the informal market in the consolidated areas.

Table 2.   Type of Predominant Residential Sub-market in the Consolidated Settlements (2006)

Country	Sub-market
Argentina	Rent
Colombia	Rent
Mexico	Sales
Peru	Rent/Sales
Venezuela	Rent
Brazil	Sales

Source: Abramo, 2006.

As discussed above, the informal sub-market in the consolidated areas is divided into two sub-markets: the commercial sub-market (purchase and sale of plots, houses and apartments) and the rental sub-market. With the impossibility of occupying land in the central areas and with the impossibility of having access to formal land, the social mechanism for the return of the poor to centrality will be the informal market for selling and renting. Recent research results on informal markets reveal the importance of the informal rental sub-market as a form of housing provision for the poor (Abramo, 2007). Table 2 shows that in many Latin American cities, the rental sub-market is the dominant sub-market in Consolidated Informal Settlements.

It is observed that in Bogotá, Caracas and some Brazilian metropolises, the rental market is dominant and plays an important role in the access of the poor to urban land. There is no doubt that the growth of the informal rental market is a recent phenomenon and the supply of that market is the result of more intensive land use in the consolidated settlements. Informal rental offers generally result from subdivisions and/or extensions of the residential unit or subdivision of the original plot. In both cases, the result is more intensive use of the land or, therefore, compaction of informal settlements.

The case of Rio de Janeiro is fairly representative of this growth. In the research carried out in 2002 (Abramo, 2003b) we verified that the share of the informal rental market represented 15 percent of the land market in the consolidated informal settlements. Within just four years, in 2006, this participation increased to 29.0 percent and the informal rental market grew in practically all the settlements (favelas) studied (Abramo, 2007). When we look at the distribution of the dominant type of product in the rental market, we see that the properties most in demand are those that consist of just one room. The predominance of small housing units in the informal rental market fuels the trend towards informal compaction. Thus, two movements feed the compaction process via the informal rental market: The first is the transformation of some settlement dwellers into informal landlords by subdividing their dwellings and/or plots to meet the growing demand for tenants in

Table 3.   Dominant Housing Product in the Rental Market by Country in Consolidated
Settlements (2006)

Country	Dominant product (%)
Argentina	1 room (89.8)
Brazil	1 room (79.4)
Colombia	2 room (42.7)
Mexico	2 room (42.2)
Peru	1 room (56.2)
Venezuela	1 room (40,3) / 2 rooms (38.4)

Source: Abramo, 2006.

consolidated informal areas. The second movement focuses on the preference of informal tenants for small units, as a consequence of their reduced
purchasing power. In general, these informal rented properties have a high
housing density, with the result that what was already unstable became even
more so (Abramo, 2007). Both the movement of informal rental supply and
demand are driving the trend towards compaction of consolidated informal
areas (Table 3).

The explanation for the growth of the informal rental market is associated with the precariousness of the labour market, but also with an inter-
generational dynamic, where the capacity for family savings is practically
non-existent and the initial capital required to acquire a land plot or a slum
dwelling simply does not exist. The story of the head of a household in Flo-
rianópolis portrays this situation in an exemplary manner (Sugai, 2007): 'I
use more than half my salary to pay rent and people here say that with that
money I could stop paying rent and buy a plot further away, but if I buy the
plot where am I going to live? I do not have the money to build a house. So, I
have to keep paying rent … even though it is so expensive'.

The story reveals that family savings are inadequate for buying a plot
and starting a progressive process of building, classic in the land plots, but
also makes it clear that one of the reasons for the inability of families to
save is related to the high price of rents in relation to their earnings. In other
words, we have an informal rental market paradox with high relative prices,
guaranteeing demand when it is not possible to switch to another informal
land sub-market, namely the plot market (Table 4).

Another factor that fuels the informal rental sub-markets is the encourage-
ment for poor households to supplement their family income by subdividing
their housing unit for renting out. In addition to that factor, we can suggest
that we also have a market stimulus. In the formal market, the profitability
of a property tends to be less than 1 percent of the market sale value of that
property. In Table 5 we can observe that the rates of profitability of informal

Table 4.   Average Rental Prices as a share of Minimum Wages in Consolidated Settlements (2006)

Country	Rent
Brazil	0.75
Argentina	0.24
Mexico	0.55
Venezuela	0.45
Colombia	0.68
Peru	0.08

Source: Abramo, 2006.

Table 5.   Profitability of the Informal Rental Market – Ratio of Average Rental Prices to Average Purchase Prices (in percentage) per Country (2006)

Country	Rent/Purchase
Brazil	2.37
Argentina	2.28
Mexico	1.09
Venezuela	0.70
Colombia	2.10
Peru	1.51

Source: Abramo, 2006.

rentals in Latin America are in general higher than the reference value of the formal neighbourhoods.

In this sense, we can affirm that there is a market stimulus in the conversion of family spaces for the purpose of offering them on the informal rental market. This perverse stimulus can reduce the indicator of habitability in informal areas and increase the compaction in informal consolidated settlements. In other words, from a land-use point of view, the growth of the rental market in informal consolidated settlements enhances the tendency of the informal market to produce a compaction of these areas.

Figure 3 also shows the mapping of the two large informal land sub-markets in the city of Rio de Janeiro. We can visualise a clear spatial distinction between the plot sub-market and the secondary land sub-market in the consolidated areas. The former is located on the urban periphery, while the latter is located in the more central areas of the city. However, the important element of this map is the one showing that the functioning of the sub-market in the consolidated settlements produces a compact structure, insofar as the functioning of the sub-market of the land plots promotes a diffuse structure.

The conclusion in terms of production of the informal territoriality that we came to verify in terms of the ways in which the informal land market functions is evident: the sub-market in consolidated settlements promotes a compact 'informal city', while the sub-market of land plots produces a diffuse 'informal city'. That is, the functioning of the informal land market for the lower-income sectors produces an urban COMP-FUSED structure (simultaneously compact and diffuse).

The Perverse Feedback Loop of the Two Informal Land Sub-Markets

Because the two informal sub-markets produce a COMP-FUSED structure, this promotes instability which affects both the habitat itself and day-to-day community life. By promoting an increasingly diffuse area of land, the informal market imposes increasing transport costs on the workers living on the land plots. In addition, when the market itself produces compaction in consolidated settlements, it promotes instability in peoples homes through increased density (property and housing) and verticalisation of buildings with all the implications for the indicators of habitability (lack of air, light, etc.) that this compaction promotes. In macro-social terms, the existence and continuity of the informal land market is linked to inequality in income distribution and the inability of public authorities to provide a massive and regular supply of housing. For this reason, we would like to continue by highlighting the perverse feedback loop of the two informal land sub-markets, an element that is not necessarily related to the increase in job insecurity or the inability to take public action, but that serves as a motor and feeds the functioning of the two informal land sub-markets.

In characterising the functioning of the two informal land sub-markets (land plots and consolidated settlements), we see that there is a feedback trend between them, where the plot sub-market generates a demand for the sub-market in the consolidated areas and vice versa, with the latter also producing a demand for the other sub-market. We have a way of operating informal land sub-markets, where one continuously promotes the demand of the other. This dynamic of informal land creates a closed system which, by generating feedback effects, results in an increased growth of the COMP-FUSED structure of informal community land.

In Figure 4 we outline the perverse feedback loop of the two informal land sub-markets. It can be observed that the operation of the informal land plot sub-market, by promoting an increasingly diffuse city, imposes an increasing cost of transport on the population that decides to live in a periphery that is ever more distant from the centre. In the same way, the precariousness of the labour market and the growth of temporary jobs requires the physical presence of this worker in some central location, imposing transportation costs that will not necessarily be compensated by their daily work. One way out for these families is to return to living centrally. But to do so, they must return

Figure 4.   The Reproduction Logic of Informal Sub-Markets: The Perverse Feedback Loop of the Two Informal Land Sub-Markets

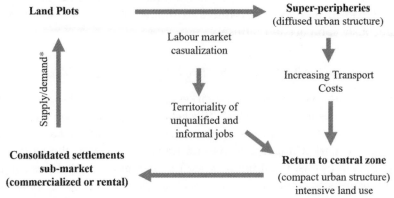

*Sellers in consolidated settlements are buyers in land plots

Source: Abramo, 2009

through the door of the informal market in consolidated areas, either through the 'hand' of the sales market, or through the 'hand' of the location market.

The operation of the plot sub-market produces a demand for the consolidated settlement sub-market in the consolidated areas. However, the growth of demand in the sub-market in consolidated areas cannot be met with a greater supply because of its relative inelasticity. Thus, the market reaction is via prices – that is, they tend to increase. With that we have an increase in families offering their properties or plots in the consolidated areas and will capitalise (or decapitalise) by buying a plot on the periphery and build houses with better (or worse) living conditions. Again, the operation of one informal sub-market fuels the demand of another, in which case the sub-market in the consolidated areas generates a demand for the sub-markets on the periphery. This feedback effect is perverse, as it produces a more compact informal urban structure in consolidated areas and a more diffuse one in urban areas; the "informal city" COMP-FUSED is a considerable cause of instability for the common home, as well as a loss of efficiency in the use of urban land. We can also affirm that the perverse feedback circuit promotes an increase in the prices of the informal land market, increasing the regressive distributions of the wealth captured in the form of land valuation.

Conclusion

The conclusion of this analysis of the relationship between the functioning of the land market and the production and reproduction of the structure of land use is to sound an alert about the risks of the return of the market as the main mechanism for collective coordination of urban land use. It has been argued throughout the chapter that both the informal market and the formal land market promote a double movement of compaction and diffusion, producing a COMP-FUSED land use structure in large Latin American cities. There is no doubt that in a city with a COMP-FUSED structure of land use, the demands of coordination and public control of the free market are essential to build a more egalitarian and fairer city in terms of access and distribution of urban wealth. Against the return of the 'overpowering' hand of the market, we have attempted to demonstrate the urgent need to fight for the return of public action to the coordination of urban land use. This must be public action renewed by the broad participation of the community in its decisions and that goes beyond the formula of modernist urban planning, where the principle of instrumental rationality delegates to the few the decisions on urban life that affect the many.

References

Abramo, P. (ed.) (2003a) *A Cidade Informal*. Sette Letras: Rio de Janeiro.

Abramo, P. (2003b) *A dinâmica do mercado imobiliário e a mobilidade residencial nas favelas do Rio de Janeiro: resultados preliminares*. IPPUR-UFRJ: Rio de Janeiro.

Abramo, P. (2006) *Mercados informais e mobilidade residencial nas favelas das grandes metropoles brasileiras*. Unpublished research report, Conselho Nacional de Pesquisa Cientifica, CNPq, Governo do Brasil.

Abramo, P. (2007) *Aluguel informal e acesso dos pobres à cidade*. Unpublished research report, Lincoln Institute of Land Policy: Cambridge MA.

Abramo, P. (2009) *Favela e mercado informal: a nova porta de entrada dos pobres nas cidades brasileiras*. Ed. Habitare-ANTAC. Caixa Econômica Federal do Brasil: Porto Alegre.

Abramo, P. (2011) *Mercado inmobiliario y la producción de las ciudades en América Latina*. Flacso-Ecuador: Quito.

Agamben, G. (2004) *Estado de Exceção*. Boitempo: São Paulo.

Alegría, T. and Ordóñez, G. (2005) *Legalizando la ciudad. Asentamientos informales y procesos de regulación en Tijuana*. El colegio de la Frontera Norte: Tijuana.

Arensberg, H., Pearson, H. and Polanyi, K. (eds.) (1957) *Trade and Market in the Early Empires, Economies in History and Theory*. Free Press: New York.

Azuela, A. (1989) *La ciudad, la propiedad privada y el derecho*. El Colegio de México: Mexico FD.

Azuela, A. (2001) *Definiciones de informalidad*. Lincoln Institute of Land Policy: Cambridge MA.

Bagnasco, A. (1999) *Tracce di comunita*. Il Mulino: Bologna.

Bruni, L. (2006) *Reciprocitá. Dinamiche di cooperazione economia e società civile*. Bruno Mondadori: Milan.

Caillé, A. (2000) *L'antropologie du don*. Desclée de Bouwer: Paris.

Duty, C. and Weber, F. (2007) *L'ethnographie économique*. La Découverte: Paris.

Fernandes, E. (2003) 'Perspectivas para a renovacao das politicas de legalizacao de favelas no Brasil' in P. Abramo (ed.) *A cidade informal*. Sette Letras: Rio de Janeiro, 173–187.

Jaramillo, S. (2001) 'La experiencia colombiana en la recuperación estatal de los incrementos del precio del suelo. La Contribución de Valorización y la participación en Plusvalias' in M. Smolka and F. Furtado (eds.) *Recuperación de plusvalías en América Latina: alternativas para el desarrollo urbano*. Editorial Eurelibros y Instituto de Posgrado e Investigación Pontificia: Universidad Católica de Chile and Lincoln Institute of Land Policy, 71–98.

Klein, J. and Harrison, D. (eds.) (2006) *L'innovation sociale*. Presses de l'Université du Québec: Sainte-Foy.

Lipietz, A. (1991) *Audácia: uma alternativa para o século XXI*. Nobel: São Paulo.

Maldonado, M. M. (2003) 'La plus-valía en beneficio de los pobres: el Proyecto Usme en Bogotá, Colombia'. *Land Lines* 15(2): 250–254.

Maldonado Copello, M. M. (2005). Operación urbanística nuevo usme: provisión de suelo urbanizado para vivienda de interés social, a partir de la redistribución social de plusvalías. Prourbana. Programa de apoyo a la políticas urbanas y de suelo en Chile, 16–24. Available at: http://www .institutodeestudiosurbanos.info//dmdocuments/cendocieu/coleccion_ digital/Ciudad_Salitre-Nuevo_Usme/Operacion_Urbanistica_Nuevo-Maldonado_Mercedes-2005.pdf

Moulaert, F., Rodríguez, A. and Swyngedouw, E. (2003) *The Globalized City – Economic Restructuring and Social Polarization in European Cities*. Oxford University Press: Oxford.

Pelligia, V. (2007) *Il paradossi della fiducia. scelte razionali e dinamiche interpersonali*. II Mulino: Bologna.

Rodríguez, A. and Sugranyes, A. (2004) 'El problema de la vivienda de los con techo'. *Eure* **XXX**(91): 53–65.

Rallet, A. (2000) 'De la globalization à la proximité geographique' in A. Rallet and A. Torre (eds.) (2007) *Quelle proximité pour innover?* L'Harmattan: Paris, 37–57.

Sabatini, F. (2003) *La segregación social del espacio en las ciudades de América Latina*. Pontificia Universidad Católica de Chile: Santiago.

Sabatini, F. (2005) *Relación entre promoción inmobiliaria y segregación residencial: giros insospechados de la Ciudad*. Lincoln Institute of Land Policy: Cambridge MA.

Smolka, M. (2007) 'Informalidad, pobreza y precios de la tierra' in M. Smolka and L. Mullahy (eds.) *Perspectivas urbanas: temas críticos en políticas de suelo en América Latina*. Lincoln Institute of Land Policy: Cambridge MA, 71–78.

Sugi, M. I. (2007) 'Relato Río Infomercado-Florianópolis' in P. Abramo (ed.) *INFOMERCADO - Relatório Final*. Finep/Habitare: Río de Janeiro.

Taylor, C. (2003) *El multiculturalismo y la política del reconocimiento*. Fondo de Cultura Económica de España: Madrid.

Williamson, O. (1985) *The Economic Institutions of Capitalism*. Free Press: New York.

2

The Pending Agenda of Property Right Formalisation in Peru: Conceptual and Public Policy Aspects

JULIO CALDERÓN COCKBURN

Universidad Nacional Mayor de San Marcos

This chapter addresses one of the most important urban policies in Peru in recent decades: the Plan Nacional de Formalización (PNF, Property Formalisation Programme), the second phase of which was developed with the Proyecto de Consolidación de los Derechos de la Propiedad Inmobiliaria (PCDPI, Consolidation of Real Estate Rights Project) supported by the World Bank (2007–2011). This project was publicly presented in March 2008, and represented a continuation of the Proyecto de Derechos de Propiedad Urbana (PDPU, Urban Property Rights Project) (1998–2004). It sought to consolidate the property rights already achieved for its beneficiaries, strengthen the land registry system, and integrate the state institutions responsible for socio-economic development and land administration.

The analysis presented here covers two levels: conceptual and public policy. To this end, it delves into the historical, theoretical and ideological foundations of the policy and tests its results against empirical evidence. Conceptual questions that emerge are: whether the results of the policy are meeting the objectives it has set; whether the connections have been made between its practical applications and the conceptual proposals that underpinned them; and its relationship with other urban and housing policies. It is concluded that the policy has met its goals but not its neoliberal objectives and, in reality, generates understandings, perceptions and uses of property in the affected families that are very different from those proposed by its promoters, based on practical aspects related more to use value of property rather than its exchange value.

This work goes beyond understanding of the needs of the Peruvian state and its public policy, to address aspects of the regularisation of the country's poor urban settlements. Given that there is almost total consensus among politicians, academics and multilateral cooperation, it is important to specify the type of policy to which the formalisation of property rights belongs. One urban tradition in Latin America consists of regularising tenure and improving habitat conditions at the same time. In Peru, however, formalisation has followed, to varying degrees, the key recommendations of Hernando de Soto (2000), the Instituto Libertad y Democracia (ILD, Institute for Liberty and Democracy) and the World Bank. This policy assumes that property rights will have a certain institutional and legal effect on the behaviour of the people affected, who are themselves regarded as, and conceived to be, free individuals and consumers in the marketplace.

Historical Genesis and Development of Formalisation

Every policy linked to a development project is subject to a logical framework analysis, which sequentially links objectives and results with activities measured in goals. So if the goals are met, it is assumed that the objectives were achieved. However, when the goals are achieved but not the objectives, there are conceptual problems in the formulation of the policy itself.

Although the PNF achieved its goals, especially in its early years, it was never able to do the same with its objectives. By 2007, the PNF had distributed 1.7 million property title deeds in cities and, by 2010, some 1.9 million (Government of Peru, 2011). According to my calculations, a total of 2.4 million titles should have been distributed by 2015. On the other hand, as the policy's promoters have pointed out, the average formalisation time has been reduced from six years to 45 days and there has been a simultaneous reduction in the costs of titling that reached US$200.00 in 2002, much less than the cost estimated by de Soto in 1986 of US$2156 (Morris, 2004: 79). However, while it is true that the quality of life of the urban poor has improved (Calderón et al., 2015), it is more realistic to understand this as an improvement in the general economic and employment situation, as well as in social policies, rather than as a consequence of the deployment of property rights, as the policy states.

In order to deepen our understanding of this misconception, we should look back to its historical genesis. The PNF proposal was first conceptualised around 1986, with the publication of the book *El otro sendero* (The Other Path) written by the Peruvian economist Hernando de Soto for the ILD. This book, as the policymakers themselves acknowledge, became the cornerstone of a proposal that, a few years later, was enthusiastically embraced by multilateral cooperation. This proposal fitted very well with the neoliberal initiatives in vogue at the time (Gilbert, 2001; Calderón, 2003; Mitchell, 2006).

Conceptually, the PNF proposal differed from previous approaches to the phenomenon of 'urban marginalisation' in the sense that social actors were no longer seen as poor people to be protected, but rather as a thriving population with a desire to improve and with a business vocation. In this framework, it was assumed that the development of private property rights would be an appropriate way to address urban poverty and informality in cities. This was established by Legislative Decree No. 803 in March 1996:

> Property ownership constitutes the major part of assets held by Peruvians of fewer resources, nevertheless, it cannot be used in the legal market because it lacks a duly registered title that confers exchange value. The procedures […] constitute a discriminatory regime that forces people to waste many years in paperwork, at great financial cost. The titles granted […] have lacked sufficient value to mobilise credit and investment in sustainable basic services. The system will increase the value of land held by Peruvians with fewer resources. Without access to formalisation, most Peruvians cannot fully benefit from economic policy. (Cited in Calderón, 2006: 186)

There are close links between neoliberalism and the proposals to develop private property rights. Neoliberalism, which emerged from a core of thinkers in the 1940s, had already been applied in a concrete manner by the military government in Chile in 1975 and then with the conservative regimes of Ronald Reagan and Margaret Thatcher in the United States and Great Britain respectively. According to the theory and model, neoliberal states should favour strong the rights to private property, the rule of law, and free market and free trade institutions as principles essential to guarantee individual freedoms (Harvey, 2007: 74). Following its acceptance by the International Monetary Fund (IMF) in the 1980s, neoliberalisation imposed a model of capital accumulation in Latin America in response to the challenge of the fiscal and energy crisis (Harvey, 2007).

When implementing neoliberal policies, the political regimes that led each country applied these conceptual principles whilst also adapting them to fit national historical, social and cultural contexts. Among the general characteristics of this intervention was the willingness of the state to shed its social burden, deregulate and make the labour market more flexible, privatise public enterprises, and support the development of financial capital, among other things. There were roll-backs of urban planning and state regulation, a reduction and elimination of public social housing programmes (with the exception of Chile), decentralisation of the state and privatisation of public utilities, and other initiatives. Peru became part of the neoliberal wave in 1990.

El otro sendero by Hernando de Soto is important because it opened an individualistic liberal approach to understanding the problems of cities and urbanisation (Duhau, 1998). In *El otro sendero*, the decades-long urban struggles of Peruvian settlers against an exclusionary state were revealed, in reality, as a long road to private property – the same one that was blocked by mercantilism. Entrepreneurial initiatives in low-income communities, some subsistence activity within the informal economy (street commerce, public transport), were revealed as entrepreneurs confronted with excessive state bureaucracy which prevented them from moving beyond simple accumulation. In spite of their traditional location in the worst parts of the cities, the housing and land on which the settlers were based was revealed to have a potential value measured in trillions of dollars, a form of dead capital that needed to be awakened through the granting of property title deeds.

The central proposal of the PNF, as has been indicated, was an extension of the thinking set out in *El otro sendero*: the land is *dead capital* that lies in the hands of the poor, without the state or the market having noticed it. The equation concludes that land and/or housing ownership is capital. Therefore – and this is the final piece of the puzzle – as poor people are rational individuals and profit-maximisers, the development of property rights will allow them to obtain economic and social benefits. The state must ensure that formalisation makes property definable, defensible and alienable (Mosqueira, 2000). In macro-economic terms, free enterprise and the market should lead the process, backed by a minimal state whose role is to facilitate the market. Property rights would provide security of tenure, access to credit and the development of secure property markets in the social world of the poor. Although over time other supposed benefits were added, these three benefits turned out to be the policy's main elements, as set out in 2000 by the Baseline of the Comisión de Formalización de la Propiedad Informal (COFOPRI, Commission for the Formalisation of Informal Property) (Apoyo, 2000).

The articulation of these three main elements (security of tenure, credit and formal property markets) converted them into a feedback loop. Titles, by affirming security of tenure, would generate greater investment in housing and infrastructure, which in turn would increase the value of property. The higher value of property, in turn, would allow greater guarantees for access to credit from private banks, the development of formal property markets, and social harmony and peace in the family and in the community (Apoyo, 2000). Mitchell (2006) has noted the paradox that while the PNF affirmed the value of the property title deeds as security of tenure and protection, it also stimulated the commodification (exchange value) of the land.

Empirical Findings

I will now evaluate two of the central planks and associated economic impacts which underpin the formalisation and use of property rights: access to credit and the development of formal property markets. The issue of security of tenure will not be addressed here; to be clear, I concur with the position of architect John Turner (1977), who affirmed the importance of security of tenure but attributed it to the public guarantee of non-eviction, rather than to private property tenure.

Since the social aspects will not be addressed here, it should be noted that in recent years some researchers have argued that property title deeds may be affecting community life in the neighbourhoods. This is because the existence of full property rights for inhabitants allows for the existence of vacant land plots in the settlements, which would be detrimental to organisational dynamics (Ramírez Corzo and Riofrío, 2006). On the other hand, there are indications that, following the systemic promotion of individualism, trafficking of land plots on the part of poor people and their leaders has increased (Pimentel, 2015; Calderón, 2016). For an overview of the impact of formalisation, see Apoyo, 2000; DESCO, 2001; Calderón, 2001, 2003, 2009; Field, 2002; SASE, 2002; ESAN, 2004; Field and Torero, 2004; Ramírez and Riofrío, 2006; Webb and Revilla, 2006; Caria, 2007.

Access to Credit

The link between property title deeds and access to credit, which I studied in 2000 at the request of the Instituto Nacional de Estadística e Informática (INEI, National Institute of Statistics and Informatics), commissioned by COFOPRI (Calderón, 2001), showed surprising results: the people who were provided with titles by COFOPRI between 1998 and 1999 did not have access to loans from private banks, but only to subsidised public credit granted by the Banco de Materiales. This financial agency, although created in 1981, grew in importance during President Fujimori's re-election campaign, and granted loans to residents whether they had title deeds or not. On the other hand, those who did not have property title deeds (neither from COFOPRI nor from any other entity) did receive loans from private banks. This shows that the lending banks opted for individuals and families with stable jobs and income capacity. The real beneficiaries of the PNF were micro-entrepreneurs willing to apply for a mortgage guarantee in exchange for investment capital (Calderón, 2001, 2003).

Although my study was played down by those advocating PNF (Morris, 2004: 140), the comparative survey in 2004 which used 2000 as its baseline (see Table 1) showed the following: 'in 2004, there was no credit preference for COFOPRI title holders. Registered titleholders were no more likely to apply for formal credit, indeed the rate of non-approval they suffered was higher than that of other groups of owners whose titles are supposedly less secure' (Webb and Revilla, 2006: 63). On the contrary, households without property title deeds (in the category of 'other document' or 'no document') were the ones that most requested credit, including those that obtained it (72 percent of the 'other document' category).

Table 1.   Households that Applied for Credit and their Approval Rate, 2004

Type of documentation	Households that applied for credit %	Credit requests approved %
COFOPRI title	25	58
Municipal title	25	54
Sale title	25	70
Other document	30	72
No document	29	58

Source: Baseline Survey 2004. Table 5.2.3–1, p. 84. Quoted by Webb and Revilla, 2006: 63.

As pointed out by Richard Webb – a reputable Peruvian economist who is by no means sceptical – those who had sale titles established by the contracting parties before a public notary had a higher approval rate than those with COFOPRI titles. While in 2000 half of the COFOPRI title holders applied for credit, in 2004 only 25 percent did so. Applications for credit did not increase with the passage of time. In 2000 the proportion of credits approved for COFOPRI title holders was 96.1 percent and in 2004 it declined to 58.2 percent. Likewise, sophisticated analyses by economists such as Field and Torero (2004), who could not be accused of opposing the PNF, confirm these assessments. In 2007, using the natural experiment technique, a young Italian economist showed that in settlements formed in around 1995 in Lima's district of Villa El Salvador, 50 percent of the owners of settlements with titles had their credit application approved, while 84 percent of the those without ownership titles benefitted from approved applications (Caria, 2007: 60).

As Table 2 shows, between 2000 and 2005 – nine years after the policy was implemented – few COFOPRI title holders had obtained mortgage guarantees. The year 2003 was the year in which most COFOPRI title holders obtained mortgage guarantees, but they only represented 1.5 percent of the total.

As of 2004, when the Proyecto de Derechos de Propiedad Urbana (PDPU, Urban Property Rights Project) came to an end, there was no connection between the property title deeds and formal private credits, especially the use of mortgage guarantees. Faced with this empirical evidence, the proponents of the PNF developed a counter-argument indicating that there was a notable increase in mortgages. This is partially true. In 2003, the Fondo Mi Vivienda (Funding my Home, a low-income housing programme based in Peru) granted 6166 mortgage loans, 7960 in 2004 and 9205 in 2005 (Calderón, 2009: 111). However, the mortgages had not increased because of the supposed benefits of formalisation, but because of something that even a New York professor of Egyptology could see: 'when a new government abandoned De

Table 2. List of Property Title Deeds, Credits and Mortgages (2000–2005)

Year	Titles	Credit	People M USD	Mortgages	Owners mortgaged Number	Average mortgage/ owner	Use of mortgage (%)
2000	1,954,607	249	154,000	66	10,000	6,600	0.9
2001	1,170,206	275	174,000	73	15,000	4,686	1.28
2002	1,294,033	314	197000	106	19,000	5,578	1.46
2003	1,364,434	372	237,000	136	21,000	6,476	1.5
2004	1,430,032	459	266,000	83	8,000	10,375	0.5
2005	1,501,332	563	299,000	NI	NI	NI	NI

Source: Unpublished COFOPRI documentation regarding graduates who have accessed mortgages.

Soto's neoliberal prescriptions and began subsidising low-income mortgages' (Mitchell, 2006: 5).

The Urban Property Rights Project ended in 2004. Between 2005 and 2007 the Peruvian state did not have a loan from the World Bank, and the Central de Información Positiva (Centre for Positive Information) project – which was supposed to provide banks with information on the credit behaviour of the poor – was abandoned. The production of information about the link between titling and credit was discontinued, with the publication of only partial information for 2005 and 2006. In 2010, COFOPRI commissioned a survey to look into the association between title and credit, but its results were not disseminated and the institution refused to provide information. Moreover, the *Programa Techo Propio* (Homeownership Programme) – a government programme created in 2002 – promoted mortgages for social housing in the settlements and actually made it unattractive for the villagers to mortgage their land in order to build their homes. The Institute for Freedom and Democracy (ILD) criticised the changes as 'counter-reformist' (ILD, 2007). In 2008, at the launch of el Proyecto de Consolidación de la Propiedad Informal (PCDPI, Informal Property Consolidation Project, 2008–2011), one of the main advisers of the policy's beginnings indicated that the issue of access to credit should be demystified, since 'it is not the most important benefit of formalisation: investment in formalised areas is' (Morris, 2008: 10).

Empirical information proves that links between titles to the urban poor and access to credit are weak. From the conceptual point of view, the link proposal was actually more the result of policymakers' desires, based on a branch of economic science, than reflecting the kind of situations that low-income and poor people find themselves in and respond to by making use of their assets and property.

The poor population which has land titles prefers (actively chooses) to use land, the most significant economic capital they own, as their residence and according to its use value. My interpretation does not deny that there is a stratum within the titled population, particularly micro-entrepreneurs, who are interested in accessing mortgage. Nor does it deny that in circumstances of *force majeure*, families and individuals from this social group dispose of their property in order to access credit. In which case, this can be very welcome. However, I maintain that what these families and individuals seek from their property is primarily shelter, and physical and psychological security: use value. These families fear losing their property to banks, which they see as impersonal institutions, and seek to avoid the insecurity and instability they have already experienced due to their informal status in the city. At the same time, private banks do not look favourably on the urban poor and are unwilling to take on debtor risks or, ultimately, to keep foreclosed homes that are difficult to place on the market (Calderón, 2003).

Formal Property Markets

The nexus between property title deeds and the development of formal property markets is another expected consequence of formalisation. In principle, a formal property market provides security for economic operators. However, the formality achieved with the title is not necessarily maintained through the forces of the property market. I maintain that, in the hands of the low-income urban groups, the property market can also lead to informality, which raises the old sociological problem of the costs of formality. The trends in the property market of titled settlements indicate that those which are well-established and consolidated, rents predominate. On the other hand, in titled settlements which are still in the process of urban consolidation, purchases and sales predominate.

In the consolidated and titled settlements of Lima, such as the old areas of Villa El Salvador and Huáscar founded in 1971 and 1976 respectively, the property rental market predominates. The owners choose to rent all or part of their homes, which benefit from the new amenities generated by the city, through rooms with common services. This situation is leading to slum formation, overcrowding and deteriorating quality of life. Moreover, transactions are rarely formal, as actors prefer to hide in the shadow of informality to avoid higher costs and taxes (Calderón, 2009). In the young and consolidating settlements, on the other hand, the property market predominates, with the sale of land without buildings or of half-built houses. Since the 1990s, various forms of illegal land plots, primary and secondary, have been consolidated, partly stimulated by the titling policy (Calderón, 2016).

The property market in the titled areas is a kind of laboratory for observing the use of property rights by lower-income sectors. Property is a social relationship full of nuances and basically consists of the right of the individual to exclude another from the use or enjoyment of a certain good or asset. Exclusion, as a social relationship, is intrinsic to property and its rights (Calderón, 2003).

The exercise of the right to property in new settlements is leading to three forms of land use. Firstly, the main use of property in the slums is as a residence – its use value. Approximately 80 percent of the land plots are used for housing (Caduceo-Caem, 2006; cited in Calderón, 2009: 53). Even those who purchase land or housing explicitly express a desire to live on it and are sceptical about the possibility of selling it (Calderón, 2009).

A second option is the non-use of land, that is, keeping it vacant, which accounts for around 20 percent of land plots (Calderón, 2009: 53). This option, which borders on land speculation from below, is almost a direct consequence of the practical application of property rights. Before mass titling, control of the local territory was held by the neighbourhood leaders, who checked that all the inhabitants actually lived there. The titling policy has undermined this organisational function by defining legal property as individual, and as definable, defensible and alienable, rather than promoting public sector guarantees or social functions. This prevents organisations from intervening in situations where the land is not inhabited. For this situation to arise, the titled homeowner must have another place to live (another property or a relative's home), which reveals filters in the beneficiary selection policy. These people look at land more as an asset, or economic capital reserve or future profit, than as territory with use value (Calderón, 2009, 2010).

A third option is to view property as imbued with exchange value. In settlements already in existence and growing for 15 years, the sales market predominates and is relatively buoyant. In some cases that I have been able to study, we can detect an annual renewal of the housing stock by 2 percent (Calderón, 2010: 646).

Therefore, one of the main benefits of the PNF, which is the development of formal property markets, corresponds in reality to only a small part of the land use that results from the actions of owners. It is true that the price of titled land (US$16 per square metre) found during my study of neighbourhoods under consolidation in Lima is three times higher than that offered for untitled land (Calderón, 2010). The titles give those selling land a US$1000 bonus compared to those vendors who do not have a title. There are social conditions that explain this economic situation: the possession of a title now signifies security and prestige. However, the higher value and price of titled land is good news for those who are selling but not for those who are buying (Durand Lasserve et al., 2007).

There is something that is not happening as predicted, though, and that is the idea that the development of the property market post-titling will become more formal. In the titled neighbourhoods, only 25 percent of the buyers in

2008 complied with the requirement to register on the Property Registry, a fact which made the registration lose relevance (Calderón, 2009). This trend towards the informality of formality (de-regularisation) had been noted by the 2004 PDPU Baseline, which verified a trend towards the non-recording of second acts. This attitude, as in the old settlements, results from the desire of the actors to avoid the costs of formality, since the requirements (public bodies, notaries) can cost between US$150 and US$250, which is expensive in relation to the average cost of real estate transaction (US$1440).

While formalisation is leading to an increase in the property market, it is not necessarily formal. There is no automatic comparison to suggest that formal property transactions will occur in titled areas and informal transactions will occur in untitled areas. Again, to imagine, once the property has been formalised, that subsequent transactions will also adhere to formal procedures reflects the good intentions of policymakers but does not correspond to the actual behaviour of actors.

The two principles of formalisation (higher land value for titles and higher formal transactions) are not logically sequential or binding. If titling increases the price of the land, there will be a part of the demand that will not reach those prices and, therefore, will be excluded from the acquisition of land. As a result, this demand will be pushed towards the purchase of untitled land in an informal property market (Calderón, 2009). This is paradoxical and logically deductible: land titling indirectly induces the development of informal markets in other settlements. At a higher level of abstraction, some economists' reasoning suggests that once all informal land plots are titled, prices will fall. But that will be the day when comprehensive policies are in place that both regularise land tenure and generate formal mechanisms for access to land, something that the markets do not seem able to do on their own.

As W. Thomas would say, if people consider something to be real, it will be real in its consequences. If people believe that the title brings prestige and economic opportunities, as the PNF has exhorted, the presence of titles raises the value and price of their properties. Logically, there are sectors of demand which, even if they wish to do so, will not be able to access certain sites because of their high price, and their exclusion will lead less wealthy buyers to purchase on the alternative, informal market, with its lack of amenities, insecurity and peripheral location. This brings us back to the old sociological issue of costs and interests (Weber): the (high) costs of formality induce the actor, in defence of his interests, to act informally and outside the law.

Pending Agenda: Involving the PNF in Wider Urban Policy

The key idea which underpins the pending agenda is that formalisation can no longer be thought of in its original terms. The PNF originated in the midst of economic adjustment and was conceived as a means which would allow the state to abandon subsidies. But since 2003, there has been a boom in public subsidies for housing in Peru, and the state itself has condemned the institutional abandonment of the sector in the 1990s.

There is, therefore, no point in considering the development of the PNF as if these institutional changes had not occurred. Formalisation has already been integrated into the housing sector and the public entities in charge of 'integrating' informal settlements in various ways (titling, basic services, roads) must converge. The decentralisation of the Peruvian state has become a core of development for the country.

The pending agenda of formalisation must be regarded from the perspective of the housing sector, not only because it is defined thus by law but because it is the best way to utilise the potential of property title deeds to improve quality of life and enhance investment. A central feature of the current housing policy is the development of public credit and subsidies, especially from 2006 onwards. At that time, the authorities realised that while the middle-class subsidy worked, the same could not be said for poor and low-income sectors. For the period 2007–2011, the Ministry of Housing established among its goals the delivery of 122,000 credits for some 600,000 people, to the tune of US$600 million (MVCS, 2006).

What is the effect of subsidised public credit on the PNF? The subsidy is aimed at those who do not have land or housing (through direct subsidies that can go up to 40 percent of the total value of the property) and those who already have land and property title deeds but require credit to improve or build housing. PNF beneficiaries are in the latter situation, receiving credit to build or improve their home. In this way, property titling is reduced to a formal requirement (filter) necessary to access the subsidy, partly moving away from the policy of linking property titling and private bank credit and inserting the state subsidy as a lever to stimulate investment. This is the case, we reiterate, with the Programa Techo Propio (Homeownership Programme), which since 2002 has offered support via subsidies and mortgage guarantees (Family Housing Bonds) for on-site construction and home improvement, obviating the need for the poor to request loans from private banks for this purpose (Calderón, 2015: 168–172).

Nevertheless, the Peruvian state seems to have lost its way with regard to its formalisation policies. Table 3 shows that the promise and delivery of property title deeds has continued, as has the discourse on the supposed benefits of such a policy, although no one really knows what this means. Titling in the twenty-first century has been lower than in the 1990s largely because new squatters did not benefit from amnesty laws.

Urban and housing policy should promote formal mechanisms to access land that reduce informal practices. So far, the 'turnkey' type of social housing

Table 3.   Distribution of Property Title Deeds in Peru (2000–2015)

Year	Titles National	Lima
2000	1,049,134	547,064
2006	495,018	113,665
2011	557,813	62,056
2015	347,544	71,538
Total	2,449,509	794,323

Source: Ministry of Housing and Construction, www.vivienda.gob.pe.

programmes are part of a free-market economy, although they are subsidised by the public sector. Part of this subsidy should be directed towards promoting municipal housing programmes, or programmes for access to land, that break the vicious circle of informality and reduce the activities of informal developers at different levels (businesses, individuals, communities). The demand subsidy must not be transformed into a supply subsidy.

Like any policy, formalisation policy must be viewed from the perspective of a decentralised state, which grants enhanced powers to municipalities. This criterion should guide the 'integration' of the informal city into the formal city by linking the sectoral public interventions along the lines of the decentralisation of the Peruvian state that is under way. Considering the trends towards informality observed in the property markets in titled neighbourhoods, the control and regulation mechanisms that operate in municipalities must be strengthened in order to contain the emergence of new slums.

The regularisation of land tenure, of which formalisation is a variant, should expand its sphere of intervention from occupied public land to land of private origin, on which informal settlements have been constituted. It was estimated that in Lima there were 329 human settlements with some 35,000 families in this type of tenure (Campaign Committee, 2006: 35), whose attention had been left to judicial jurisdictions. Since its founding law (Decree Law 803 of 1996), the PNF has authorised the regularisation and formalisation of occupied public land. In 2006, Article 21 of Law 28,687 opened the door to the expropriation of privately owned lands, but its regulations only governed aspects concerning the reconciliation of conflicts between the occupants of land and the owners of property rights, as well as declaration of ownership by means of a claim to *prescripción adquisitiva de dominio* (adverse possession). In February 2009, Law 29,320 was issued, authorising the expropriation of privately owned land, but this has not had much effect. Moreover, dealing with land acquired by housing cooperatives and communal lands also constitutes a legal vacuum. Similarly, there are difficulties in regularising downtown areas of the city where slums exist, whose unregistered occupants and/or owners cannot access the financial benefits offered by the state.

The policy of regularisation – formalisation of property – must therefore consider not only its social and economic impact on families but also the connections between the 'communal system' and the 'government system'.

Conceptual Aspects

The experience of formalisation has left lessons to be learned. The concept that a poor person with property title deeds is, or should be, transformed into a rationally profit-maximising individual (*homos economicus*) has vanished, to be replaced by a public policy which affirms that it is investment in settlements which will raise people's standard of living and, in so doing, increase use value and exchange value. The funding that drives this investment come from two sources. On the one hand, the resources of the families themselves, obtained through savings and loans from relatives which they then use to invest to develop their family strategy. On the other hand, the subsidised public credit granted by institutions such as the Ministry of Housing's Homeownership Programme (Calderón et al., 2015). One task that remains outstanding is to identify the role that private and business investment can play in this process.

Subsidised public credit expands investment in infrastructure in low-income settlements, improves living conditions and symbolically affects the way that the poor develop their life strategies. The poor do not have to mortgage their homes to meet their basic needs. My view is that the strength of the subsidy somewhat placates the deployment of free market principles in the population. The poor, unlike other groups and social classes, are relatively less dependent on market mechanisms. In its reproduction strategies, the presence of the state (subsidiary, clientelistic, populist) and its own resources have prevailed. The urban poor currently have subsidies for water and sanitation, construction and improvement of housing, food and property title deeds and even, in a recent development, electricity.

Less dependence on the market also implies that its logics penetrate less, with more dependence on contributions from the state and the community. This is something that public policies should take into account. The poor and low-income sectors act according to reasonable (not rational) calculations in a context of deprivation which conditions how they weigh up their involvement in the worlds of formality and informality in which they are embedded, and the land on which they are registered. The acceptance of goods via commercial channels, or the assumption of a total cost, is only acceptable so long as they can afford it, and it is clear that the state has no particular interest in providing that good. This is not to say that the promotion of free markets and 'possessive individualism' – the curious perception of individuals, promoted by the state since 1990, that they 'owe nothing to society' (McPherson, 2005: 15) – has had no effect on how the poor enter the market. It has had an effect, but not necessarily via notions of formality devised by policymakers.

Neoliberalist assumptions (Harvey, 2007) propose a competitive society with winners and losers, decided by the successes and mistakes of individuals. Although according to official statistics the economic model has reduced poverty and increased the middle class, even in 2016 there are still one million poor people in Lima without drinking water at home. There is nothing to say that the losers of the system cannot share the dominant discourse, nor that they should opt for rebellion or communitarianism. Anomie, the mismatch between a cultural structure that sets normative values which govern behaviour, and individuals' socially structured capabilities, can lead to innovation and to a rejection of institutional practices, whilst preserving cultural goals (Merton, 1984: 241, 256).

From this perspective, economic and urban informality is a form of anomie. The discourse of possessive individualism and the free market has led to a greater inclination amongst the poor to participate in informal property markets. This is evidenced not only by the titling by COFOPRI of empty land plots subject to market speculation, but also by the current processes of urban low-income expansion in which the poor have gone from being squatters to land-traffickers. In contrast to patterns of occupation a few decades ago, people no longer squat on a single land plot in order to live there, but rather eight or ten lots are taken in order to be sold later, reflecting an income-generating strategy carried out by 'autonomous subordinates' (Pimentel, 2015). Trafficking in land plots, which coexists with other illegal land markets conducted by informal leaders or companies, could not function without the complicity of clientelism carried out by local authorities and political operators (Calderón, 2016). In the new settlements, there is a tendency to create a rather weak social fabric which leads to the demand for common goods through clientelistic relations and not through collective action or social movements.

The consideration of social policy formalisation, or of land regularisation more generally, within comprehensive urban and housing policies, should aim not only to increase investment in formalised areas, as is happening thanks to subsidies, but also to channel the genuine use of property rights to improve the quality of life of individuals, families and settlements. It is worth putting to one side the economic bias that sees property as a guarantee of credit or exchange value, and assuming that it also plays a role by providing psychological and symbolic security, and use value. Likewise it is worth questioning the idea that the market necessarily generates optimal results and that the summation of individual actions leads to collective improvements in the quality of life of the settlements. Rather, criteria should be applied which acknowledge the social function of property and promote public guarantees against the excessive application of individual property rights.

Land ownership has a use value, not just an exchange value, which allows access to other use values such as infrastructure, location, proximity to friends, social networks for self-protection, etc. (Logan and Molotch, 2007: 17–23). The sum of these use values improves life quality, and the right to claim such use values belongs to all the city's inhabitants.

References

Consultoría, A. (2000) *Encuesta de línea de base. Reporte final.* Proyecto Derechos de Propiedad Urbana-COFOPRI: Lima.

Caduceo-Caem Consorcio (2006) *Información resumen del censo participativo Lima Centro.* Caduceo: Lima.

Calderón Cockburn, J. (2001) 'Análisis comparativo de la población beneficiada y la no beneficiada por el Plan Nacional de Formalización' in Instituto Nacional de Estadística e Informática *¿Ha mejorado el bienestar de la población?* INEI: Lima, 63–92.

Calderón, J. (2003) *Propiedad y crédito: la formalización de la propiedad en el Perú.* PGU-Hábitat: Quito.

Calderón Cockburn, J. (2006) *Mercado de tierras urbanas, propiedad y pobreza.* LILP-SINCOS: Lima.

Calderón Cockburn, J. (2009) 'Títulos de propiedad, mercados y políticas urbanas'. *Revista Latinoamericana y del Caribe de Centros Históricos – OLACCHI* **3**: 7–62.

Calderón Cockburn, J. (2010) 'Titulación de la propiedad y mercado inmobiliario'. *Estudios Demográficos y Urbanos* **25**(3): 625–661.

Calderón Cockburn, J. (2015) 'Las políticas de vivienda social: entre la vivienda nueva y la construcción en sitio propio' in T. Bolívar, M. Rodríguez and J. Erazo (eds.) *Ciudades en construcción permanente ¿Destino de casas para todos?* ABYA-AYALA, Universidad Central de Venezuela and CLACSO: Quito, 147–178.

Calderón Cockburn, J. (2016) *Democracia, individualismo y clientelismo.* Un contra-ejemplo en Perú'. International Sociology Association Conference: Vienna.

Calderón Cockburn, J., Quispe, J., Lucci, P. and Lenhard, A. (2015) *On the Path to Progress: Improving Living Conditions in Peru's Slum Settlements.* ODI: London.

Caria, A. (2007) *Títulos sin desarrollo: los efectos de la titulación de tierras en los nuevos barrios de Lima.* DESCO: Lima.

Comité de Campaña por el derecho a una vivienda digna (2006) *El Plan Nacional de Vivienda 2006–2015: cómo incluir a los sectores más vulnerables.* CENCA: Lima.

de Soto, H. (1986) *El otro sendero.* ILD: Lima.

de Soto, H. (2000) *El misterio del capital: por qué el capitalismo triunfa en occidente y fracasa en el resto del mundo.* El Comercio: Lima.

DESCO Centro de Estudios y Promoción del Desarrollo (2001) *Estudio de cultura registral*. PDPU-COFOPRI: Lima.

Duhau, E. (1998) *Hábitat popular y política urbana*. Prorrúa-UAM-A: Mexico FD.

Escuela de Administración de Negocios para Egresados ESAN-IMASEN (2004) *Segunda encuesta de hogares para la medición del impacto del proyecto de derechos de propiedad urbana en el bienestar de la población*. COFOPRI: Lima.

Field, E. (2002) 'Entitled to Work: Urban Property Rights and Labour Supply in Peru'. *Princeton Law and Public Affairs*, Working Paper 02, October.

Field, E. and Torero, M. (2004) *Do Property Titles Increase Credit Access Among the Urban Poor? Evidence from a Nationwide Titling Program*. Working paper. Cambridge: Harvard University.

Gilbert, A. (2001) 'On the Mystery of Capital and the Myths of Hernando de Soto: What Difference does Legal Title Market?' NAERUS (Network Association of European Researchers on Urbanisation in the South): Leuven. https://pdfs.semanticscholar.org/0fc7/ae14c674fbf716a03a3e4c7c91ddfa98ba40.pdf [accessed 6 July 2019].

del Perú, G. (2011) *Obras para el pueblo. Así avanzó el Perú: cinco años invirtiendo en los más pobre*. República del Perú: Lima.

Harvey, D. (2007) *Breve historia del neoliberalismo*. Editorial Akal: Madrid.

Instituto Libertad y Democracia (2007) *La guerra de los notarios*. ILD: Lima.

Logan, J. and Molotch, H. (2007) *Urban Fortunes: The Political Economy of Place*. University of California Press: Berkeley.

Macpherson, C. B. (2005) *La teoría política del individualismo posesivo: de Hobbes a Locke*. Editorial Trota: Madrid.

Merton, R. (1984) *Teoría y estructura social*. FCE: Mexico FD.

Mitchell, T. (2006) 'The Work of Economics: how a Discipline makes its World'. *European Journal of Sociology* **45**(2): 297–320.

Morris, F. (2008) 'Promoción de la inversión y crédito: Agenda del Segundo Proyecto (PCDPI)'. *Seminario de Lanzamiento del 'Proyecto Consolidación de los Derechos de Propiedad Inmueble*. March: Lima.

Morris, F., Endo, V. and Ugaz, R. (2004) *Develando el misterio. La formalización de la propiedad en el Perú*. COFOPRI-Banco Mundial: Lima.

Mosqueira, E. (2000) 'Las reformas institucionales para la creación de un sistema de derechos de propiedad' in R. Abusada, F. Du Bois, E. Morón and J. Valderrama (eds.) *La reforma incomplete*. Universidad del Pacífico-Instituto Peruano de Economía: Lima, 107–169.

Ministerio de Vivienda, Construcción y Saneamiento, MVCS (2006) *Plan Nacional de Vivienda 2006–2015*. MVCS: Lima.

Payne, G., Durand-Lasserve, A. and Rakodi, C. (2007) '*Social and Economic Impacts of Land Titling Programmes in Urban and Peri-urban Areas: a Review of the Literature*'. World Bank Urban Research Symposium, Washington, 14–16 May.

Pimentel, N. (2015) *Subalternos autónomos: tráfico de tierras en Carabayllo*. Unpublished doctoral dissertation, Universidad Nacional Mayor de San Marcos, Lima.

Ramírez Corzo, D. and Riofrío, G. (2006) *Formalización de la propiedad y mejoramiento de barrios: bien legal, bien marginal*. Estudios Urbanos, DESCO: Lima.

SASE Instituto (2002) *Estudio sobre la dinámica de los asentamientos humanos.* PDPU-COFOPRI: Lima.

Turner, J. (1977) *Todo el poder para los usuarios. H.* Blume Ediciones: Madrid.

Webb, R., Beuermann, D. and Revilla, C. (2006) *La construcción del derecho de propiedad: el caso de los asentamientos humanos en el Perú.* Colegio de Notarios: Lima.

3

The Limitations of Land and Social Housing Policies in Overcoming Social Exclusion: The Bogotá Experience

MARÍA MERCEDES MALDONADO COPELLO

National University of Colombia, Bogotá

Introduction

This chapter examines the obstacles encountered in the implementation of Law 388 of 1997 in the city of Bogotá, an urban reform law that provides a series of tools for municipal governments to intervene in the land market. The paper focuses on the mechanisms which facilitate the production of social housing accessible to low-income families, bearing in mind that this continues to be one of the main unresolved problems of Latin American cities. It is also a key issue in the long process associated with the country achieving a majority to pass a law of this nature in Congress.

The chapter also looks at the gap between the formal adoption of constitutional and legal norms, sometimes resulting from long-term social demands, and their effective implementation. Recent Latin American constitutional reforms have been generous in the formal expansion of rights but are not always accompanied by concrete mechanisms to make them effective. The Colombian case shows that the implementation of these mechanisms is accompanied by tensions that prevent the achievement of minimum objectives like social inclusion and solidarity.

For sixteen years (2000–2015), four governments in the city of Bogotá attempted to implement land and land use legislation. They applied different mechanisms to regulate the land market and faced or replicated various obstacles, including the design of national housing policies. Despite these efforts, difficulties remain in terms of serving the poorest families who have had access to housing through informal means, especially in the last few decades, through the rental of self-built units in land plots purchased from informal developers in the preceding years. Despite their apparent capacity to rethink the rules of the game on the distribution of land incomes, land policies have not succeeded in reversing the existing order and improving the conditions of access to land (and, more generally, to the city) for those people traditionally excluded and particularly affected by economic crises, and by the expansion of structural unemployment or work outside the wage economy.

The first part of this chapter broadly examines the evolution of national housing policy and then discusses the experience of applying land policy instruments in Bogotá. This chapter is an updated version of the text 'The Limitations of Land and Social Housing Policies in Overcoming Social Exclusion. The Bogotá Experience' published in 2012 in Mexico City under the editorship of Clara E. Salazar. It is a work that includes research carried out at the Institute of Urban Studies and the formulation of recommendations for the Colombian Constitutional Court. Above all, it is a reflection and elaboration of my own recent experience as Secretary of Planning and Housing in the municipal government of Bogotá, from 2012 to 2014.

National Housing Policies: Economic Promotion Over Social Policy

After 40 years of repeated attempts, an urban reform law was passed in 1989 (Law 9). There was no strong social movement behind these efforts, rather it was shaped by liberal congressmen, urban planners and experts from national bodies. Nevertheless, a significant statement on land policies was achieved and further fleshed out in the 1997 Law 388, following a constitutional reform produced within the framework of one of the peace agreements the country signed. Like much of urban reform in Latin America, it combines the redistributive mechanisms of land rent and the commitment to democratising access to land ownership and, above all, housing.

The approval of the urban reform law, however, was followed by a shift in national housing policies towards the promotion of the construction sector, given its recognised capacity to stimulate the economy and incorporate market mechanisms into housing production. The new policy was reduced to a unique mechanism – the direct demand subsidy – which seeks to enhance the ability of low-income families to pay for housing produced by private agents. According to data from the Departamento Nacional de Estadística (DANE, National Department of Statistics) and the National Planning Department's poverty missions, a family is assumed to be below the poverty line when its monthly income is less than US$400 for a family of four. By the time these reforms were adopted, more than 50 percent of the country's population was below the poverty line although there have been significant improvements over the last twenty years in terms of multidimensional poverty reduction.

In 1991, the national bodies responsible for the production of social housing, including land management and credit supply, research into technologies and support for community management processes, were dismantled. These were replaced by a financial fund to manage the resources allocated to family subsidies, which are distributed at the territorial level and via programmes, on the basis of criteria that varied over time. Years later, a Ministry of Housing was created which so far has not taken a comprehensive view of housing policies and has maintained its emphasis on financial aspects. Indeed, the national government showed an almost total lack of interest in the implementation of the urban reform legislation, did not make much effort to strengthen the management capacity of municipal governments, and for years it was assumed that the private sector would be more efficient in advancing land management.

For around fifteen years, both the individual amount of family benefit (at most, 40 percent of the legal ceiling for social housing) and the budgetary allocation remained low. Difficulties in accessing credit, persistent financial poverty and the scarce supply of private sector housing led to benefits being allocated to families, but years went by without them being able to use the benefits and they became invalid (for detailed analysis from different perspectives on national housing policy over the long term, see Chiappe de Villa, 1999; Maldonado, 2010; Maldonado and Alviar 2012; Ministry of Housing, City and Territory, 2014).

The poor performance of housing policy in terms of families' effective access to adequate housing was particularly evident in the massive influx into the cities of people displaced by the internal armed conflict. The first wave of rural–urban migrations had taken place in the 1960s and 1970s, and gave rise to informal settlements and the emergence of housing agents known as 'pirate developers'. The pirate landlords subdivided and sold off relatively large tracts of land in the peripheries of cities without providing any type of services or infrastructure, and outside urban planning regulations, thus gaining significant profits from land rent. Even so, this form of urban spoliation was accompanied by certain solidarity mechanisms and clientelist networks which provided access to infrastructure and social services, and alleviated unstable conditions. The effects of recent forced displacement to the cities due to the armed conflict (when guerrillas, paramilitaries and even the army caused sustained displacements) demonstrated the limitations of a public policy reduced to the management of demand subsidies to solve the problem of widespread access to housing.

In 2004, the Constitutional Court brought together in a single case numerous writ actions filed throughout the country for the protection of constitutional rights, brought to court either individually or by organisations of the victims of displacement. The court adopted the decision to 'declare the state of institutional affairs'. It then began to press, through orders to public bodies, for a change in national housing policy, and for the greater involvement of municipal governments in improving the effectiveness of the policy. The volume of resources in the national budget was increased, yet without any structural change in policy being implemented.

The response of the national government, echoing the demands of private builders, was to conceive of land policies derived from urban reform legislation as an obstacle to the mass production of housing by the private sector. It began to dismantle them with a number of measures which pursued one main objective: how to speed up the conversion of rural land into urban land, and how to make social housing projects financially attractive to the private sector. In particular it promoted large-scale projects in peripheral zones of cities which lacked sufficient access to transport or places of employment, much less to the facilities and services of urban life.

There are several stages in the evolution of the relationship between housing policy and land use planning, and land policies. It is important to bear in mind that social housing is defined in Colombia, above all, by legally established price ceilings. Initially, these ceilings were implemented to require that certain percentages of the private loan portfolio be allocated to this type of housing, then in relation to housing and land policies. Currently, the regulations include priority housing (*Vivienda de Interés Prioritario*, VIP), with a ceiling of 70 legal monthly minimum wages and social housing (*Vivienda de Interés Social*, VIS) with a monetary ceiling equivalent to 70 legal monthly minimum wages (the monthly minimum wage is around US\$300). However, there is no quality criterion linked to this price limit, which has led to the construction of very small, low-quality housing, except for a few isolated efforts by municipal governments to promote better living conditions.

In 2004, a National Decree (No. 2060) was issued that reduced the minimum land plot for social housing, bypassing municipal standards. A land plot of 35 m^2 was allowed for single-family housing, 70 m^2 for two-family housing and 120 m^2 for multifamily housing, with concessions no greater than 25 percent for public space and amenities. It was adopted as a measure aimed at stimulating private housing construction, which mostly favoured the landowners, with one of the lowest sub-division standards in the world. This led to higher and higher population densities, precisely for those sectors of the population where access to public space and common amenities is most necessary. In 2012, this measure was repealed after the belated recognition that it had been ineffective in increasing social housing construction and, on the contrary, had contributed to the rise in land prices.

In 2010, 'Macro-projects of National Social Interest' were established, a device that allowed the Ministry of Housing to approve housing projects proposed by private developers directly and expeditiously, with the possibility of even repealing the rules associated with municipal land use planning and weakening the powers of municipal governments. The aim was to reduce the demands and expedite the formalities required to convert rural land into urban land, while the national government took control of project management in the long term. The aim was to promote the large-scale production of housing in increasingly remote areas, facilitated by the use of rural land and with little urban planning; this allowed the appropriation of capital gains by private developers.

The result is that the minimum infrastructure requirements, such as access to water and sewerage, are barely met. Moreover, the supply of social services such as education and health or social protection and integration programmes is foisted onto the municipal governments, without them necessarily agreeing to (or being involved in) the decision, not to mention the difficulties imposed on families in terms of transport. We will explore these issues later in an analysis of Soacha, a municipality in the capital city of Bogotá, where national policies have concentrated the production of social housing.

In 2012, the supply subsidy was adopted by Law 1537, which included an important change that recognised the weaknesses of leaving the supply of social housing almost exclusively in the hands of private builders. This law was the basis for a highly publicised national programme of free or full subsidy housing (see Gilbert, 2014). With this law the national government began to allocate quotas to different territorial bodies and put out calls to private builders or create agreements with municipal public bodies for the construction of housing. In land management, this law establishes that each development project (or the incorporation of rural to urban land) that is executed anywhere in the country must allocate 20 percent of that housing at a value of US$20,000. In addition, it provides a framework to allow for express modifications to urban plans Programa de Ordenamiento Territorial (POT, Territorial Regulatory Programme) in order to expand the supply of rural land. Moreover, the design of the calls for proposals envisaged by the law favours large-scale projects, as well as builders of a significant size, because such initiatives require previous experience in terms of the large number of square metres to be built and payment is made at the end of the project.

The free housing programme was first implemented in large cities, where just over 100,000 homes were built between 2012 and 2015. However, its effectiveness, in terms access to quality housing and its impact on conditions of poverty and vulnerability, has not yet been comprehensively assessed. In any case, only 40 percent of the families displaced by armed conflict had access to these houses, despite the fact that their humanitarian situation was what led to the policy change in the first place. A second version for smaller cities and rural municipalities, launched in 2014, has been developed more slowly. Fiscal constraints have led the national government to re-emphasise demand-side subsidies and interest rate subsidies, which are largely absorbed by landowners or private financial institutions (see Sabatini and Brain (2006) for analysis of the impact of housing subsidies on land prices). As a next step, we will now compare the relation between this national housing policy and land policies in the city of Bogotá.

The Bogotá Experience

Bogotá is a city of almost eight million inhabitants and around 2 million dwellings, whose urban area occupies some 40,000 ha. Twenty percent of this urban area was developed from informal occupations where today 40 percent of the population lives in high density. During the second half of the twentieth century 160,000 social housing units were built under public management mechanisms, most of them national, according to data taken from Saldarriaga Roa (1990, records of the Municipal Housing Secretariat). A smaller number were built through community self-management, with progressive development housing.

More recently, the behaviour of the informal sector has changed towards greater densification as a result of self-building on land purchased from pirate developers (generally 72 m^2), where up to four flats are built by its occupants, creating a significant supply of small and precarious housing for rent. However, this supply of affordable rental housing compensates for the lack of formal housing (public or private) being produced and is generating an unequal city, some of it very densely populated.

In 1988, the popular election of municipal mayors began in Colombia, followed in 1990 by the implementation of urban plans, under the guidelines of the urban reform law. The mechanisms that have been applied are: the land bank; the association with owners through land readjustments; the use of public land; the mandatory provision of a proportion of land for social housing or priority housing; and the obligation to develop and build on vacant land within the city (or land designated by the development plan as suitable for urbanisation) within a period of two years (Table 9). If the land is not developed and/or built on by its owners, a state agency can conduct auctions in favour of builders interested in constructing social housing, and the owner is paid a price within the established limits of around US$20,000 or US$38,000.

As indicated in the introduction, the analyses and data contained here have been taken from research I conducted at the Institute of Urban Studies of the National University of Colombia on 'Monitoring Land Policy in Relation to the Formal and Informal Housing Markets in Bogotá' (the results of which have not been published), as well as from the information produced during my tenure as Secretariat of Planning and Secretariat of Housing of the Bogotá Mayor's Office, 2012–2014. The number of social housing units built in the last fifteen years (Table 9) contrasts with those built during some 40 years of

Table 9.   Social Housing Built according to the Instruments Used, 1999–2015

Instrument/agents	Size	No. and type of houses built	Period
Municipal land bank - Metrovivienda	4 projects 397 hectares	46,000 VIP	1999-2015
Mandatory % of land for social housing	Around 1,000 hectares are mixed with other types of housing and uses.	40,000 on site, VIS and VIP in partial plans 6,000 moved to other areas	2002-2014
Mandatory development and construction on vacant land	158 hectares mixed with other uses	15,000 VIS 1,000 VIP	2009-2014
Use of public lands in good locations	6 hectares approx.	3,400 VIP	2012-2015
Public procurement for small-scale projects	5 hectares	1,200 VIP	2013-2015
Private management by different mechanisms	N.D.	68,000 VIS	2000-2015
Total		199,600	

Source: prepared by the author based on information produced by the Planning Secretariat of Bogotá on partial plans, the information system of the Secretariat of Housing and its management reports.

national management. This may indicate the effectiveness of the urban reform law's mechanisms on the one hand, but also suggests that certain builders are moving into this segment of the market, encouraged in particular by the availability of subsidies and tax exemptions. Moreover, it also shows that the lowest priced housing (up to 70 minimum monthly wages) is only built as a result of strong state intervention. When an interest rate subsidy is available from public sources, so-called social housing (with a ceiling of 135 minimum wages) is quite attractive to private builders, because it reaches households where at least one of the members has a formal job, so long as demand in cities like Bogotá is high enough to ensure sales.

From the point of view of urban planning policies, the relationship (sometimes a tension) between the national government or municipal government, builders and families mainly revolves around the following aspects:

a. ease and/or speed of incorporation of low-cost land for medium and large-scale operations;
b. scale of projects;
c. location, including ease of access to the city centre and urban life;
d. social mix and integration;
e. suitability of social housing to the socio-economic conditions of families.

The land bank met builders' expectations regarding the availability of land, insofar as it tried to provide land at the periphery of the city, though within the political-administrative limits of the municipality. In such sites the municipal government assumed all the formalities and risks of land acquisition (including expropriations) carried out the general urban planning works and then sold this urbanised land to the builders in plots from one hectare upwards. However, larger building companies have been most attracted to the flexible approach to urban planning rules which allow them to incorporate rural land and begin development from the start of the chain, from land purchase to construction, albeit with state support in terms of infrastructure. Flexibility implies that few demands are made of the construction companies in terms of comprehensive urban planning, such as access to schools, health facilities, recreation and comprehensive social services. This results in lower living standards for families living in such sites and additional responsibilities for the municipal government.

One of the problems faced by the land bank was that it did not fully apply the logic of this mechanism, in terms of creating a territorial reserve that anticipates the rise in land prices. The price difference results from the purchase of decontaminated land destined for urban use, and makes it possible to finance the costs of urban planning. By not achieving sufficient control over land prices, the selling prices of developed land were not necessarily attractive to developers, especially at an early stage.

One advantage of the land bank, and of the public control of the land, is that, over time, conditions were imposed on the builders creating better housing standards, especially in increasing the size of the houses somewhat. The great disadvantage of this instrument, though, as well as the necessary regulatory flexibility, is that it concentrates a large number of families with similar socio-economic characteristics together (because of the same size of housing, the same criteria for access to state programmes, the same housing financing conditions). This reinforced the residential segregation that characterises Latin American cities.

Since 2003, two different lines of policy have been proposed which emphasise the protection of environmental zones and the management of land for social housing, alongside the efforts of successive Bogotá city governments which have tried to comprehensively apply the mechanisms engendered in Laws 9 of 1989 and 388 of 1997. The national government, meanwhile, has tried to weaken these instruments, which were assumed to be an obstacle to real estate activity, leading to the reinforcement of segregation and inequality. The strongest instance of this tension was the decision by the Ministry of Housing to promote the construction of social housing in Soacha, a municipality bordering on Bogotá, whose population is around 500,000. Soacha has one of the highest concentrations of poverty and informality in the country, and is home to a high percentage of families displaced by the armed conflict. This decision was imposed on a municipality that does not have the institutional

Figure 5.   Location of Social housing Projects in Soacha, Colombia

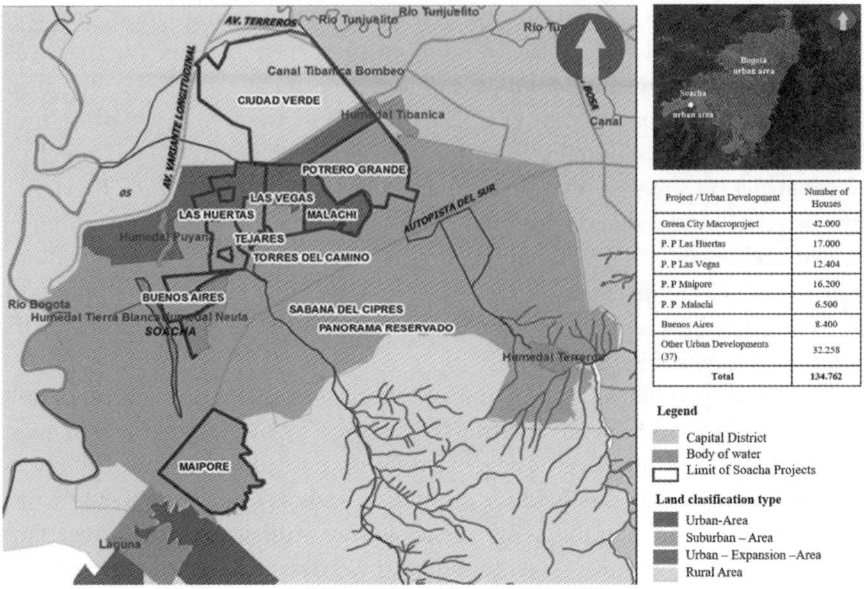

Project / Urban Development	Number of Houses
Green City Macroproject	42.000
P. P Las Huertas	17.000
P. P Las Vegas	12.404
P. P Maipore	16.200
P. P Malacki	6.500
Buenos Aires	8.400
Other Urban Developments (37)	32.258
Total	134.762

Legend

    Capital District
    Body of water
    Limit of Soacha Projects

Land clasification type

    Urban-Area
    Suburban – Area
    Urban – Expansion –Area
    Rural Area

Source: Empresa de Acueducto y Alcantarillado de Bogotá, 2014.

or fiscal strength of Bogotá, and led to the creation of formal projects which, while they were built quickly and are of good quality, lack the social infrastructure and transport linkages needed by members of these households who work mostly in Bogotá.

Among the Macro-projects of National Social Interest previously referred to, the one with the largest number of dwellings is located in Soacha (Figure 5). In a single 328-hectare project (run by just a few building companies), 49,000 social housing units are being built on rural land converted directly into urban land. This project resulted from a resolution of the Ministry of Housing, and was subsidised by national and Bogotá financing which funded the construction of water and sewage infrastructure. In other words, public financial reserves were used to create significant capital gains for landowners. However, even today when a large part of the project has been built and there are serious problems with the functioning of mass transport (given that this suburban area does not yet have a metro and depends exclusively on the Rapid Transit Bus), the ministry's attitude has been elusive in the face of such problems.

Ciudad Verde (the Green City macroproject) was initiated in 2009 and the national government supported other private projects around it over the next few years building about 140,000 homes, almost all of them social

Table 10. Amount of Housing built in Bogotá and Soacha 2004–2015

Year	Bogotá				Soacha			
	VIS	VIP	Another type	Total	VIS	VIP	Another type	Total
2004	8,600	4,381	15,060	28,041	432	342	14	788
2005	5,882	8.938	19,071	33,891	342	970	9	1,321
2006	8,621	11,418	22,740	42,779	1,466	928	20	2,414
2007	10,925	8,380	26,587	45,892	3,153	2,043	156	5,352
2008	7,372	6,413	22,693	36,478	1,542	1,480	15	3,037
2009	9,239	5,204	16,044	30,487	1,693	413	15	2,121
2010	12,184	5,468	23,993	41,645	3,909	549	9	4,467
2011	12,158	2,793	25,485	40,436	12,299	1,090	242	13,631
2012	7,455	4,381	23,323	35,159	7,821	1,900	102	9,823
2013	5,683	1,710	24,417	31,810	12,240	5,410	272	17,922
2014	6,425	7,672	21,255	35,352	6,793	2,350	460	9,603
2015	8,355	5,359	19,582	33,296	8,306	743	885	9,934
Total	102,899	72,117	260,250	435,266	59,996	18.218&$$$;	2,199	80,413

VIS: social housing, up to 135 monthly minimum wages; VIP: priority housing, up to 135 monthly minimum wages; another type: non-price-controlled housing. Minimum monthly wage around US$280.
Source: National Department of Statistics (DANE),

housing or priority housing. All told, this will double the population of the municipality. Most of Bogota's large construction companies acquired land within the macroprojects encouraged by the offer of land that already met construction standards, as opposed to the slower approval processes of partial plans. The latter, in accordance with urban reform laws, sustains the readjustment of land with an equitable distribution of burdens and benefits, and requires landowners to partly finance the required infrastructure. As a result of these projects, the proportion of social housing initiatives in Soacha began to increase, as shown in the Table 10.

From an average of 4000 homes under construction per year in Soacha up to 2010, the number of homes under construction per year increased from 2011 and reached a peak of around 18,000 dwellings in 2013 (Table 10). Moreover, in just three years, the construction of more than 41,000 homes began, a situation that only started to reverse in 2014, as a result of the policies of the government of Bogotá in the period 2012–2015 – another source of tension with the national government.

The central aim of the Bogotá city government's housing policies (and indeed of its government programme in general) was to combat social segregation, including residential segregation, and it sought to improve social housing locations and reduce the scale of housing projects in favour of social mixing. I witnessed these discussions first hand, when I was Secretary of Planning and Housing. To this end, the city government used various mechanisms, such as: compulsory construction on vacant land within the already built-up urban landscape of the city, subject to a forced sale by public auction; the use of fiscal assets (public property) to initiate demonstration projects in good locations which would break the pattern of segregation present in the city; the mandatory use of proportions of land for social housing; and partnerships with landowners and builders, to support the management of those projects developed from partial plans where their promoters agreed to leave the land for priority housing in the same project, without moving it to other areas of the city. This had a double effect, not only in terms of resources, but also in improving the possibilities of social mixing. This mechanism was important because previously those leading projects in zones which could be put to profitable use would often transfer their mandatory obligation to build priority housing to other zones and projects where social housing dominated. Alternatively, they would pay an equivalent monetary sum to the municipal body operating as a land bank (called Metrovivienda) to develop the projects elsewhere.

The government programme, called 'Bogotá Humana' (Alcaldía de Bogotá DC, 2012), went further than the national government and imposed the mandatory proportion of land destined for priority or social housing, not only on land destined for urban expansion, but also for projects linked to the renewal and densification of the city. This implied a commitment to greater social integration and the breaking down of resistance to the proximity of poorer social groups in a country with one of the highest levels of inequality in the world. It also meant having a significant impact on the urban land market, reducing prices by 20 percent in the first year and by 30 percent in the second year for housing valued at 70 minimum monthly wages.

The first objective to be achieved with this range of mechanisms was to return responsibility for social housing in Soacha that had been in the hands of the national government back to Bogotá. It also aimed to insert small-scale social housing projects into the existing urban fabric right across the city. All this took place within the framework of the National Programme for Free Housing (this policy is analysed from different perspectives by Gilbert, 2014; Correa et al., 2014; Giraldo Isaza, 2014; Carreño Fuentes, 2016). A significant number of quotas were allocated to Soacha and a total of 8100 were assigned within Bogotá. This project was managed by the Metrovivienda land bank but the Ministry of Housing wanted to develop all the housing in Campo Verde located at the border with Soacha and in an area which had recently experienced flood threats. The government of Bogotá decided to withdraw the Campo Verde project until new studies on flood threat and mitigation were carried out, and asked the national government for support in developing a number of small projects within the city, in line with its local government programme.

The timing of revitalisation projects does not coincide with the timing of elections, though, when what matters are campaigns and inaugurations, not the durability and long-term effects of housing. Nor are revitalisation projects in sync with the timescales of the major builders, who enter the market in social housing, as already indicated, according to the regulatory and financial possibilities of developing large projects which offer significant economies of scale.

The aim of the government's 'Bogotá Humana' programme was not only to reduce the scale of housing projects for the poorest families who require priority housing, but also to support small and medium building enterprises, as a way of diversifying and strengthening those builders who had always been reluctant to participate in social housing production. It also allowed for the revival of popular housing organisations which had been disadvantaged and weakened by the system of direct subsidies, such as community-based mechanisms and the self-management of housing production. All this clashed with national policy.

In response to the decision of the municipal government of Bogotá to establish mandatory proportions of social housing throughout the city, the Ministry of Housing issued a national decree that established obstacles which worked against the application of this measure in areas other than urban expansion. There was no other explanation to account for the ministry's refusal to intervene in the land market, which they considered to be too strong, and their reluctance to introduce social housing in areas intended for social groups with a greater capacity to pay.

Changes in the Location of Priority Housing Projects in Bogotá

In Figure 6 we can see that the development of major projects was located outside the expanded centre, that is, in the periphery of the city. The projects in the western zone, promoted by the Metrovivienda land bank, and those in the northeastern zone created a concentration of up to 15,000 social housing units. In contrast, the aforementioned mechanisms encouraged social housing projects to be dispersed throughout the urban area, allowing poor families access to the various infrastructure, equipment, work and lifestyle opportunities offered by the city.

However, one valuable opportunity which arose due to this change in orientation of housing policy at both national and municipal levels became a point of partisan confrontation between two governments with very different political orientations. This project was created following the order of the Constitutional Court to protect the rights of the population displaced by the internal armed conflict. However, the two levels of government were unable

Figure 6.   Location of Priority Housing Projects in Bogotá, Colombia

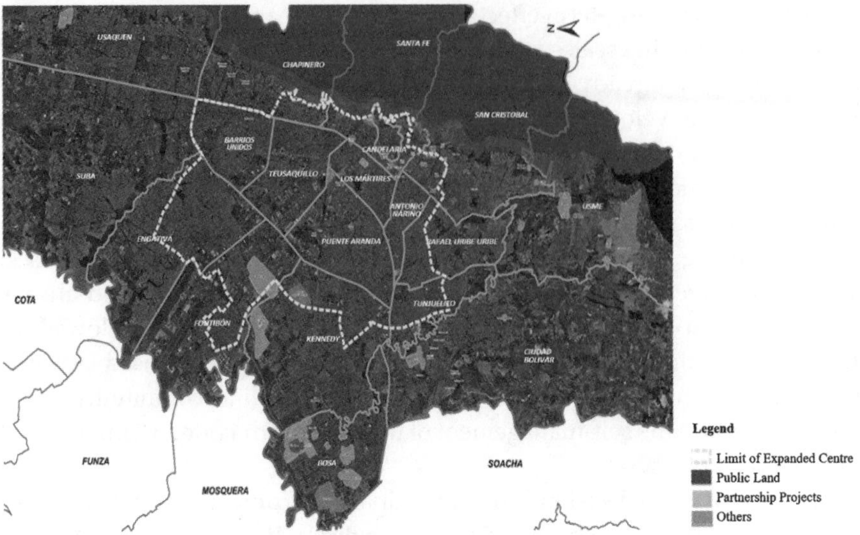

Source: prepared by the author based on information produced by the Planning Secretariat of Bogotá on partial plans.

to create sufficient consensus to articulate their strategies and instruments in favour of families with urgent needs for access to housing. Even so, the construction of 20,000 units of priority housing began and projects were planned for another 10,000, the most significant located within private developers' partial plans. Thanks to the management and financial support provided by the government of Bogotá, these developers agreed to leave the housing for low-income families in place despite the probable impact on property prices, which is a common cause of defiance.

The resistance to housing programmes committed to social integration came not only from the national government but also from the media and from neighbours, even in low-income and middle-income sectors. It was necessary to develop long consultation programmes and hold sustained discussion with the neighbourhood residents in order to reduce opposition to the arrival of the projects. Also, it was crucial to create community building and cohabitation programmes for families with a history of poverty and exclusion who came to live in a heterogeneous property zone, and buildings, where problems of violence and insecurity easily arise (see, as an illustration of this, the journalistic note on the subject: Correa et al., 2014).

There was an episode that exacerbated tensions and tested both the capacity of the government of Bogotá to build consensus and the capacity of society to allow spatial transformation. It also opens the door to questions about the possibilities and limitations of social mixing. One of the instruments of the housing policy was the use of fiscal property land to develop demonstration projects. In around 2014, the availability of four land plots emerged which until then had been destined for public car parks, located in areas of high population income and profitable usage. Since the government programme is mandatory during the mayor's four-year term, the municipal entities began to manage the project. The reaction against it, especially from the media, was excessive, given that the actions of the mayor's office had been strongly contested, with accusations of populism which typifies leftist governments of the region. The leaders of those targeted by the media campaign emerged, full of dignity, to explain to the media that they and their families were people like any other, and that they were capable of taking on the challenge of social mixing. In the midst of the controversy, a councillor of the same political party as the Minister of Housing managed to obtain the suspension of the projects in a legal action motivated by the alleged negative impact on the state's assets, given that the land allocated for priority housing could be utilised more profitably, thus devaluing the land.

The position of those private developers who agree to build projects that include social mixing and set out to develop commercial development (offices and shops) as well as housing for middle- and high-income groups, and priority housing is thus refreshing. The idea is to build homes with similar exterior features, but priority housing homes would have simpler internal finishes and be home to people in more difficult social situations. This addresses the twin challenges of changing the association between poor people and the Latin American slums that dominate Latin American cities, and also of changing entrenched segregation mentalities.

It should be noted that it is not easy to implement the building of houses worth a controlled price of around US$20,000 in areas of profitable use and high-income population. The dilemma will always exist, of projects that are not large enough to generate ghettos or so small that they are easily absorbed by the environment or give rise to situations of social tension. These are government dilemmas and social dilemmas that have no easy answers. However, they were part of a government programme aimed at dispersing such housing throughout the urban area, in small and medium-size projects, so that one day any inhabitant of the city would have a priority housing project about twenty minutes from their home. It was proposed with the objective of social transformation in one of the most complex aspects of urban life.

On the other hand, the government of Bogota began the work of creating and strengthening social housing organisations, most of whose members were victims of the armed conflict. The local government allocated its own land with the purpose of adding the municipal subsidy to the national subsidy and created other special repair funds for these families. Progress was made in the management of six projects of around 1000 homes, but the Ministry of Housing delayed the release of their financial contribution, which made finalising the finances impossible and made organisation very difficult, adversely affecting families uprooted by the conflict.

In October 2015, the elections were won by a mayor whose party was in alliance with that of the Minister of Housing, and the now Vice-President of the Republic. In other words, after sixteen years, the vision of land use planning and housing policy in both the national and district governments finally fully converged. The mayor's term began in January 2016. His government programme eliminated the municipal housing subsidy so that the financing and, consequently, the orientation of the policy, has been left entirely to the national government.

Some of the policies which advanced social housing and integration still remain, such as the mandatory proportions of land earmarked for social housing in urban expansion projects, which should lead to a certain level of social mix in large urban projects such as the one planned for the northern part of the city. The land reallocation scheme which entails the equitable distribution of burdens and benefits also allows for the allocation of proportions of land for social housing, while owners receive an average land price that also includes land for more profitable uses. However, the mayor has announced major projects in Soacha and Mosquera (another smaller neighbouring municipality), and it is to be hoped that most of the lower-priced social housing will be sent to these surrounding municipalities, with the adverse effects in terms of infrastructure and services already noted, zones that have not yet been able to form a metropolitan authority. Moreover, an official from the Mayor's Office sent a message out to the displaced persons organisations, saying that while they will seek solutions, they cannot continue with the populist policy of building socially mixed housing as it is unsustainable.

Conclusion

This assessment of the key components and central points of conflict associated with both national and city-wide housing policies in Bogotá demonstrates some of the challenges linked to this vital issue in Latin America's urban agenda. They include: the availability of sufficient fiscal resources; the type of mechanisms deployed; and the effect that they generate in terms of both owners and financial institutions. Scant attention is paid to land use planning policies and, therefore, to the problems associated with the location of housing and, more specifically, of the place of low-income people and their families in urban life, as well as the environmental and social impact of major housing projects located on the periphery of cities. The political decision-maker thinks little about what life is like for a teenager in a family with a monthly income of US$300 in a house of 40 m² or less in an enclosed complex, without nearby access to a library, a film club, or a community cultural project. This question is hardly ever asked when it comes to housing policies, despite their lasting effects on the integration of young people to social and political life or, a matter at the forefront of urban concerns, to crime and security.

The spatial distribution of social groups and disputes over urban space occurs outside the housing policy design, except for slow changes charted here as a result of residential segregation or the improvement of housing location. The informal city was seen for years by some as an escape valve created by low-income people, given that the system as unable to provide sufficient and adequate housing. For some urban theorists, it was interpreted as a way out, a form of resistance and creativity in the face of exclusionary public policies. The problem has existed for years, and following periods of repression or rejection policies moved towards legalising of land tenure and neighbourhood improvement programmes as the best way to formulate a social housing policy. Indeed, national and municipal governments in many cities have made significant investment in public services and transport infrastructure, social facilities and green areas. But cities will always be indelibly marked by areas with lower urban standards, stigmatised, seen as different and dangerous. Some low-income areas, due to the growth of cities, end up occupying good locations, and their occupants must resist the pressures of gentrification and expulsion by public action or the market.

Yet the question remains about how to deal with the problems that arise in the large housing zones peripheral to cities built by developers where they have constructed social housing but not the necessary amenities essential to urban living. Integrating such sites will be much more difficult than in the neighbourhoods that developed informally where, from the beginning, there was much greater diversity – in architecture, in the residents, in the streets, in neighbourhood life, and in patterns of solidarity. There are also other aspects that have an impact on daily life, even when governments are committed to overcoming segregation. There is the widespread practice of housing people in buildings (sometimes high towers) or in groups, due to the scarcity of land that substantially transform the daily life. Moreover, housing production is at the centre of one of the processes that creates the greatest tensions within capitalist development – the distribution and appropriation of urban rents. Speculative processes are so powerful that it is hard for environmental demands or social needs in the city to take precedence. Whether they are organised or not, people end up having to adapt to the conditions of exclusion and segregation that speculative processes impose.

It may take as long, or even longer than the four decades of Colombia's legal reforms for land use planning mechanisms to achieve these urgent social objectives, such as better conditions of access to and enjoyment of the city by low-income groups. First of all, it will be a difficult task to overcome the traditional conception within urban planning or regulation that land use be understood in terms of land value. More generally, that real estate is understood in relation to the mechanisms of distribution of land use based on control, separation and segregation and the allocation of the right to build, with the aim of maintaining high land prices, on the assumption that everyone can participate in this form of wealth through private property. On the other hand, we should bear in mind the strong ideological and institutional resistance to such understandings, and the counter-logics which emphasise access to, and enjoyment of, housing in the community. Also important are the inhabitants' economic rationales, which are shaped by a context of reduced income for the majority of the population and the structural weakness – if the term can still be used – of wage relations. In fact, all of this is evidence of the crisis of a model of social policies based on an increasingly weak and reduced wage ratio. The idea of public action and the welfare state itself, in which resources were mobilised for the 'reproduction of the labour force' as well as wages, has less and less capacity to ensure the survival of the low-income groups.

Low-income inhabitants in Latin American cities have demonstrated their capacity to mobilise resources – monetary, technological, social, legal, organisational – and to build their homes in the long term, as a life project that gives them security. These practices combine the relations of neighbourliness and proximity, based on small-scale economies (both in terms of volumes and distances). These are combined with those of the state which are linked to a generalised market, in many cases mediated by the relations that Polanyi (1944) calls redistribution. These appear due to the concentration of authority in the hands of certain actors and the distribution of competition via territorial networks that ensure the circulation of products and resources, and maintain relations with the outside world. It remains to be seen how these relationships operate when the supply of formal housing grows, within a structure that prioritises the economic activation of the construction sector and that ensures a distribution of resources that reinforces inequality. As Zigmunt Bauman suggested, one of the strongest and most agonising expressions of the modern civilising project is the attempt to destroy the plurality of ways of life on the basis of the profound conviction that we are building a way of life that is clearly superior to any other, known or imaginable, and that its triumphant expansion is in itself assured by its own intrinsic power of attraction.

Housing is a need that is neither expendable nor replaceable, which protects human beings from the conditions of the environment and provides them with a space to carry out their daily activities that correspond to the sphere of privacy. A lack of housing is thus a mark of extreme marginalisation and has a permanent impact on living conditions and as a consequence creates ruptures in the social bond. Moreover, housing contributes to the construction of urban space and is an essential factor in the organisation of territory. For all these reasons, the provision of this necessity is assumed in almost all societies to be a responsibility of social effort, or, seen in another way, as part and parcel of solidarity commitments. But the way that this premise is translated into concrete mechanisms, such as those discussed in this chapter, may reaffirm these objectives or impose distortions and contradictions.

So how can we achieve better living conditions and social integration in the midst of a weakened workforce society and its mechanisms of redistribution, but also of control and discipline? How can we control the tendency to insert the community's needs and practices, viewing them as merely one more resource in the wider market? At a time when alternatives for social transformation other than social reforms have disappeared (and, therefore, the hope for better living conditions which depend on them) the scant response of Latin American elites and governments is worrying.

References

Álvarez, L. F., Perpiñan, F., David, S. and Saucedo, M. (2014) *Análisis de la ejecución del programa Locomotora de Vivienda entre los años 2010–2013 propuesto por el presidente de Colombia, Juan Manuel Santos*. Unpublished master's dissertation, Universidad EAFIT: Medellin.

Alcaldía de Bogotá D.C. (2012b) 'Plan de desarrollo 2012–2016, Bogotá humana'. [WWW document]. URL http://oab2.ambientebogota.gov.co/es/documentacion-e-investigaciones/resultado-busqueda/plan-de-desarrollo-2012-2016-bogota-humana [accessed 31 January 2019].

Brain, I. and Sabatini, F. (2006) 'Los precios del suelo en alza carcomen el subsidio habitacional, contribuyendo al deterioro en la calidad y localización de la vivienda social'. *PRO* 4: 2–13.

Carreño, F. C. (2016) 'Evaluación de la política pública de vivienda gratuita: ¿Hacia una disminución del déficit?' Available at: https://www.researchgate.net/publication/301957233_Evaluacion_de_la_Politica_Publica_de_Vivienda_Gratuita [accessed 31 January 2019].

Chiappe de Villa, M. L. (1999) 'La política de vivienda de interés social en Colombia en los noventa'. *Serie Financiamiento del Desarrollo* 80. CEPAL: Santiago de Chile. https://repositorio.cepal.org/bitstream/handle/11362/5287/1/S995336_es.pdf [accessed 31 January 2019].

Corporación Colegio de Villa de Leiva, Universidad Nacional de Colombia. Sede Medellín. Centro de Estudios del Habitat Popular CEHAP (1996) *Estado, ciudad y vivienda. Urbanismo y vivienda estatal en Colombia 1918–1990*. INURBE: Santa Fe de Bogotá.

Correa, P., Cuevas, A., Silva, S. and Baena, P. (2014) 'La otra cara de las viviendas gratis'. *El Espectador,* 4 octubre, Bogotá. Available at: https://

www.elespectador.com/noticias/nacional/otra-cara-de-viviendas-gratis-articulo-520618 [accessed 31 January 2019].

Dávila, J. et al. (2006) 'Suelo urbano y vivienda para la población de bajos ingresos. Estudios de caso: Bogotá-Soacha-Mosquera, Medellín y Área Metropolitana: informe final'. Development Planning Unit (DPU), University College London: London. [WWW document]. URL http://discovery.ucl.ac.uk/1328432/1/Davila_DPU_2006_Suelo_Urbano_y_Vivienda_Cities_Alliance-DNP_Minvivienda.pdf [accessed 31 January 2019].

Gilbert, A. (2014) 'Free Housing for the Poor: An Effective Way to Address Poverty?'. *Habitat International* **41**(1): 253–261.

Giraldo, F. (2014) 'Las "casas gratis" del gobierno no son como las pintan'. *Razón Pública*, 27 October. [WWW document]. URL http://www.razonpublica.com/index.php/politica-y-gobierno-temas-27/8005-las-casas-%E2%80%9Cgratis%E2%80%9D-del-gobierno-no-son-como-las-pintan-i.html [accessed 31 January 2019].

Maldonado, M. (2009) '¿Cómo garantizar el derecho a la vivienda? Acceso y disfrute de una vivienda digna por parte de la población en condición de desplazamiento' in C. Rodríguez (ed.) *Más allá del desplazamiento. Políticas, derechos y superación del desplazamiento forzado en Colombia*. Universidad de los Andes Ediciones, UNIANDES: Bogotá, 146–222.

Maldonado, M. (2012) 'Limitaciones de las políticas de suelo y vivienda social para superar la exclusión social. La experiencia de Bogotá' in C. Salazar (ed.) *Irregular. Suelo y mercado en América Latina*. El Colegio de México: Mexico FD, 159–212.

Maldonado, M. and Alviar, H. (2012) 'Recomendaciones para avanzar en el goce efectivo del derecho a la vivienda' in M. J. Cepeda (ed.) *Desplazamiento forzado: reflexiones para salir de la encrucijada*. Universidad de los Andes Ediciones, UNIANDES USAID, OIM: Bogotá, 52–106.

Maldonado, M. and Hurtado, A. (2014) 'La declaratoria de desarrollo y construcción prioritarios (sujeta a venta forzosa en pública subasta) en Colombia: La experiencia de Bogotá, 2008–2012' in M. Smolka and F. Furtado (eds.) *Instrumentos notables de políticas de suelo en América Latina*. Lincoln Institute of Land Policy: Cambridge, 103–108.

Polanyi, K. (1944) *The Great Transformation. The Political and Economic Origins of Our Time*. Beacon Press: Boston. [WWW document]. URL http://inctpped.ie.ufrj.br/spiderweb/pdf_4/Great_Transformation.pdf [accessed 31 January 2019].

República de Colombia (2012a) *Ley 1537. Diario oficial* No. 48.467, 20 January. [WWW document]. URL https://docs.supersalud.gov.co/PortalWeb/Juridica/Leyes/L1537012.pdf [accessed 31 January 2019].

República de Colombia (2004) Ministerio de Ambiente, Vivienda y Desarrollo Territorial. *Decreto 2060*, 24 de junio. [WWW document]. URL http://www.minvivienda.gov.co/Decretos%20Vivienda/2060%20-%202004.pdf [accessed 31 January 2019].

República de Colombia, Contraloría General de la República (2006) *Evaluación de la política pública de vivienda social*. Contraloría Delegada para el Sector Infraestructura Física y Telecomunicaciones, Comercio Exterior y Desarrollo Regional: Bogotá.

República de Colombia, Ministerio de Vivienda, Ciudad y Territorio para el Séptimo Foro Urbano Mundial (2014) 'Colombia: 100 años de políticas habitacionales' ['Colombia: 100 Years of Housing Policies']. Ministerio de Vivienda, Ciudad y Territorio para el Séptimo Foro Urbano Mundial: Bogotá. [WWW document]. URL https://es.slideshare.net/Minvivienda/libro-100-aos-de-polticas-habitacionales [accessed 31 January 2019].

Universidad Nacional de Colombia, Instituto de Estudios Urbanos, Proyecto Debates de Gobierno Urbano (2010a) 'Plan de Ordenamiento Zonal del Norte: Áreas protegidas, financiación de infraestructuras y vivienda de interés prioritario'. Workshop No. 1, Bogotá. [WWW document]. URL http://www.institutodeestudiosurbanos.com/descargas/cat_view/147-eventos/182-debates-de-gobierno-urbano/184-talleres.html [accessed 31 January 2019].

Universidad Nacional de Colombia, Instituto de Estudios Urbanos, Proyecto Debates de Gobierno Urbano (2010b) 'La formación de los precios en relación con las decisiones de ordenamiento territorial en el borde norte de Bogotá'. Workshop No. 2, Bogotá. [WWW document]. URL http://www.institutodeestudiosurbanos.com/descargas/cat_view/147-eventos/182-debates-de-gobierno-urbano/184-talleres.html [accessed 31 January 2019].

Universidad Nacional de Colombia, Instituto de Estudios Urbanos, Proyecto Debates de Gobierno Urbano (2010c) 'Operación Nuevo Usme'. Workshop No. 4, Bogotá. [WWW document]. URL http://www.institutodeestudiosurbanos.com/descargas/cat_view/147-eventos/182-debates-de-gobierno-urbano/184-talleres.html [accessed 31 January 2019].

4

Cure or Vaccinate, Two Contrasting Policies:.Regularisation vs. Land Reserve in Sustainable Urban Development

CARLOS H. MORALES SCHECHINGER

Erasmus Universiteit, Rotterdam, Netherlands

Introduction

If Plenty of Urban Land is Available for Housing, What is the Problem? A Critique of Official Diagnosis and Remedies.

The Programa Sectorial de Desarrollo Agrario, Territorial y Urbano 2013–2018 (PSDATU, The Sector Plan for Agrarian, Territorial and Urban Development) indicates that in 131 cities of more than 50,000 inhabitants, of which 59 are metropolitan areas, 495,000 hectares of vacant land were identified, 85,000 of which are vacant intra-urban plots (SEDATU, 2013: 1). This means that approximately 19.8 million homes could be housed on this land (at a density of 40 dwellings per hectare) of which 3.4 million could be located within the current urban area. In addition, and according to the Registro de Reservas Territoriales Públicas y Privadas (RENARET, Registry of Public and Private Land Reserve), of a sample of 110,000 hectares of land reserves, 59 percent are within the current urban areas, that is, 64,900 hectares. The Directorate of Economic Housing Studies of the *Sociedad Hipotecaria Federal* (SHF, 2016: 1:3, Federal Mortgage Society) estimated that the demand for new-build housing, is 320,774 homes, plus an additional 716,168 to cover the housing shortfall. This equates to a total housing demand of 1,036,942 homes in 2016. Assuming that similar levels of demand will be generated over the next twenty years, which would amount to 20.7 million dwellings, it is possible to assume that the current vacant area would be sufficient to meet the housing requirement for most of the next two decades.

What makes the vacant land suitable for housing is not entirely clear-cut, but given that the PSDATU 2013–2018 indicates that the estimated vacant land is intra-urban, it implies that it is located in at least one of the perimeters of urban containment. These are: Urban Type 1, consolidated urban areas with access to employment; Urban Type 2, areas in the process of consolidation; and Urban Type 3, areas adjacent to the urban area. Vacant land located in Urban Types 2 and 3 also implies proximity to infrastructure and urban facilities, as well as being close to urban activities.

In short, it can be said that the urban land available for housing physically exists, that an important section of it has infrastructure and that there is no legal impediment for it to be designated for housing use; suitable land is not 'scarce'. Since 1992, the land belonging to *ejidos* (land held in common by a specific community) and *comunidades* has been eligible to enter the formal market, although before that date this was also possible by means of expropriation. In these circumstances, it is difficult to argue that the problem of Mexican cities is scarcity of urban land, although the official view continues to consider it so. In the 2013–2018 PSDATU, the federal government stated that: 'A significant number of urban development plans establish areas of urbanisable land far in excess of long-term needs, which makes it difficult to move towards compact city models and promotes land speculation' (SEDATU, 2013: 73).

To solve this problem, the same programme proposes as a strategy: 'to foresee the need for land reserves for the development of human settlements, population centres and metropolitan areas' and proposes six specific lines of action. These are: to identify, register, quantify and evaluate public and private land reserves acquired for housing purposes; to coordinate the development of projects with the public, private and social sectors; to constitute land reserves and offer land for urban development; to guarantee the sustainability of regional development in population centres (SEDATU, 2013: 85, 86). The creation of land reserves implies that the aforementioned land is set aside and that the reserves are used to promote the orderly growth of the city, regardless of its tenure regime. While this does not require land to be government property, this possibility is not ruled out. In fact, in strategy 2.2. of the same plan, which refers to the control of urban expansion, one of the lines of action indicates that actions at the three levels of government and the social and private sectors should be coordinated and encouraged in order to promote land management.

In a different vein, the *Comisión para la Regularización de la Tenencia de la Tierra* (CORETT, Land Tenure Regularisation Commission) considers that in Mexico 90,000 plots are subdivided 'irregularly' per annum (SEDESOL, 2010, cited in DOF, 2013: 78). According to the Housing Research and Documentation Centre and the Federal Mortgage Society (CIDOC and SHF, 2010: 87), these subdivisions are presumably not suitable for urban development. The state agencies link this lack of suitable land to the failure to comply with urban and building regulations; to the illegal encroachment or sale of land; to inappropriate topography; to the lack of services, infrastructure, facilities, roads and transport; and to the site's remoteness from consolidated urban areas. Thus, at least 14 percent of housing is dealt with informally. CORETT has regularised land tenure in these subdivisions for 43 years and has done so at a rate of 58,140 plots per year, that is, it only regularises two-thirds of the dwellings built via the informal sector each year. Although the organisation has focused mainly on Informal Settlements (ISs) on land belonging to agrarian communities, other agencies have done so for other types of tenure, yet there is a significant backlog accumulating.

At present, the Programa Sectorial de Desarrollo Agrario, Territorial y Urbano 2013–2018 (PSDATU, Sectorial Programme for Agrarian, Territorial and Urban Development) continues to include lines of action related to the issue, but the regularisation of the ISs has been weakened, as Salazar's chapter in this volume indicates. Yet the land policy in Mexico seemingly continues to adhere to Hernando de Soto's approach (2000), which maintains that the granting of legal documents of ownership will allow access to financial resources for the households, since '[...] it adds value to the family wealth and offers guarantees that support its eventual sale' (CIDOC and SHF, 2007: 42). The programme continues to focus on the modernisation of Public Property Registries (RPPs), aiming to promote spatial planning as a means of enhancing people's wellbeing and achieving efficient land use. This objective is supported by the following strategies: (1.1) promoting inter-institutional and intergovernmental coordination with local authorities and society to improve land planning and management; (1.2) providing tenure security through regularisation and certification of ownership; (1.3) modernising the RPPs and the National Agrarian Registry, that is, registries at state and municipal levels, and the national rural property registry; (1.4) regularising informal human settlements according to land use planning; and (1.5) granting legal certainty for those holding *ejido* land and communal land tenure, in order to guarantee the rights of agrarian individuals (DOF, 2013).

Although, parallel to this, programmes for housing improvement subsidies do exist, it is not always possible for ISs settlers to obtain them due to the prerequisite that their land tenure status needs to be resolved. There are also programmes that improve the urban infrastructure of these settlements; in this case, the allocation of public resources for water, sanitation, electrification and transport is separate from the regularisation of land tenure.

In short, there is enough suitable land in cities, but it is not used to address the demand for residential use. Access to land is therefore obtained, at least partially, through informal means. Current land policy measures include, on the one hand, correcting the legal status of informally occupied land by regularising it and, to some extent, by providing it with services. On the other hand, and to a lesser extent, they are preventing informal occupation through direct state intervention in growth areas and inducing settlement in existing urban areas. Both policies operate via the same framework, the exchange and distribution of land through the market. On the supply side, owners – private, agrarian communities and government agencies – request payments, in currency or in kind, for giving up the use of their land. On the demand side, users or intermediaries make outlays, in currency or in kind, to gain access to such land. Users can be households, cooperatives, or public entities that buy a plot of land, while developers act as intermediaries, buying large tracts of land to develop housing, or public entities acquire land reserves.

The curative policy of regularisation of urban land tenure, together with the processes and institutions established in Mexico to implement them, have basically created a land transfer system which operates outside any administrative system of public distribution. The preventive policy recognises the role of the market, as it focuses its strategy on the development of housing estates where the commercial logic dominates, as well as the public acquisition of land reserves, according to the prevailing market. The compensation paid for public acquisitions – even in the case of expropriations – and its sale to developers and users are based on observing market behaviour.

Both formal and informal markets are thoroughly integrated. Competition for locations within the city takes place in the same forum: the market. The informal and the formal are opposite ends of a spectrum where, on the one hand, legal provisions are fully complied with and, on the other, none are complied with. The 2013–2018 PSDATU has been an attempt to articulate existing programmes that treated curative and preventive policies as if they operated independently, as if the application of one did not affect the other. However, this initiative has not generated new approaches. The policy of regulating land tenure is not new, and despite its limitations it remains central to official discourse. The policy of land reserve has been rather cyclical and its impact has been much smaller. To know whether these policies can interact and, more importantly, have an effect on the pattern of housing, it is necessary to reflect on how the urban land market operates and how public policies can influence it. The following sections are devoted to this.

Understanding the Anatomy: Some Peculiarities of the Urban Land Market

As referred to by several authors, land trading has unique characteristics (see Ricardo, 1963 and Alonso, 1964; and later authors such as Eckert et al., 1990; Smolka, 2002, 2003; Jaramillo, 2003; Morales 2004, 2006; Cagmani, 2005; Needham, 2006). Among them, the relative irreproducibility of land stands out, not only because of the difficulty of creating land as a physical support for activities in general, but also because its character and location within the wider environment and society cannot be exactly replicated. Also various land buyers tend to concentrate their preference on a few locations – as is well known in the world's cities – but the creation of similar locations requires a slow and costly collective effort. As cities are not built overnight, land supply is inelastic, i.e. structurally scarce. Additionally, the characteristics of a specific location are very difficult to destroy because their duration is very long term, even when the physical conditions of a place deteriorate over time without the owner having intervened. For example, a disaster can destroy land improvements, whether they be infrastructure or buildings, but not spatial relationships; the latter often lead to reconstruction on the spot.

It is also important to note that the actors involved in the land market have particular characteristics. On the supply side, for example, there is usually a distinction between public, private and social owners, yet other categories are also recognised: (i) the owner-occupant who, when offering their land or property on the market, seeks to recover at least enough money to buy another property with similar characteristics to enable them to continue to occupy property; (ii) the owner-investor, who acquires land or property to resell or develop in order to obtain at least a profit at the average rate that similar capital yields for the economy as a whole; and (iii) the inheritor landowner, who accesses the land or property without paying for it, who does not need to use it, and who retains it while there is no pressure to sell it. Of these three types, the owner-investor is the one who tends to act with economic rationale and is the one who economists tend to keep in mind when explaining the fundamental concepts of the operation of the land market. The owner-occupant and inheritor landowners are the ones who make the study of the land market much more complex than that of other markets so it means we have to involve other disciplines such as law and politics to help us address the topic.

Understanding the economic rationale of owners is useful in explaining some of the forces governing the market, but it is also necessary to understand the notion of ownership with which the market operates. It is difficult to find pure examples of each type of owner in the real world and each land transaction combines behaviours that characterise at least two types. This depends on the legal environment and the extent to which the market complies with it. For example, where the law grants and defends unrestricted property rights, withholding land does not pose a significant risk to the owner, so market supply of land tends to be low, and so they relax their behaviour and reinforce their inheritance conception of property. Unlike places where the law imposes tax obligations and/or burdens on property if not used, withholding land involves risks and/or costs that puts pressure on the owners to use it or offer it on the marketplace. This environment rationalises their behaviour and reinforces the investment conception of property. In the case of Mexico, the owner-occupant would be represented by a household that acquires a plot for the purpose of living on it; the owner-investor would be the housing developer who acquires land as an investment; and the inheritor owner would be the rights holder of communal land (or *ejido* land) who maintains ownership of land in the urban periphery, but has ceased to farm it.

Since the land is not reproducible, it does not have a reproduction cost that determines a minimum price the owner can demand. The price is therefore essentially determined by the pull of competing buyers. They do not require land to consume it, but to carry out activities on it; in this sense, they will be willing to compete for it according to the profit or satisfaction that such activity represents. Therefore, the demand for land derives from the use that can be made of it (Smolka, 2002: 5). To dedicate the land to urban use requires transformation or improvement, and this can be done by the user himself or with the support of a builder. In many cases, this requires a significant amount of capital, which leads to the emergence of new agents specialised in financing and property development. The agent demands land as an intermediate input to add infrastructure and buildings and sell it on the property market. The intermediation of real estate development between the original owner and the end user further exemplifies the concept of derived demand: the demand for land is strongly linked to the demand for an ultimate property product. If we use our typology of Mexican users, we would have: (1) households that have a certain capacity to pay and represent the derived demand; (2) rights holders of *ejidatarios* (communal) land that can only ask from poor households whatever money they can afford; and (3) developers that act as intermediaries and add capital to the land, whether this is a large amount (infrastructure and housing in the case of a housing estate) or only small (improvements such as street layout to access land plots in the case of an irregular subdivision, or, if preferred, clandestine subdivision).

An owner-investor of a housing development starts from the maximum price that the buyers – the families – are willing to pay in the market. The price includes the cost of building the dwelling and the infrastructure that serves it. This cost is the capital needed for construction, calculated at least at the average profit that encourages the investor to build the dwelling. The remaining amount, after deducting the construction cost from the price of the dwelling, is known as the residual value of land and it will represent to the investor an additional profit, over and above the aforementioned average profit. However, the investor will have to share such additional profit with the landowner, who will not otherwise cede the right to use of the land. The residual value of the land will exist even if an owner-investor is not involved in the construction of the improvement, for example when it is carried out by the land user, i.e., by self-building the dwelling. The residual effect is independent of the nature of the agent leading the demand. In the first case, it comes from an investor developer building a housing complex and in the second case, an informal sub-divider selling irregular plots to self-builders.

The extent to which the residual value is divided between the agent of the demand and the owner will depend on many factors, but generally, the likelihood that the owner will keep all of it is high. The wide competition between buyers and the scarcity of land supply favours the land owner; this allows him to choose the buyer who is willing to give up the entire residual value. Thus, the residual value is transformed into what is known as 'land rent'. The main schools of economics recognise that the owners demand a rent for themselves from the land users without adding an equivalent value to the economy. Therefore, in the economic accounting of a country, land purchase and sale operations are considered transfers, not increases in gross product. In Mexico, the tax system does not consider this to add value and the purchase and sale of land does not incur value added tax.

The concept of 'land rent' was developed by classical economists to explain that portion of society's product that owners demanded from agricultural producers in order to cede the use of their land to them (Ricardo, 1963; Smith, 1976). In each agricultural cycle the producer must pay a part of his product to the owner. When a producer wants to acquire land so as to stop having to pay rent, the owner will demand, as a selling price, a capital of such magnitude that allows him to invest it at an average rate of return that yields cyclically and in the future the same income he currently receives (Marx, [1867] 2009). In other words, the price of land is essentially nothing more than a capitalised expression of land rent. Of course, if there is a possibility that the rent on a specific plot of land will be higher in the future, the owner will capitalise this higher rent in the price; that is, he will anticipate that future profit.

This is most evident in the urban environment where a new land use may potentially be in demand years after the sale and could yield a higher rent that can be anticipated in the price by the original owner. The rent that will determine the price of the land will not be that of the current use but that of the potential use. The scarcity and long-lasting characteristics of the land allow the owner to ask that the selling price of the land should correspond to the user who can pay the most money. The best example of this mechanism is that of the market price of vacant land in a city; it is not sold at the price derived from the rent of the current use, which would be zero, but at the price derived from the rent of potential future use. Where there are several future uses, the selling price will be what is often referred to as the 'highest and best use'. This phenomenon is also observed in the periphery of cities (Rabello de Castro, 2012; Smolka, 2013: 8). The owner of a piece of agricultural land, including the rights holder of communal land, sells the land at a price higher than the current use value because he knows that the expectation is that it will eventually be given an urban use that will pay more. Somehow, the recognition of this phenomenon is reflected in Mexico's land policies. There, a regulatory and fiscal stimulus to the occupation of vacant land is recommended for the urban area; for the periphery, direct intervention through the acquisition of land reserves is compensated at prices higher than the agricultural value.

The rent of the land, or its capitalised sale price, is observed in different modalities. One of these is differential rent, defined, for example, by the difference in production and transport costs required for agricultural land to produce the same product; in this case, rent depends on the differences in fertility of each plot of land and its location in relation to consumer markets. A variant of this differential rent is one that depends on the intensity of the capital invested to increase the productivity of the land and generate an even greater rent. Other more complex modalities include absolute rent, which explains the amount of money that a landowner, even under the worst conditions, can demand to transfer the right to own the land; and monopoly rent, which allows a landowner to demand additional amounts for land with characteristics highly desired by the demand. An example of this is the difference in prices between rural and urban land. The scarcity of urbanised land in many of the country's cities creates price differences of between five and six times between rural land and urbanised land (CIDOC and SHF, 2008).

Rent patterns are more clearly expressed in rural areas than in urban areas, and therefore their understanding is often initiated by studying the former. In the countryside, agricultural products are cultivated from the land, and the consumer is not concerned about where they originated. In the city, buildings remain anchored to the land while they are being 'consumed', once the construction process is complete. The landowner is related first with the owner-investor, during the production stage of a building, and second, with the end user. In some societies the original owner leases the land to the owner-investor on a long-term basis, who sells only the construction to the end user, transferring the lessees' obligations to him. In other societies, future land rents are capitalised in advance through the price paid by the owner-investor to the original owner for acquiring the land. Once the building has been constructed, the land, together with the construction, is sold to the end user who becomes the owner-occupant. Between these two extremes are countless variations in ownership that become more complex as financial institutions intervene to support them with large sums of money that supply-and-demand stakeholders need to build and acquire property.

The modalities of urban land rental are involved in all this complexity and arise both in the direct relationship between owners with builders, and in the indirect linking of the former with the end users. The most recognised form of rent in the urban sphere is the differential rent per location, observed in the decrease in the price of land the further it is from the most desirable areas of the city, for example from its centre. In essence, a household that has a fixed amount of money to spend on its location in the city may choose a central location to spend less on transportation, but has to pay the difference on more expensive land; alternatively, it may choose to pay less for a peripheral location, but pay the difference in transportation to the centre. In addition to the forms of rent mentioned above, there are other less recognised modalities (Jaramillo, 2003).

The complexity of urban rent gives rise to the diverse spatial structure of cities. Sociologists, economists and geographers have described this diversity by referring to distributions in concentric circles (Park and Burgess, 1925), in sectors (Hoyt, 1939), or in multiple nuclei (Harris and Ullman, 1945). Sociologists have described processes of filtering into lower social groups or of 'gentrification' into higher groups (Caulfield, 1989; Florida, 2003). They have also identified many other processes of valuation, displacement and so on (Wacquant, 2008). In addition, they have described, along with economists, the formation of property sub-markets each bringing together various stakeholders, land uses and very diverse selling modes (Liu et al., 1990). The way each market competes for space explains the various structures and the resulting land price profiles of cities. Underlying all of them is the logic that derives from the unique characteristics of land that we have been describing, and it is the theory of land rent that explains to a large extent the way in which cities are structured.

The land market is in a process of constant motion. Its dynamic is typically characterised through the amount of land offered at a given time, the speed at which it is absorbed by demand, and the price that is agreed. But explanations beyond these indicators are needed to understand the market. For example, at the general level changes in the interest rate of the capital market affects the capitalisation rate that mediates between land prices and land rents. At the specific level, changes in zoning regulations increase land prices only where such change happened. There are also increases that depend on fluctuations in investment opportunities between various capital markets, such as availability of mortgages or housing subsidies. These increases fuel speculation from investors seeking to become owners and capitalise on these advantages. Sometimes they fuel speculation by passive inheritor landowners, who do not have to do anything for their land value to increase. Sometimes it is the owner-investor who lobbies for more profitable land uses.

The market operates with rules that are consolidated into laws. There is a tendency to emphasise the legal framework governing land ownership in a world that increasingly relies on the market as a mechanism for allocating goods and services. Multilateral organisations widely promote the adoption of legal regulations on property, but these must achieve political and social recognition for the market to operate for the benefit of all. When the outcome does not satisfy the population as a whole, parallel rules emerge with which the market operates, often called informal. It should be emphasised that informal land markets share several of the rules of economic logic that we have been describing: irreproducibility, inelasticity, indestructibility, the residual nature of land rent, its capitalisation into price, and the logic of maximum and best use. Hence, the formal and informal markets are intimately linked. The nature of these rules and the links between the two markets should also be explored.

Understanding the Physiology: Some Explanations of Urban Land Market Behaviour and Price Formation

All land markets are connected throughout the city. For the given piece of land, several different land uses compete, the owner pursues the maximum and best use, privileging some uses over others according to the ability and willingness of each user (Smolka, 2003). At the top of the scale are usually corporate offices, especially at high densities, and shops, particularly with a high turnover of goods sold. Social housing is at the lower end of the scale, and lower still are public and environmental uses with very low direct profitability. The low ability to pay makes social, public and environmental uses uncompetitive, resulting in low rates of return compared to those that would be achieved with other land uses; this keeps the owner or investors from focusing on those land uses … unless they adopt the informal development strategy.

Informality in urban uses with low ability to pay is increasingly becoming a strategy of profit maximisation. Such is the case of cities with large poor areas. Owners and investors come to these markets offering lower quality plots in order to lower costs and increase the rate of return (Pírez, 2014: 489). The reduction in quality is achieved in at least four ways: poor location, no infrastructure, no facilities, and risky land. The costs of subdividing land is thus reduced, and not only are the profit rates made equal to the formal land development, but they are even surpassed. This reduction in production cost does not translate into lower prices for the poor; instead, plots are sold at high prices that require buyers to use their maximum ability to pay. Due to the scarcity of land, the competition of supply is low, essentially inelastic, and the end result is that the rate of profit is higher. This activity has made distant, unserviced, risky, and unsuitable land more profitable, therefore attracting more owners and investors into these markets. This explains the growth of informal markets and the fact that it has recently started to reach not only the poorer sections of the population, but also the middle sections that in previous decades had only gone to formal property markets (Smolka, 2002).

For this trend to continue, agents who benefit from it need laws and authorities to reduce property obligations. Attracting subdivisions in poorly located land can be done by erasing urban borders or by relaxing the zoning regulations. Subdividing land without infrastructure is achieved by reducing street widths, service networks, and requirements for facilities and parks in development regulations. Eliminating risk of eviction is achieved by tolerating occupation and regularising land that could flood or collapse. Bringing unsuitable land to the market is achieved by tolerating the withholding of suitable land, that is, not forcing the owners to develop and sell their land to fulfil current demand within a specific time limit.

The above situation creates vicious circles where an owner or an intermediary investor (clandestine land developer) sells plots without authorisation, without services, without land titles and in inadequate areas, which are then titled by the public authority and services are introduced. This way of creating ISs makes the scheme more profitable and attracts more informal land supply and less formal land supply. It also encourages agents to lobby for greater tolerance, and expand title regularisation programmes and subsidies to introduce services. One might think that this vicious circle of informality and regularisation would lead to a virtuous cycle, since titling plots allows households to get a mortgage facilitating access to capital plot. However, in countries where informal plots have been massively titled, such as Mexico, there has been no impact on mortgage applications, that is, the vicious circle has not become virtuous (Smolka, 2003; Morales, 2006).

Another vicious circle that has formed is that which exacerbates municipal fiscal weakness and leads to the misapplication of resources in the following ways: by sacrificing taxes to stimulate, but not achieve, the use of land served; by sacrificing taxes to informality with the intention of easing the burden on the pockets of the poor, without managing to do so; and by subsidising the introduction of services, without recovering said subsidies from the owners who benefit. On the one hand, this feeds the vicious circle of speculation where the best strategy of the owners is to retain the land served in order to be able to charge a premium. This creates a scarcity for that particular land of that quality and at that price; moreover, withholding the land from sale only serves to feed that scarcity.' In addition, a tax exemption is requested in order to stimulate investment in services, which, however, only reinforces the retention of land. On the other hand, there is the vicious circle of the informal land market to which those who are excluded from the land market have to turn, putting pressure on them to increase the prices of informal land, thus squeezing the income of those who are excluded and to whom the respective subsidies are eventually granted.

The vacant land and services resulting from these processes represent open and deliberate speculation on the part of the owner, especially if he is a property investor. In the case of the inheritance owner, his speculation may or may not be conscious, obeying a cultural context where a right to free disposal prevails without obligations, with a low tax burden and consent to sell when required. Sometimes, this owner is an institution that is not aware of the effect it produces, nor does it have the risk of not being aware of it, that is, it does not have any tax burden or obligation to develop with defined uses and timescales (Smolka and Sabatini, 2000).

In order not to wait for the maximum and best land use to arrive, the owner could sell at a price equivalent to future use capitalised at present value; that is, he can anticipate the expectation. In the event that the transaction comes to fruition, the new owner will have to maintain the expectation until it is fulfilled, until the demand for that maximum and best use for that land arises. Thus, the shortage of land in the market does not arise so much because there is not enough land, but because those areas that are well located, served, without risk and in a timely manner are few. Likewise, it does not depend on whether its use or sale is authorised, but rather on whether it is in the interest of the owner to retain it; the best economic strategy is to retain it, and so the prevailing scarcity is that caused by the owners' own economic logic.

Land retention behaviour depends on the balance of the owner's rights and obligations on the land. The balance depends on the way in which these rights and obligations are expressed in law, on the contradictions between them, on legal practice through administrative applications and judicial interpretations, on tolerance for legal compliance and on the institutionalisation of mechanisms that regulate what is tolerated. What is exchanged in the land market is not the specific object but the set of rights and obligations relating to that object. The terms of the exchange are influenced by this set of rights and obligations; if the law and its practice minimise the obligations, the buyer's desire will increase and he will be willing to pay more for a piece of land without obligations. Likewise, the seller's profit will increase not only because the price increases, but because the expenses that the obligations could incur are reduced; the effect is to increase the gap between the price and cost of the property.

On the other hand, it is necessary to distinguish between builders and owners: both operate in the construction industry but are actors with different motivations (Jaramillo, 2010: 390–396). The builder creates goods that can be used by society, he obtains a profit from this activity, is subject to competition from other builders who can multiply if demand increases, forcing him to be efficient and lower his rate of profit. He competes for capital to which he must offer a competitive rate, which tends to be equal to the competitiveness of other productive branches. The owner controls an indispensable basic input: the land. The possibility of competition is restricted to other owners with similarly located land, and there are no production costs. These and other characteristics make it difficult to reconcile the interests of the two players: especially if the owner is a wealthy person, less so if he or she is an investor.'

The connection between owner-investor and builder is through global capital that makes various investment niches compete and that flows to those who offer the highest returns. To the extent that investment in land involves low initial expenditure (low price for land in difficult terrain in predominantly rural locations), low costs (few taxes for retaining ownership and few obligations to donate some of the land for public use, and introduce services), and high selling price (even for peripheral land and without services for less profitable uses), the return will be very high, even higher than investment in construction which requires high levels of investment, competitive selling prices and modest levels of profit. The greater the gap between the two investment sectors, the greater the migration of capital from construction to land investment.

The implicit process is the generation of high land incomes (capital gains) through internal rearrangement, the growth of the city and its provision of services; also, the authorisation of specific owners to use their property according to the collective needs of the city's inhabitants. These rents essentially benefit the owners; the city recovers them only to the extent that it can make a payment, in cash or in kind, payable to the owner for the privilege of benefiting from the rents created by the city. The benefits to the owner, through rent appropriation, will increase if the city administration adopts policies of tolerance and subsidisation of access to land, as these reduce costs and increase prices and, consequently, profits. But the gains can be reduced by increasing obligations to provide services and contribute to public spending, so that the city can encourage improvements and redistribute capital gains.

Understanding Whether the Patient Is Healthy or Not: Some Effects of Urban Land Market Rules

The land market operates under rules that do not necessarily follow the orthodox assumptions of the market economy of other commodities. The land market works differently because the characteristics of the land goods do not allow a fully competitive and rational supply and demand. The effects of this particular market on the socio-economic and spatial structure of cities have persistent negative outcomes such as urban sprawl, segregation and lack of services. These unsatisfactory results are often attributed to state intervention, which is identified as market distorting when setting taxes and regulations (Alterman, 2012). It is argued that an increase in property taxes increases the price of land and that the delimitation of the area of expansion of the city in regulatory urban plans decreases supply and pushes up prices (Smolka, 2011: 108). Assuming that both policies are responsible for the fact that large sections of the population do not have access to adequate space, various societies have implemented policies that tax and deregulate the land market to make it work better, without achieving this. Latin America is an interesting laboratory for observing the extent to which land markets operate with and without orthodox rules. One of the characteristics of the region is the large informal land market that has accumulated an inventory of ISs in virtually every city regardless of size. It has been said that this is due to over-regulation of the market. The reverse interpretation argues that it is the broad tolerance of non-compliance with regulation that is conducive to such an informal market. The debate seems to oscillate between considering ISs as a product that emerges outside the formal market and aspires to operate freely, and observing them as the best example of the free market. One interpretation or another has far-reaching implications for the definition of urban policies.

Formal land markets have gone through stages of high regulation and deregulation. In Latin America there are examples of deregulation that have hoped for an adequate and efficient allocation of land use in the city as an effect, that is, that it will be acceptable to the entire population. It has also been hoped that this will release land to the market and, as a result, lower prices so that more people can afford it, and improve the location and quality of urbanisation and housing. Evidence questions the benefits of such deregulation (Borrero and Morales, 2007); it appears to formalise the rules under which the informal land market operates and produces expensive, poorly located land without services.

Thus, the liberation of land markets can present contradictions such as an increase in their availability, as well as an increase in their price. The explanations can be found in the very logic of the atypical functioning of this market (Abramo, 2011: 168–178). If one thinks of the scarcity of properly located land, there is a physical scarcity in not only absolute but also relative terms. This scarcity can be increased if government regulations prevent some of the land that is well located from being sold for urban use. This happens, for example, when urban plans limit expansion zones, bring changes from housing to commercial use, or announce an urban project on specific land. In addition to physical and regulatory scarcity, there is also economic scarcity, namely the scarcity that economic agents cause when they decide not to sell a piece of land, in the hope of a greater and better future use that will yield a higher price, and there is no law that prevents them from retaining it. This type of shortage can also be caused by the presence of other factors such as the reduction of taxes that punish the retention of land, and in the following situations: when the shortage of well-located land is compounded by the scarcity of infrastructure and services among the city's land; when the cost of introducing services is low, because it is not required by law, resulting in an increase in profit; and/or when illegal sales, i.e., without paying taxes and infrastructure costs, are rewarded with the delivery of titles and the subsequent introduction of services with government subsidies.

Land retention is an example of asset-owning behaviour in which all types of owners participate when the market environment is deregulated and tax-deductible. The implications of the behaviour of landowners, atypical of that of owners of other goods, make it necessary to look with caution at an environment of liberalisation; this may be useful for other markets, including the construction market, but is counterproductive for the land market.

Cure or Vaccinate? a Brief Conclusion

In light of the above concepts, the policies of regularisation and constitution of territorial reserves will inevitably interact in the formation of Mexican cities with effects that are not necessarily desired. The longstanding curative policy of regularisation of land obtained through an informal market has sent a message to landowners and buyers that this is the way to operate and that land rent can be capitalised by those asset owners and/or by intermediaries who divide up the land outside the law in order to reduce investment and maximise profit. The incipient policy of reserve acquisition is subject to this logic, and will find it difficult to compete against informality unless mechanisms are put in place to reduce expectations of capitalising on the future revenues of asset owners and investors. Expectations of profit in the periphery are very high, probably higher than in the interior of the city even though the prices are lower.

The retention of vacant land within the current urban area of the city is another effect of inadequate medicine. The profit expectations of the owners inside the city have accumulated and it will be difficult for them to give them up. They will tend to keep the land vacant, if incentives are established, by reducing the costs of ownership (reduction of taxes and of urban and building obligations) and giving them greater rights (such as increasing densities for free), rather than encouraging them to offer their land at affordable prices for less profitable uses.

In the creation of land policies in Mexico, understanding the links between the formal and informal market is still uncertain, otherwise official documents would prioritise one policy over the other. That is to say, on the one hand the informal market should no longer be regularised a posteriori, but should be actively prevented, in order to send the message that it is not profitable. On the other hand, a wide range of land should be promoted, and owners and developers should be required to comply with requirements that cover what a household is going to pay for anyway, that is, for that payment to be applied to building the infrastructure and housing itself, and not to increase the price of land.

Urban land policy in Mexico must face a similar challenge to that faced by public health policies: it is better to vaccinate than to cure, otherwise the cure absorbs all resources without sustainably solving the problem in the long term. To favour the supply of land with infrastructure over regularisation is not simple, but it is not impossible either. In the 1980s and early 1990s, the government of Aguascalientes adopted a strong preventative policy and practically abandoned a curative policy. This had encouraging results, substantially reducing the informal market. When at the end of the decade it withdrew the massive offer of land plots with infrastructure and resumed a curative policy on old ISs, the informal market grew again (Jiménez, 2000).

References

Abramo, P. (2011) *La producción de las ciudades latinomanericanas: mercado inmobiliario y estructura urbana.* Quito: Municipio Metropolitano de Quito, Olacchi.

Alonso, W. (1964) *Location and Land Use: Towards a General Theory of Land Rent.* Harvard University Press: Cambridge.

Alterman, R. (2012) 'Land Use Regulations and Property Values: the "Windfalls Capture" Idea Revisited' in N. Brooks, K. Donaghy and G. Knaap (eds.) *The Oxford Handbook for Urban Economics and Planning.* Oxford University Press: New York, 755–786.

Borrero Ochoa, O. and Morales Schechinger, C. (2007) 'Impacts of Regulations on Undeveloped Land Prices: A Case Study of Bogotá'. *Land Lines* **19**(4): 14–17.

Camagni, R. (2005) 'La renta del suelo urbano' in A Bosch (ed.) *Camagni Economía Urbana.* Antoni Bosch Editor: Barcelona, 163–197.

Caulfield, J. (1989) 'Gentrification and Desire'. *Canadian Review of Sociology and Anthropology* **26**(4): 617–632.

Centro de Investigación y documentación de la Casa, A.C., CIDOC and Sociedad Hipotecaria Federal SHF (eds.) (2007) Estado actual de la vivienda en México 2007. Mexico FD.

Centro de Investigación y documentación de la Casa, A.C., CIDOC and Sociedad Hipotecaria Federal SHF (eds.) (2010) Estado actual de la vivienda en México 2010. Mexico FD.

de Soto, H. (2000) *The Mystery of Capital: Why Capitalism Triumphs in the West and Fails Everywhere Else.* Basic Books: New York.

Eckert, J., Gloudemnas, R. and Almy, M. (eds.) (1990) *Property Appraisal and Assessment Administration.* International Association of Assessing Officers: Chicago.

Florida, R. (2003) *The Rise of the Creative Class: and How its Transforming Work, Leisure, Community and Everyday Life.* Basic Books: New York.

Harris, C. D. and Ullman, E. L. (1945) 'The Nature of Cities'. *Annals of American Academic on Social Science* **242**(3): 7–17.

Hoyt, H. (1939) *The Structure and Growth of Residential Neighbourhoods in American Cities.* Federal Housing Administration: Washington

Jaramillo, S. (2003) *Los fundamentos económicos de la 'participación en plusvalías'*. CIDER, Universidad de los Andes and Lincoln Institute of Land Policy: Bogotá, Colombia and Cambridge.

Jaramillo, S. (2010) *Hacia una teoría de la renta del suelourbano*. Universidad de los Andes: Bogotá.

Jiménez, E. (2000) *El principio de la irregularidad: mercado de suelo y vivienda en Aguascalientes, 1975–1998*. Universidad de Guadalajara, Juan Pablos Editor y Centro de Investigaciones y Estudios Multidisciplinarios de Aguascalientes: Mexico FD.

Liu, C. H., Hartzell, D. J., Greig, W. and Grissom, T. V. (1990) 'The Integration of the Real Estate Market and the Stock Market: Some Preliminary Evidence'. *Finance and Economics* 3(3): 261–282.

Marx, K. ([1867] 2009) *El capital: crítica de la economía política*. Tomo III. Siglo XXI editors: Mexico FD.

Morales Schechinger, C. (2004) 'Políticas de suelo urbano, accesibilidad de los pobres y recuperación de plusvalías' in *Cuarto seminario internacional: innovando los procesos de acceso al suelo. July 2004. CD-ROM Programa Universitario de Estudios sobre la Ciudad, Coordinación de Humanidades, Universidad Nacional Autónoma de México*. Mexico City: Lincoln Institute of Land Policy.

Morales Schechinger, C. (2006) Apuntes sobre conceptos desarrollados por Martim Smolka respecto del mercado del suelo y el impuesto a la propiedad en América Latina. Lincoln Institute of Land Policy. [WWW document]. URL https://es.scribd.com/document/257333188/SAPUNTES-SOBRE-CONCE PTOS-DESARROLLADOS-POR-MARTIM-SMOLKA-RESPECTO-DEL-ME RCADO-DEL-SUELO-Y-EL-IMPUESTO-A-LA-PROPIEDAD-EN-AMERI CA-LATINA-DOCUMENTO-DE-T [accessed 7 July 2019].

Needham, B. (2006) 'Planning, Law and Economics' in *An Investigation of the Rules we Make for Using Land*. Routledge: London and New York.

Park, R. and Burgess, E. (1925) *The City*. University of Chicago Press: Chicago.

Pírez, P. (2014) 'La mercantilización de la urbanización. A propósito de los "conjuntos urbanos" en México'. *Estudios Demográficos y Urbanos* 29(3): 481–512.

Rabello de Castro, S. (2012) 'Faculty Profile'. *Land Lines* 24(1): 18–19.

Ricardo, D. (1963) *The Principles of Political Economy and Taxation*. R. D. Irwin: Homewood Ill.

Secretaría de Desarrollo Social (SEDESOL) (2010) *Diagnóstico sobre la falta de certeza jurídica en hogares urbanos en condiciones de pobreza patrimonial en asentamientos irregulares*. [WWW document] URL http://www.sedesol.gob.mx/work/ models/SEDESOL/Sedesol/sppe/dgap/diagnostico/D_PASPRAH_2011 .pdf [accessed 5 February 2019].

Secretaría del Desarrollo Agrario, Territorial y Urbano (SEDATU) (2013) *Programa Sectorial de Desarrollo Agrario, Territorial y Urbano 2013–2018*, DOF, 16 December. [WWW document] URL http://www.dof.gob.mx/nota_detalle .php?codigo=5326473&fecha=16/12/2013 [accessed 5 February 2019].

Smith, A. and Cannan, E. (1976) *An Inquiry into the Nature and Causes of The Wealth of Nations*. University of Chicago: Chicago.

Smolka, M. (2002) 'Regularización de la ocupación del suelo urbano: el problema que es parte de la solución, la solución que es parte del problema' in *CD-ROM Curso profesional sobre mercados informales, regularización de la tenencia y programas de mejoramiento urbano*. Lincoln Institute of Land Policy: Cambridge.

Smolka, M. (2003) 'Informalidad, pobreza urbana y precios de la tierra'. *Land Lines* **15**(1): 4–8.

Smolka, M. (2011) 'Precios elevados (e inaccesibles) de la tierra urbana habilitada' in M. Á. Porrúa (ed.) *Periurbanización y sustentabilidad en grandes ciudades.* CONACYT, Instituto de Geografía (UNAM) y Cámara de Diputados: México City.

Smolka, M. and Furtado, F. (2013) *Implementing Value Capture in Latin America. Policies and Tools for Urban Development.* Lincoln Institute of Land Policy Cambridge, 83-117.

Smolka, M. and Sabatini, F. (2000) 'The Land Market Deregulation Debate in Chile'. *Land Lines* **12**(1): 1–3.

Sociedad Hipotecaria Federal (SHF) (2016) *Demanda de vivienda 2016.* [WWW document] URL https://www.gob.mx/cms/uploads/attachment/file/146194/Demanda_2016.pdf [accessed 5 February 2019].

UN HABITAT (2008) *Secure Land Rights for All.* UN HABITAT: Nairobi.

Wacquant, L. (2008) 'Relocating Gentrification: The Working Class, Science and the State in Recent Urban Research'. *International Journal of Urban and Regional Research* **32**(1): 198–205.

5

New Procedures, Persistent Failures: Entitlement Practices in Mexico's Informal Settlements

CLARA SALAZAR

El Colegio de México

Introduction

Two types of land-holding and two patterns of property rights overlap on the periphery of Mexican cities: *ejidos* (land held in common by a specific community) and the informal settlements (ISs) located on them. Both are subject to formalisation of land tenure: the *ejidos* are covered by the Programa de Certificación de Derechos Ejidales y Titulación de Solares, (PROCEDE, Programme for the Certification of Communal Land Rights and Urban Land Plot Titling) implemented since 1993 by the agrarian ministry; the ISs have been subject to the regularisation programme carried out by the Land Tenure Regularisation Commission (CORETT, Comisión de Regularización de Tenencia de la Tierra) since 1973. Thus, since the early 1990s, two government agencies have been handing over 'urban land plot' titles located in *ejidos* on the periphery of cities. This has implied an overlap of functions between two organisations whose mandate is to serve two different target populations: CORETT must offer legal certainty to the settlers of ISs located on *ejidos* (*avecindados* or settlers), while the National Agrarian Registry (RAN, Registro Agrario Nacional) must offer it by law and free of charge to the *ejidatarios* (people who are rights holders in *ejidos*). Although the Agrarian Law recognises the *avecindados* as agrarian subjects, they have not been endowed with the same property rights as the *ejidatarios*. The legal reforms of 1992 gave legal status to the *ejidos* and recognised the *ejidatarios* as landowners where the land was endowed to them, even though that land had been sold outside the law and is now, *de facto*, occupied by other settlers. The law also allows private actors to participate in the ISs regularisation process, and has created new instruments to transfer land from the agrarian regime to the civil or common regime. Until 1992, this process was used solely by CORETT, however, and paradoxically the new process of recognising property rights in the urban peripheries serves to hamper and complicate the process.

The objective of this chapter is to reflect on how the change to formal rules has generated new dynamics in the titling process of those who inhabit plots on *ejidos* in the urban periphery of Mexico. We maintain that the reconfiguration of relationships between old and new actors has given rise to new alliances in the name of the law, as well as resistance to its implementation. This has led to unforeseen conflicts over the regularisation of the ISs in the urban periphery. We start from the premise that the positions occupied by the social actors in any social field are defined by the capital they possess, by their capacity to modify how functions are distributed and in the relationship of subordination or domination that they manage to impose on others (Bourdieu, 1993; Bourdieu and Wacquant 2003). As a result, the new legal framework that has given the agrarian jurisdiction to formalise social ownership has also weakened CORETT's capacity to act, institutionalised since the early 1970s. In addition, we show that this has stimulated the incorporation of private agents into the regularisation process, restricting the capacity of IS settlers to formalise their property.

Analysis of official data from CORETT and the National Agrarian Registry (RAN) helps to reveal both the achievements and setbacks of the IS regularisation process. In other studies, we have analysed the impact of PROCEDE on urban expansion (Salazar, 2009, 2011) and on communal land liberalisation processes for the market (Salazar, 2010). In this chapter, we focus on how the field of IS regularisation has changed since 1992, and to do so carried out fieldwork in the San Cristóbal Ecatepec *ejido* located in the Mexico City Metropolitan Area (MCMA). There we identified and interviewed both old and new actors involved in the regularisation process and we reveal our findings about how they interact and the nature of alliances or conflicts. These sources are complemented by analysis of the current legal rules, as well as case files provided by the settlers, which chart their dealings with different authorities, in their search for legal certainty of their property.

Context: *Ejidos*, the Formation of Informal Settlements (ISs) and their Regularisation between 1973 and 1992'

The institutionalisation of *ejido* rights in Mexico has been in existence for over a century. The awarding of land to agrarian communities and the creation of *ejidos* dates back to 1915, when, in the context of the Mexican revolution, an agrarian law was passed in Veracruz that marked the most extensive agrarian reform in Latin America (Kouri, 2015). Those agrarian communities which could provide supporting documents were awarded land while landless peasants were given land formerly belonging to large estates or *haciendas*, under the name of *ejidos*. Both lands were declared inviolable and inalienable, which means that they were excluded from the land market.

The endowment of land was consolidated during the period that Lázaro Cárdenas was in office (1935–1940), but the policy followed by Avila Camacho (1940–1952) mainly favoured the private agricultural sector, meaning that much of the distributed land lacked the resources required to make it productive. By 1940, this situation, together with the industrialisation project and its concentration in specific urban centres (Garza, 1985), had generated a new phase of economic growth and stimulated a process of rural–urban migration (Alba, 1989: 23). Within this, the new settlers were located in 'rural islets' (Adler, 1978: 47) located on the urban peripheries that were often *ejidos* and state-run (Schteingart, 1989). For example, *ejidos* came to represent 70 percent of the surface area of Mexico City (Cruz, 2001: 86).

In a context in which the majority of migrants had, for economic reasons, migrated from the countryside to the city where there was no housing supply available (Adler, 1978: 57), the continuous occupation of *ejidos* without property title deeds and without basic infrastructure reached unexpected levels, creating what we have called informal settlements (ISs), until it became the predominant form of low-income urbanisation for people without access to a loan. According to Duhau (1998), about 70 percent of Mexican cities were formed as ISs. In response to social demand, and in order to provide legal security to the settlers who had their homes themselves on *ejido* land, the federal government created the Land Tenure Regularisation Commission (CORETT) in 1973.

It was not until the early 1990s, in the context of the structural reforms imposed by the World Bank, that the Mexican state considered need to regularise land tenure for the *ejidatarios*. As we have mentioned, since their creation, the *ejidos* had been recognised as 'limited' owners of the lands they had been endowed with or acquired by other means. That is to say, since their formation it was established that they would be governed under a community regime: property rights would be limited to the use, exploitation and consumption of the resource, but *ejidatarios* had no right to dispose of the land (sell); and the exercising of their rights would be decided on a joint basis by all the members of the *ejido*, and not on an individual basis.

One of the reasons why settlers of the ISs located on *ejidos* do not have legal security of ownership is that they accessed the property as *'avecindados'* or squatters. The agrarian regime, which limits the property of *ejidatarios* by preventing them from selling, assigning, transferring, leasing, mortgaging or encumbering the land, has never prevented the *ejidatarios* from providing a plot of land for other settlers who serve the community (Federal Agrarian Reform Act, 1971). However, as can be seen from the research carried out by Varley (1985), having been accepted as an 'settlers' did not in most cases mean that they had also been granted legal rights over the land plots they were occupying. The other reason is that while *ejidatarios* were explicitly prohibited from selling the land, this did not imply that they did not do so. In violation of the law, and in the context of rural–urban migration that characterised the process of rapid urbanisation between the 1940s and 1970s, large expanses of *ejido* land located on the outskirts of Mexican cities began to be divided into plots by the *ejidatarios* themselves, who sold the undeveloped plot to low-income settlers. The latter occupied the plots without demanding property title deeds and built their homes on them, forming the so-called ISs.

The process of ISs regularisation, carried out by CORETT before 1992, frequently began with the publication of an expropriation decree in its favour, which implied that this organisation became the temporary owner of the expropriated property. Prior to this, the agency had contacted the *ejidatarios* to agree on the terms of the expropriation and on the amount of compensation, thereby reducing the risk of writs of *amparo* by the *ejidatarios*. Once the decree was published, the agency carried out a census of settlers, measured each property, delimited the areas restricted to urbanisation, set aside the land to be given up, identified the risk zones, assigned the land use according to current urban regulations, and presented a proposal to the corresponding municipality to regularise the settlement. Once this proposal was approved by the competent local authority, CORETT then recognised the settlers who could prove their legitimate possession of the property by presenting one of the following documents: a certificate of right to urban land, a rights transfer contract, a private contract of sale, an *ejido* record, or a notarised certificate of information, in addition to official identification papers. Although some of these documents lack legal validity, the agency had always accepted them as legitimate proof that they possessed land, so that once these requirements had been met, the regularisation process was completed by registering them in the Registro Público de la Propiedad (RPP, Public Property Register), in the name of each of the accredited owners.

We are not claiming that the regularisation carried out by that body was infallible. In fact, it was an ineffective mechanism in quantitative terms because the provision of property rights never succeeded in reducing demand. Between 1973 and 1992, CORETT was the only agency authorised to regularise the ISs, and in that period it delivered nearly 1.1 million deeds to IS settlers throughout the country. Following amendments to the law, the agency has delivered another 1.3 million deeds. Thus, in 43 years it has delivered a total of 2.5 million deeds to IS settlers, yet it is estimated that there are at least three times as many in the country's metropolitan area alone (Salazar, 2011). Likewise, the process is inefficient; it requires an excessive amount of time to be completed, taking on average seven or eight years (Ibarra, 2012).

The regularisation policy has thus had its limitations as a mechanism to resolve the persistence of informal access to land and to poverty reduction (Calderón, 2006, 2010; Fernandes, 2008), but it cannot be denied that the policy has allowed millions of settlers in Latin American countries to have a place to live. In Mexico, where poor people have gained access to land primarily through informal buying and selling rather than through land invasions, CORETT has played the role of mediator between the parties, avoiding conflicts between sellers (*ejidatarios*) and buyers (settlers) of land. One of the reasons for this relative harmony is that the state had established a *de facto* social agreement with all actors: that of tolerance. In other words, the *ejidatarios* were not sanctioned for illegal land sales, nor were the settlers punished for having participated in a process that could be described as fraudulent; in fact, after the creation of CORETT, evictions practically disappeared. The other reason is that, in a clientelistic way, the local urban authorities usually negotiated with the settlers of the ISs for the installation of basic services, long before the delivery of the property title deeds was completed. In addition, recourse to expropriation allowed the land to be transferred to CORETT as owner, which meant that the *ejidatarios* lost any ownership rights over it, so the agency could integrate all the steps of the regularisation procedure under its command, from the designation of beneficiaries to the delivery of public deeds. The new legal framework has destroyed this institutionalisation, however, creating conditions of uncertainty regarding the formalisation of property and giving way to new mechanisms that are neither more effective nor more efficient.

Changes to the Formal Rules in 1992 and their Effect on Corett's Regularisation Process

Although the reforms to Article 27 of the Constitution and to the Agrarian Law were carried out with the aim of ending agrarian distribution and making it easier for *ejido* land to become commodified, they were also justified from an urban perspective. Part of the Explanatory Memorandum presented by the Federal Executive argued that the narrowness of the formal property market, together with the ban on incorporating *ejido* land into urban development, contributed to the proliferation of irregular settlements. In addition, it was said that the *ejidatarios* did not enjoy equality in the market because there was no legal framework that favoured the legal sale of *ejido* land and its incorporation into urban development. Consequently, there was a need to offer legal security to peasants in order not to reproduce their poverty. As a result, mechanisms were created so that the *ejidos* could have a legal framework that would allow them to individualise community ownership, that is, privatise it by transferring it from the agrarian regime to the common law system, and incorporating it within the legal land market. Likewise, and prioritising the private property regime recently granted to the *ejidatarios*, the *Ejido* Assemblies were empowered to intervene in the regularisation of the ISs (Salazar, 2014: 71–72).

Perhaps the elements that had the most significant impact on the transformation of IS regularisation were Articles 9, 56 and 87 of the Agrarian Law published in the Diario Oficial de la Federación (DOF, Official Gazette of the Federation) on 26 February 1992. The first recognises the 'legal status and assets of the *ejidos*'; the second states that 'the *Ejido* Assemblies, the highest representative body of the *ejido*, may regularise the tenure of [the land of] the owners or those who lack the corresponding certificates'; and the third authorises the *ejidatarios* to 'benefit from the urbanisation of their lands'. Since 1992, the *ejidatarios* have interpreted these statements to mean that they can carry out at least four actions: (i) obtain full control over the land that was endowed to them or that they acquired by any other title, i.e., they can legally sell it and speculate on it; (ii) decide in the *Ejido* Assemblies which of the people living on ISs located on *ejidos* will be registered as *avecindados* or 'recognised settlers', and consequently will enjoy legal rights over the land they occupy; (iii) undertake the procedures for regularising these properties without the presence of CORETT; and (iv) appropriate the added value generated by the settlers during years of occupation through the process of transforming the land from rural to urban.

In effect, with the new Agrarian Law the Mexican state withdrew from CORETT its exclusive power to regularise the ISs in *ejidos*, and shifted to individuals, the *ejidatarios*, the capacity to designate who is a legitimate owner of plots in ISs. In addition, it eliminated the fact that expropriation is practically the only mechanism by which it is possible to sub-divide *ejido* land to regularise the ISs. As a result, expropriations in favour of CORETT have decreased, and consequently its regularising actions have also decreased. According to information provided by CORETT, between 1975 and 2015 it had pursued a total of 1971 expropriation decrees in *ejidos*, executed 1773 of them and expropriated 1328 million hectares. From the analysis of the database we have carried out (Figure 1) it can be concluded that the number of expropriations carried out by CORETT peaked during its institutionalisation period (1970–1976) and during the Carlos Salinas de Gortari administration (1989–1994), which, being the executor of the constitutional and agrarian reforms, facilitated the expropriations and also promoted the regularisation of ISs as a form of legitimation. In the following presidential periods, expropriation decrees decreased substantially and consistently. In parallel, the area expropriated on behalf of the organisation has also decreased. Obviously, the decrease in expropriations has also been affected by the 198 expropriation decrees not executed as a result of the protections pursued by the *ejidatarios*.

Figure 1.   Expropriation Decrees and Expropriated Area in Favour of CORETT to Regularise ISs Located in *Ejidos*, according to Presidential Period (1970–2016)

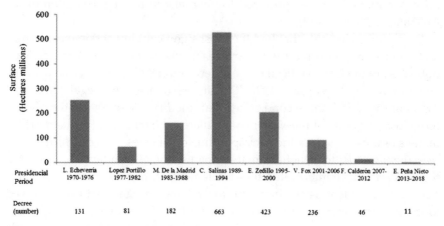

Source: own calculations based on CORETT (2016).

Although writs of *amparo* filed against the expropriation decrees are not a recent phenomenon (Varley, 1985), they have led to IS settlers in those *ejidos* not being able to obtain legal certainty about the property they occupy. There is no updated information on the number of land plots pending regularisation in the *ejidos*, but in 2006 it was estimated that the number of land plots not regularised due to writs of *amparo* reached 215,596 (El Colegio Mexiquense, 2006).

The decrease in expropriation decrees can also be explained by other reasons. Firstly, in 1999 CORETT moved from the agrarian sector to the Secretaría de Desarrollo Social (SEDESOL, Ministry of Social Development), and this restricted its powers to acquire, manage and alienate land in favour of urban development (El Colegio Mexiquense, 2006). Secondly, after 1992 the process of approving expropriation decrees became more complex. CORETT officials mentioned that after the Salinas de Gortari administration (1989–1994), and in order to advance the formulation and approval of an expropriation decree, the agency required not only the *ejido*'s consent, but that this consent be ratified each time that the *ejido*'s representative bodies changed, which occurs every three years. This meant that the execution of each expropriation decree for CORETT was conditioned by the *ejido*'s internal elections and the expectations of its new representatives.

Thirdly, the Registro Agrario Nacional (RAN, National Agrarian Register) was empowered to separate out the urban land plots from *ejido* land and to register them in the RPP. This has resulted in a decrease in CORETT's activity in regularisation. Between 1993 and 2015, the RAN issued 2.58 million titles

Table 1.   Registered Agrarian Subjects and Title of Urban Plots Managed between 1993 and 2015 According to the two State Agencies

Registered Subjects[*]	Number	Percent
Holders of ejidos	4,210,830	52.0
Owners	1,442,807	17.8
Settlers	2,447,226	30.2
Total	8,100,863	100.0

Titles of Urban Land delivered by organisation	Number	Percent	Surface Total (hectares)	Surface Average Land Plot (m^2)
RAN[**]	2,589,722	65.1	379,738.8	1,500.0
CORETT[***]	1,387,752	34.9	73,728.9	500.0
Total	3,977,474	100.0	453,467.6	

Source: prepared by the author based on:
* Instituto Nacional de Estadística, Geografía e Informática (2007) (INEGI, National Institute of Statistics, Geography and Computing); ** RAN, 2015; *** CORETT, 2016a.

on urban plots (*solares urbanos*), while CORETT delivered around 1.38 million (Table 1). This means that in the same period of time, the RAN completed twice the number of actions executed by CORETT. In principle, it could be concluded that the new attribution granted to the RAN expedited the titling of urban plots to the settlers of the ISs. But this process is far from complete. On the one hand, it is necessary to keep in mind that the RAN is an organisation of the agrarian sector, and its main function is 'to provide legal certainty to social property in Mexico, through the control of land tenure and the rights consti-tuted with respect to *ejidos* and communities'; that is, to provide legal certainty to *ejidatarios* and communal land owners. In contrast, CORETT's function is to regularise the land tenure of the IS settlers located in *ejidos*, that is, men and women who live in the *ejidos* but do not have communal land rights. In other words, the target population of each organisation is different.

In addition, the 2007 Agricultural Census indicates that at the national level, 4.2 million *ejidatarios*, 1.4 million owners (people who own a plot but are not *ejidatarios*) and 2.4 million 'settlers' had been registered. RAN data indicate that this agency had delivered about 2.6 million urban land titles by 2015. This means that the urban land titles processed by RAN cover only one out of every three agrarian subjects. Although neither of the two sources offers information on the nature of the beneficiary of the title of the plots, it is safe to assume that the vast majority of them are *ejidatarios* and not IS settlers. This is because the Agrarian Law states in Article 68 that all *ejidatarios* have the right to receive a free urban plot of land (and consequently a title of ownership to the property), but it does not establish these rights for ISs settlers within *ejidos*. In order for the latter to obtain legal rights over the property they inhabit, the same law specifies that they must be recognised in *Ejido* Assemblies as 'settlers of *ejidos*', their names must be registered in the minutes of the Assembly, and they must be submitted to the RAN for the corresponding procedure. This means that the RAN is obliged to apply for titles to urban plots of land for all *ejidatarios*, but not for ISs settlers. The titling of a property in favour of the latter depends on the decision of the *ejidatarios*, and the RAN only processes it at the express request of the *ejidatarios*. As we will see later, the *ejidatarios* do not always make the request, which leaves the ISs settlers in limbo. Going back to Table 1, it can also be observed that the number of subjects registered as *ejidatarios* is almost double that of those declared as 'settlers'. As is widely known, the number living within *ejidos* is far greater than the number of *ejidatarios*. This is simply because until 1992, the *ejidos* were not authorised to increase the number of members beyond those assigned by law; upon the death of an *ejidatario*, they could only cede their *ejido* rights to one member of the family. This means that a significant proportion of IS settlers have not been recognised as *ejido* settlers.

Another fact that shows the gradual dismantling of CORETT is its decreasing activity. In the first three years of legal reform, the RAN delivered nine out of ten titles of urban land, while the CORETT delivered only one in ten (Figure 2). The intensive action of the RAN in this short period was possible thanks to the implementation of PROCEDE for free, which has allowed the individualisation of communal land plots to take place, but has not had a positive impact on the titling of the urban plots in favour of the settlers.

It is important to note, however, that between 1993 and 2015 both agencies substantially reduced the number of titles to urban plots. In the case of the RAN, the downward trend in titling is not worrying because it is practically a standard procedure: the *ejidatarios* are registered as such in the RAN and their property rights are explicitly recognised in the law. In addition, the demand for titles has not increased, because the number of *ejidatarios* does not increase. Consequently, it is possible to meet the goal of legally certifying the plots. In the case of CORETT, the downward trend of actions is alarming: there is a historical delay in the titling of land in favour of IS settlers, and their property rights are not protected by any law. In addition, poor households continue to have access to land on an informal basis so demand is always growing. Although the Programa de Apoyo a los Avecindados en Condiciones de Pobreza Patrimonial para Regularizar Asentamientos Humanos Irregulares (PASPRAH, Programme for the Support of Settlers in Conditions of Material Poverty to Regularise Irregular Human Settlements) has existed since 2008, its scope has been very limited. In the seven years that the PASPRAH has been in operation, 204,600 grants have been awarded at national level, with an average of nearly 23,000 per year. But it is estimated that there are more than 7.5 million plots of land yet to be regularised in the country's 56 metropolitan

Figure 2. Number of Urban Plot Deeds Delivered by the RAN and CORETT, National (1993–2015)

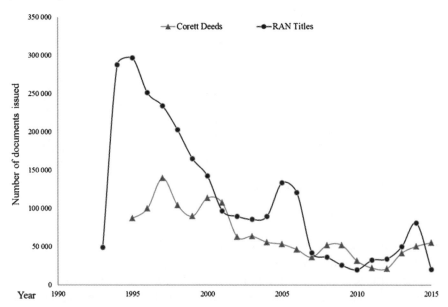

Source: prepared by the author based on: * Registro Agrario Nacional (2015) (RAN, National Agrarian Registry); ** Comisión de Regularización de Tenencia de la Tierra (2016a) (CORETT, Land Tenure Regularisation Commission).

areas alone (Salazar, 2010: 98). It is also important to note that the budget allocated to the programme has not increased, indeed it has tended to decrease, while the costs implicit in its implementation have risen, leading at the same time to a substantial decrease in the number of grants awarded (Table 2). The low priority given to the budget is consistent with the gradual dismantling of the organisation and the double discourse on the need to grant legal security of tenure when it comes to dealing with the poor.

The New Field of Regularisation: The Case of the San Cristóbal Ecatepec Ejido

The San Cristóbal Ecatepec *ejido* is located in the municipality of Ecatepec (Figure 3), which is one of the 59 municipalities in the Mexico City Metropolitan Area (MCMA). In 1993, when the process of measuring *ejidos* known as PROCEDE was carried out, the *ejidos* had a total area of 972.32 hectares. Of these, 580.23 were delimited as an area for common use and 392.10 hectares were earmarked for human settlement (RAN). The number of registered

Table 2.   Budget and Subsidies Granted through the PASPRAH to Formalise Property (2008–2016)

Year	Budget granted (million)[a]		Number of subsidies
	MXN$	US$	
2008	302.1	16.6	38,258
2009	337.6	18.6	33,592
2010	236.2	13.0	24,016
2011	203.4	11.2	21,177
2012	101.4	5.6	11,443
2013	178.4	9.8	17,305
2014	124.0	6.8	14,266
2015	318.8	17.5	28,465
2016	182.7	10.1	18,269

Source: prepared by the author based on unpublished information from CORETT (2016b).
[a] Amount granted. Deflated values as of January 2016.

beneficiaries was 154 *ejidatarios* (communal landowners), two *posesionarios* ('possessors of land plots') and no *avecindados* (settlers living there). This is in spite of the fact that according to municipal authorities, there are currently six ISs in the *ejidos* (San Cristóbal, San Andrés, San Francisco de Asís, Del Carmen, Del Carmen II, and Emiliano Zapata), with around 8000 non-regulated properties. According to data from the 2010 Population and Housing Census, there are 38,661 people living in these colonies. These settlements began to take shape during the 1970s, when low-income people bought land of around 800m^2, without basic infrastructure, and built their own homes there. At present, most of these land plots have been subdivided, some into up to four sections, to be shared with relatives or sold to other settlers, beginning a process of redensification. An estimated 12,000 households are located there. Despite not having been regularised yet, the ISs have piped water, electricity and telephone connections, and most of the streets are paved. Work on this infrastructure was mainly carried out by local residents and financed with their own resources, while the municipality of Ecatepec provided technical advisors.

The irregularity of these settlements continues to this day because the *ejidatarios* of San Cristóbal Ecatepec filed a writ of amparo against the expropriation decree, published in favour of CORETT in 1993 for 158.76 hectares, in order to regularise the ISs. According to interviews with the *ejido* authorities, the writ of amparo was filed because the *ejidatarios* considered that the compensation payment agreed with the Mexican state was well below the market price of the land. This was despite the fact that the *ejidatarios* had already received a payment from the IS settlers when they bought the properties twenty years earlier. Starting in 1992 and buoyed by the fact that the

Figure 3. The San Cristóbal Ecatepec *Ejido*. Located in the Mexico City Metropolitan Area

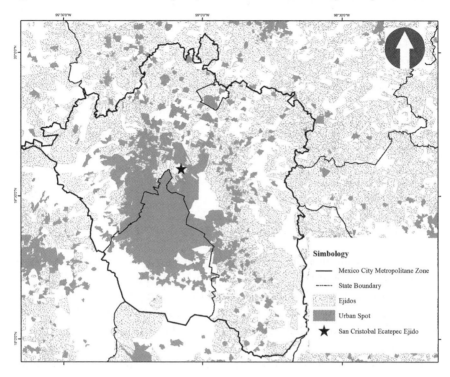

Source: prepared by the author.

law had granted them the power to regularise urban plots without the presence of CORETT, the *ejidatarios* saw the chance to subordinate the completion of expropriation in favour of more profitable economic interests. Thus, in the expectation of obtaining greater economic benefits than those derived from compensation, the *ejidatarios* decided in the *Ejido* Assemblies to unilaterally contract a private company which would carry out the formalities to regularise the IS settlers' properties.

Alliances and Conflicts over the Regularisation of ISs in the San Cristobal Ecatepec Ejido

In our interviews with them the IS settlers stated that at the end of 2003 the representatives of the San Cristóbal Ecatepec *ejido* informed them that the *Ejido* Assembly had agreed to begin work on the titling of urban plots. Through flyers, the *ejidatarios* called on the residents to go to *La Casa del Campesino* (*ejido* headquarters) to receive information about the procedure they needed to follow in order to regularise their plots. They were also

Table 3.   Cost of Regularisation According to Private vs. Governmental Administration (Deflated Values as of January 2016)

Use of land plot	MXN/m²	USD/m²
Private*		
Housing or fallow land	50.1	2.8
Commercial or mixed	100.2	5.5
Commercial or mixed with services	150.3	8.3
Average cost		
Average cost (800 m², Option A)	40,079.50	2,205.70
Updating of rights	2,505.00	137.8
Issuance of deed	3,339.90	183.8
Total	45,924.40	2,527.30
CORETT**		
Average cost	16,699.80	919.1
PASPRAH grant	−13,359.80	−735.2
Total	3,340.00	183.8

Sources: author's own calculations based on *on-site interviews and ** CORETT, 2016b.

told that the Asamblea de Delimitación, Destino y Asignación de Tierras (ADDAT, Land Delimitation, Destination and Allocation Assembly) would be held in August 2004. For the IS settlers, this was evidence that the *ejidatarios* had begun to implement a regularisation process without the presence of CORETT. Until then they had been aware that the expropriation decree regularising their plots had been published, and they were confident that it would be executed, disregarding the writ of amparo filed by the *ejidatarios*. The unilateral decision by the *Ejido* Assembly to hire a private company to regularise its properties made it clear that they would be affected. On the one hand, they were losing the certainty that the Mexican state had offered them, which recognised their legitimate right to housing, as expressed in the Mexican Constitution. On the other hand, the poorest households could no longer benefit from the PASPRAH, a programme which could provide a grant to help with the payment of the certification formalities because this was only available for households living on *ejidos* expropriated by CORETT. The conflict between the *ejidatarios* and the settlers stems from the choice of a private administrator to handle the regularisation. The alliance between the *ejidatarios* and a consultancy firm which did not know the IS settlers, was an affront to them. Now they had to pay for the regularisation of their land plots at the market rates specified on the flyers, valued per square metre and according to land use (Table 3).

With the new managers, the price of the private regularisation service rose much higher than that which the IS settlers would have owed to CORETT. For example, for an average land plot of 800m² and with the specified rate for housing use, the settlers had to pay the private company approximately US$2205 (MXN$40,079) for the regularisation formalities. These included not only the technical work (the IS plan and plot measurement) and the collection of all necessary documents, but also the legal and administrative advice given to the *ejidatarios* in order to deliver a complete set of records to the RAN. In addition, the settlers would have two other expenses: the payment for updating the proof of possession issued by the *Ejido* Assemblies, and the document registering the property in their name in the RPP (Table 3). The total costs with a private administrator were more than double those incurred with CORETT, and are extremely high if we consider that at that time the monthly minimum wage (MMW) was equivalent to US$114.5 (MXN$2080.6) in January 2016, and that 24 percent of the economically active population earns up to 3 MMWs, and another 60 percent earns between 3.1 and 5 MMWs (INEGI, 2010).

When the workers of several private companies were questioned about the costs of regularisation, they stated that there was no official criterion for assessing the first two economic considerations, that each communal land had its own rate and that each company made its own calculation. The officials interviewed confirmed that the final price of the regularisation carried out by them was indeed much higher than the one established by CORETT, but they responded that the process was much faster. The ability of CORETT to charge lower costs is related to its expertise; the political work and partnerships established with state and municipal governments, as well as local notaries, is what allows the organisation to avoid market rates.

Although the regularisation process might be quicker, data from the interviews suggests that the effectiveness and efficiency achieved by the private managers could be questioned. This depends on several factors: on the one hand, the capacity of the *ejidatarios* to reach an agreement with the settlers on the procedure to be followed; on the other hand, the ability of the company to comply in a timely manner with the procedures required, as well as the expertise to convince the settlers to adhere to their proposal. The failed actions in these stages of the process have led to the extension of regularisation indefinitely.

In the case in point, the company's administrator stated that he had contacted the *ejidatarios* through their networks and offered them a service that promised to reassert their position *vis-à-vis* the 'settlers', as well as producing, in a shorter period of time, higher economic returns than those they would obtain from the compensation. The services offered to the *ejidatarios* included advice about regularisation in three areas: legal, technical, and administrative. With respect to the first, they offered guidance on compliance with the federal, state, and local regulations required to meet the qualification conditions. At the technical level, they promised to re-measure the boundaries of the PROCEDE zone, to make a general plan of the IS and to measure the plots within the general layout. At the administrative level, they offered to combine the documents and plans to be submitted to the municipal authorities and later to the RAN as appropriate. Moreover, they made an attractive economic offer linked to the profits. Estimating the number of properties to be regularised, they offered to pay the *ejidatarios* between 20 percent and 25 percent of the fee that they would charge the IS settlers for the regularisation process.

The plan failed from the outset because they did not adequately inform the settlers about the procedure, so they resisted participating in a private regularisation process. Once the *ejidatario* had been confirmed as the legitimate owner of the land, the company began convincing the settlers of ISs by appealing symbolically to their hopes and fears. They played on people's desire to provide security for their families through having property title deeds, but also included messages in the pamphlets which preyed on the IS settlers' fears, using phrases such as 'leave illegality behind' or 'avoid losing your assets'. They also added pressure through verbal threats, suggesting that if they did not accept the proposal their lands would be titled in the name of the *ejido*. But these tactics were unsuccessful. In July 2007, the San Cristóbal Ecatepec communal land had submitted a list of 572 subjects entitled to urban land to the RAN, but this list included only 7 percent of the irregular plots of *ejido* land. Those who did comply tended to be the most vulnerable people, such as older adults and single female heads of household, who accepted the terms of land regularisation without the presence of CORETT. Those who decided to hire the private regularisation service explained that they had done so because they 'don't want to leave problems for their children to deal with' or 'are afraid of losing everything'.

The strategy of intimidation, in addition to being a clumsy manoeuvre, also had devastating effects on the management. The majority of the 'settlers' reacted negatively, perceiving the proposal as an ultimatum and an act of abuse by the *ejidatarios*. The ISs settlers said they refused to participate because, apart from the high cost of the fee they had to pay to the company, they would have to pay the *ejidatarios* another US$137.8 (MXN$2505.00) to update the 'transfer of rights' for the property they inhabited, which implied that they were disregarding what were appropriate documents obtained when they bought the urban plot. In addition, they would have to make yet another outlay of US$183.8 (MXN$3339.90) for the issuance of the final document, that is, for the property title deed issued by the RPP.

What we want to highlight is the lack of skill in creating a new foundation for social relations that treated IS settlers as clients to be taken advantage of, who could be charged twice for a commodity that has already been paid for, used and transformed. Ultimately, this was the death knell of the strategy. By the end of 2014, negotiations between the *ejidatarios* and the consultancy firm had stalled. The refusal of the settlers to enter into this private regularisation process prevented the company from obtaining the expected profit and, as a result, from deriving the dividends offered to the *ejidatarios*. This generated disagreements among these partners and divisions within the *ejido*. In the middle of that same year, new *ejido* authorities had been elected, who, given the company's failure to comply, were in favour of resuming the regularisation of the ISs with CORETT. Groups opposed to this refused to acknowledge their authority and asked for their dismissal. At the same time, the new *ejido* authorities informed the 'settlers' that they were in talks with CORETT, but because of the internal conflicts in the *ejido* they refused to inform them of the content of the talks with the organisation. As a result, the IS settlers went to the CORETT offices to get more information about the situation, whereupon officials told them that the negotiations had stalled. The *ejidatarios* had demanded an adjustment to the compensation, which was not possible. The decree of property expropriation under the *ejido* or communal regime had already been published, with the amount being the responsibility of the Instituto de Administración y Avalúos de Bienes Nacionales (INDAABIN, Institute for Administration and Appraisal of National Assets) and not of CORETT. Up to July 2016, the two mechanisms had been immobilised; neither the company nor CORETT had made progress in the titling of the urban plots for the 'settlers'. In this case, the expectation that the regularisation would be accomplished more quickly has not been fulfilled, nor has the promise of offering legal security for the properties.

In addition to the vision that motivated these reforms to the land tenure system, the ambiguity and loopholes contained in the Agrarian Law have also affected regularisation. These have generated ambivalent situations in the designation of the urban plots to the settlers, as well as in the mechanisms to regularise their property. A crucial point has been the non-recognition of any rights for the settlers of ISs over the urban land they occupy and the degree of discretion with which an *Ejido* Assembly makes its decisions. As already explained, among the 'settlers' are children and relatives of *ejidatarios*, as well as neighbours and migrants in general. As a general trend, the former obtain land through land transfer and without economic intermediation, while the latter do so through purchasing processes not registered with any competent authority. Similarly, when relations are cordial, the *Ejido* Assembly often reserves the right to recognise or grant children and relatives of *ejidatarios* the certificate of right to the urban land they occupy for free, but establishes a fee for non-family neighbours. Although the latter may possess suitable documents that would accredit them as legitimate owners of the urban plots of land before CORETT, the freedom granted to the *Ejido* Assembly to endorse them in exchange for financial compensation makes it difficult to continue with the regularisation process.

In this context, the recognition of land ownership rights in favour of the settlers of ISs has become a currency of exchange that recreates practices which, because they are not regulated, are permitted and not punished. In other words, the formalisation of property rights in private hands has added to the arbitrary and illegal management mechanisms that characterise access to *ejido* land. This highlights the contradiction behind the constitutional change: the promise that progress would be made in offering legal security of property, with the aim of ending poverty. The gradual destruction of CORETT and the injection of business interests into IS regularisation are proof that the reforms to the *ejido* tenure system have not been able to 'turn freedoms into something more than mandates, that is, into authentic political conventions that are the foundation of social coexistence' (Cordova, 2010). Recognising the legitimate possession of urban plots of land, based on categories that grant differentiated rights to *ejidatarios* and other 'settlers' and exclude IS settlers from the population of the *ejidos*, has resulted in a new discriminatory phenomenon. This is contrary to the principle that has governed CORETT since its creation, which has been to include all the settlers in the list of owners of a property, regardless of their relationship with the members of the communal land.

Conclusions

Observing the shift that the formalisation of property has taken in the ISs implies reflecting on how the modification of formal rules reconfigures the field of objective relations, transforming not only the objective for which it was created, but also destroying the entire institutional system involved, that is, the social mechanisms which regulated more cooperative behaviour before the 1992 reforms. This is because the new legal framework is aimed at supporting 'economic freedom', the driving force behind business logic, rather than consolidating the legal security of property for the poor.

Picking up Bourdieu's (1993) point, the reforms to the Constitution and the Agrarian Law fail in their objectives of achieving legal certification, since social actors have imposed a new structure of relations, with differentiated incentives and restrictions. Supported by the new agrarian legal framework, the *ejidatarios* have been able to adjust their position in the game of transferring land ownership in order to more successfully mobilise their social capital and exercise control over the property rights of other citizens. The reformed legal framework allows them, on the one hand, to appropriate a power that the state had reserved for itself before the 1992 reforms and, on the other, to use community institutions to adjust individual interests and practices. In other words, the law allows them to appropriate 'the economic and political resources that give the State power over all the games and the rules that govern them' (Bourdieu, 1993: 66). In this context, actors such as CORETT and the settlers of the ISs, who had been central to the regularisation process, now find new barriers – both formal and informal – to participating in conditions of equity in the recently defined field of relations. It looks like it will generate further exclusion and discrimination and is generating social conflicts that did not exist before the reforms. As owners with full rights, and stimulated by the institutional agrarian framework, they speculate on the costs implicit in the regularisation procedures and pressure the IS settlers to enter the unjust game of the market.

The data presented also supports the view that the constitutional changes and the omissions in the Agrarian Law offer a broad spectrum of interpretations of property rights, which delays and complicates the regularisation of the ISs in the urban periphery. It is becoming increasingly evident that the policy of regularisation is an instrument incapable of providing 'legal certainty'. The *ejidatarios* seem less willing to accept the expropriation decrees that allowed CORETT to give legal certainty to the settlers, while the dismantling of CORETT and the presence of private managers generates suspicion and uncertainty among the settlers, forging distrust between neighbours and creating new social conflicts among them.

References

Adler de Lomnitz, L. (1978) *Cómo sobreviven los marginados*. Siglo XXI: Mexico FD.

Alba, F. (1989) *La población de México: evolución y dilemas*. El Colegio de México: Mexico FD.

Bourdieu, P. (2003) *Las estructuras sociales de la economía*. Anagrama: Barcelona.

Bourdieu, P. and Wacquant, L. J. D. (1993) *Respuestas: por una antropología reflexiva*. Grijalbo: Mexico FD.

Calderón Cockburn, J. (2006) *Mercado de tierras urbanas, propiedad y pobreza*. SINCO editores/Lincoln Institute of Land Policy: Lima.

Calderón Cockburn, J. (2010) 'Titulación de la propiedad y mercado inmobiliario'. *Estudios Demográficos y Urbanos* 75: 625–661.

Córdova, A. (2010) 'Qué es la Constitución'. La Jornada, 16 May. [WWW document]. URL https://www.jornada.com.mx/2010/05/16/opinion/019a1polhttps://www.jornada.com.mx/2010/05/16/opinion/019a1pol [accessed 7 July 2019].

CORETT (2016a) 'Decretos de expropiación y áreas Expropiadas a favor de CORETT'. [Database on CD-ROM] [Update: December 2016].

CORETT (2016b) 'Presupuestos y subsidios otorgados a través de PASPRAH para regularizar la propiedad 2008–2016. [Database on CD-ROM] [Update: December 2016].

Cruz, M. S. (2001) *Propiedad, poblamiento y periferia rural en la Zona Metropolitana de la Ciudad de México*. UAM-Azcapotzalco/ Editorial de la Red Nacional de Investigación Urbana: Mexico FD.

Duhau, E. (1998) *Hábitat popular y política urbana*. Porrúa-UAM-A: Mexico FD.

El Colegio Mexiquense (2006) *Análisis de los Impactos de las Acciones de la Comisión para la Regularización de la Tenencia de la Tierra (CORETT)*. Unpublished report presented to Dirección General de Evaluación y Monitoreo de los Programas Sociales (DGEMPS). Secretaría de Desarrollo Social: México.

Fernandes, E. (2008) 'Consideraciones generales sobre las políticas públicas de regularización de asentamientos informales en América Latina'. *Revista Eure* *XXXIV* **102**(1): 25–38.

Garza, G. (1985) *El proceso de industrialización en la Ciudad de México 1821–1970*. El Colegio de México: Mexico FD.

Ibarra, L. (2012) *Una política pública entrampada. La regularización de los asentamientos humanos Irregulares en suelo de origen social en México*. Unpublished master's dissertation, Facultad Latinoamericana de Ciencias Sociales: Mexico FD.

Instituto Nacional de Estadística, Geografía e Informática INEGI (2007) *Censo Agropecuario 2007*. [WWW document]. URL http://www.beta.inegi.org.mx/app/biblioteca/ficha.html?upc=702825292867 [accessed 1 February 2019].

Instituto Nacional de Estadística, Geografía e Informática INEGI (2010) *Censo de Población y Vivienda*: Aguascalientes. [WWW document] URL https://www.inegi.org.mx/programas/ccpv/2010/ [accessed 7 July 2019].

Kouri, E. (2015) 'La invención del ejido'. *Nexos* **37**(445): 54–61.

México (1992) 'Constitución Política de los Estados Unidos Mexicanos'. *Diario Oficial de la Federación*, 28 January. [WWW document] URL http://www.ilo.org/dyn/natlex/natlex4.detail?p_lang=en&p_isn=27837 [accessed 1 February 2019].

México, Secretaría de Desarrollo Agrario, Territorial y Urbano (2014) '*Reglas de operación para el Programa de Apoyo a los Avecindados en Condiciones de Pobreza Patrimonial para Regularizar Asentamientos Humanos Irregulares (PASPRAH)*'. *Diario Oficial de la Federación*, 28 December. [WWW document] URL https://www.dof.gob.mx/nota_detalle.php?codigo=5377551&fecha=28/12/201 [accessed 1 February 2019].

México, Secretaría Desarrollo Agrario, Territorial y Urbano (2016) *Registro agrario nacional: padrón e historial de núcleos agrarios (PHINA)*, updated to July 2016. [WWW document] URL http://www.ran.gob.mx/ran/index.php/sistemas-de-consulta/phina [accessed 1 February 2019].

México, Secretaria de la Función Publica (2004) 'Ley General de Bienes Nacionales'. *Diario Oficial de la Federación,* 20 May [WWW document] URL http://www.diputados.gob.mx/LeyesBiblio/ref/lgbn/LGBN_orig_20may04.pdf update1 June 2016. [accessed 1 February 2019].

México, Secretaria de la Reforma Agraria (1971) 'Ley Federal de la Reforma Agraria'. *Diario Oficial de la Federación*, 16 April. [WWW document] URL www3.diputados.gob.mx/camara/content/download/.../ley_reforma_agrarisa_1971.pdf [accessed 1 February 2019].

México, Secretaria de la Reforma Agraria (1992) 'Ley Agraria'. *Diario Oficial de la Federación* 9 April. [WWW document] URL [accessed 1 February 2019].

México, Secretaria de la Reforma Agraria (1993) 'Reglamento de la Ley Agraria en materia de certificación de derechos ejidales y titulación de solares'. *Diario Oficial de la Federación*, 6 January [WWW document] URL http://www.diputados.gob.mx/LeyesBiblio/regley/Reg_LAgra_MCDETS.pdf [accessed 1 February 2019].

México, Secretaría de la Reforma Agraria, Registro Agrario Nacional (2003) *Programa de certificación de derechos ejidales y titulación de solares (PRO-CEDE)*. [WWW document] URL http://www.sct.gob.mx/obrapublica/MarcoNormativo/3/3-3/3-3-5.pdf [accessed 1 February 2019].

Registro Agrario Nacional (RAN), Dirección de Titulación y Control Documental (2015) 'Títulos de Solares Urbanos'. [Database on CD-ROM] [Update: December 2015].

Salazar, C. (2009) 'La disponibilidad de suelo social en las áreas metropolitanas del país'. *Estudios Agrarios* **41**(2): 125–144.

Salazar, C. (2011) 'La privatisation des terres collectives agraires dans l'agglomé ration de Mexico. L'impact des réformes de 1992 sur l'expansion urbaine et la régularisation des lots urbains'. *Tiers Monde* **206**(2): 95–114.

Salazar, C. (2010) 'La oferta potencial de suelo social en la Zona Metropolitana del Valle de México. Una lectura a partir de la certificación ejidal' in: A. Iracheta, and E. Soto (eds) *Impacto de la vivienda en el desarrollo urbano. Una mirada a la política habitacional en México*. Memorias del Tercer Congreso Nacional de Suelo Urbano. El Colegio Mexiquense: Mexico FC, 307–332.

Salazar, C. (2014) 'El puño invisible de la privatización'. *Territorios* **30**(2): 69–90.

Schteingart, M. (1989) *Los productores del espacio habitable: estado, empresa y sociedad en la Ciudad de México*. El Colegio de México: Mexico FD.

Varley, A. (1985) 'La zona urbana ejidal y la urbanización de la Ciudad de México'. *Revista de la metrópoli mexicana* **15**(6): 71–95.

6

Informal Settlements in the Age of Digital Cartography: Insights from Mexico City

PRISCILLA CONNOLLY
Universidad Autónoma Metropolitana-Azcapotzalco, Mexico City

'Informal' housing settlement has been responsible for a substantial propor-tion of twentieth-century Latin American urbanisation. François Tomas (1996) suggested that between one-quarter and two-thirds of all urban residents in the region live in some form of informal settlement. Since the 1970s, it has been widely held that the *colonias populares* comprise at least two-thirds of all resi-dential growth in Mexico City (Ward, 1976; Connolly, 1977). This percentage is much higher in smaller Mexican towns and villages, but substantially less in some other medium-sized cities, such as Aguascalientes or Mérida (Jiménez, 2000; Eibenshutz and Benlluire, 2009).

Is this informal settlement process a permanent feature of cities in Latin America and other regions, as Mike Davis (2006) suggests, or is it a twentieth-century phenomenon that will give way to new forms of producing housing engendered by neo-liberal policies, globalised financial markets, information technology and the socio-demographic transformations of the new millennium? This chapter addresses this question by observing the effect of recent policies and economic trends on the dynamics of informal housing production in Mexico City between 1990 and 2010. It also seeks to raise issues related to the definition of 'informal' and methodological approaches to the subject in the era of digital technology.

In the Mexican case, there are several factors that could have affected the production of housing in informal settlements over the past two decades. Without claiming to provide an exhaustive list, these factors can be conve-niently grouped under five headings:

(a) socio-demographic transformations of urban society
(b) national and local housing finance policy
(c) macroeconomic stability, access to mortgage and rising land values
(d) the differentiated and uneven application of land use and other regu-lations regarding both formal and informal urban development and

(e) the end of the Agrarian Reform and changes in the regulation of communal property.

Context

Socio-demographic Transformations in Urban Society

The multiple socio-demographic factors influencing informal settlement formation and development may be condensed into five interrelated trends: the city's population growth rate, migration flows, family size and the role of women, and employment. From its explosive growth in the mid-twentieth century, Metropolitan Mexico City's total population grew at a sedate average rate of 1.7 percent per annum between 1990 and 2000 and 0.9 percent between 2000 and 2010, less than the national average. In the same decade, the mean annual demographic growth rate of Mexico City proper – called the 'Federal District' or DF until January 2016 when its name was changed to 'Ciudad de México' – was only 0.3 percent, but considerably higher (1.3 percent) in the surrounding metropolitan municipalities (CONAPO, 2012). Although these figures might seem to indicate a relatively stable housing demand, they translate into a population increase from 15.5 million in 1990 to 21.1 million in 2010. Furthermore, given the change in the age pyramid and family structure – from an average of five persons per dwelling to 3.5 in 2010 – this additional population has generated an increase of over two million dwellings, or more if you count empty houses. The demographic transition also means that women are having fewer children and are more actively involved in the workforce, which means less time to embark on the lengthy and time-consuming process of self-build housing.

The slowing down of population growth is due not only to lower birth rates but also to the increasingly negative net migration from Metropolitan Mexico City over the past decades. For example, between 2005 and 2010, there were 160,000 more emigrants from the city than immigrants. Most immigrants do not now come from rural areas or smaller towns and cities but from other metropolitan areas (Pérez and Santos, 2013). Thus, people needing new homes do not come from rural backgrounds, accustomed to living without urban services and building their own houses; rather, they have grown up in the city, are connected to the social networks and have a basic education. However, education, even a university degree, no longer guarantees a job with a steady wage and social benefits. At a national level, informal employment, defined as jobs in micro businesses, unprotected by labour legislation, without social benefits and the self-employed, oscillates between 57 and 60 percent of total employment (ILO/FORLAC, 2014: 5), slightly less – 48 percent – among residents of Mexico City proper (STPS, 2016: 4). Informal employment is not necessarily low paid, although much of it is part-time and precarious. It also tends to be 'counter-cyclical' to both business cycles and formal employment, acting as a kind of buffer in times of crisis, such as after 1994 and 2009 (Fernández and Meza, 2015). Independently of income, informal employment is a serious barrier to obtaining a mortgage or other housing credit, which explains why so many relatively well-off families can only make a home in informal settlements, building a house as their economic situation allows. New families with low or unstable incomes often do not have any other option than to continue living with their parents, either in the same house or, as is common in informal settlements, in separate dwellings built on the same plot as the family home (Ortega-Alcázar, 2007; Ward, 2016). Access to housing credits, of course, also depends on their availability, a condition that radically changed after reforms to the major financial institutions in the 1990s.

Local and National Housing Policy

'Housing policy' in Mexican government discourse has referred almost exclusively to mortgage finance for new construction. Before the 1990s, the housing finance institutions did not supply enough credits to satisfy their effective demand. Most of those entitled to housing credits had to resort to informal solutions for lack of other options, even though they qualified for a mortgage. During the period that concerns us here, these institutions radically altered their rules of operation, so that from the second half of the 1990s the supply of mortgage loans nationwide increased dramatically, financing a yearly average of nearly 700,000 developer-built homes during the first decade of the new century. Between 2000 and 2010, this boom supplied more than half a million mortgage for purchasing new houses located in large-scale projects in outlying metropolitan municipalities of Mexico City (CONAVI, 2016). During the same period, nearly 100,000 new apartments in condominiums of five units or more were also built within Mexico City proper (DF). After 2010, the housebuilding boom was affected not only by the global financial crisis, but also by the saturation of effective demand, made up of employees with low and middle incomes in urban areas (Topelson, 2006: 34; Connolly, 2006a: 129). Since then, regulation has relaxed even more, allowing second home purchasers to benefit from national housing funds, as well as the combination of mortgage to cover higher value properties. At the same time, the availability of credits and subsidies geared to lower-income demand, such as loans for secondhand homes, home improvements and extensions have increased.

A predictable effect of this explosion in formal housing supply, especially in the cheaper market located in peripheral municipalities, is that it would absorb part of the solvent effective demand that was traditionally met by informal settlements. However, formal production still leaves unattended between 40 and 50 per cent of the metropolitan population with the lowest and/or with non-verifiable incomes, who have little alternative but to seek the 'self-build' solution in informal settlements.

For the poorest third of the population in Mexico City proper, some options are provided by two housing programmes implemented by the local Housing Institute. The first programme funded the construction of almost 175,000 new apartments between 2001 and 2010, providing mortgages for families with incomes below five minimum wages (INVI, 2016). Hypothetically, this type of programme should retain some low-income population in central areas.

The second programme aims at strengthening the consolidation and improvement of housing in informal settlements. During the same period, it provided almost 175,000 credits for the improvement or construction of new housing in areas of 'high or very high marginalisation indexes' (INVI website). Here the expected impact of these credits would be to bolster the normal densification of regularised settlements within Mexico City proper, due to investments made for the improvement, expansion or replacement of existing housing.

Macroeconomic Stability, Access to Mortgage Credit and Rising Land Values

The restructured housing finance system would have been totally ineffective without the macroeconomic stability achieved after the 'tequila crisis' of December 1994. By the end of the decade, inflation, currency exchange and interest rates had all been brought under control resulting in an exceptionally favourable economic climate for the real estate sector during the first eight years of the new millennium. The resulting housing boom and availability of credit caused land prices to rise in Mexico City and elsewhere between 2000 and 2010. Inflated land prices in central areas have been attributed to the ban on new development in peripheral areas of Mexico City between 2001 and 2006, mentioned below (Benlliure 2005). However, the increase has been general and continuous in the whole of Mexico City proper and the more centrally located metropolitan municipalities (Guadarrama, 2007).

Following research into previous effects of economic cycles on Metropolitan Mexico City's expansion and densification (Connolly, 1988), I would have expected that an increase in land prices would limit urban expansion, especially formal urbanisation, with the corresponding densification of previously both formal and informally urbanised areas. As we shall see, this did not happen.

Differential Planning Policies

In the past, opposing policy restrictions for new developments in the two states that constitute Metropolitan Mexico City have determined complementary growth patterns. It is generally accepted that the limits imposed by the DF's mayor Ernesto Uruchurtu (1953–1966) contributed to urban expansion in municipalities in the State of Mexico to the north and east (Cornelius, 1975: 203; Moreno, 1979: 163; Stolarski, 1982: 36). For the period considered here, we could predict that the ban on new housing developments in some parts of the DF between 2001 and 2006, and the ongoing policy on 'recycling' and 're-densifiying' central areas would have a similar effect. This policy, first outlined in the Urban Development Programme of the Federal District in 1997, was legally enacted in the '*Bando 2*' proclaimed by Andrés Manuel López Obrador on 7 December 2000, a few days after taking office as mayor. The measure was implemented by withholding authorisations for new water mains connections except in the central districts; here, housing construction was actively encouraged by the simplification of the building permit procedures (Esquivel, 2007: 256).

New informal urban development has also been discouraged in the DF by new planning practices that complicate the normal regularisation processes (see Salazar in this volume). Before any land titling can take place, informal settlements inside the DF need to obtain a change in their land use status, an extremely complicated and drawn-out procedure which is seldom fully completed (Wigle, 2013; Connolly and Wigle, 2017).

The restrictive policy pursued in the Federal District contrasts with the relatively permissive practice concerning new housing development in metropolitan municipalities. As in the 1960s, it was predictable that the combination of restrictive and permissive planning policies would push recent urban development towards the outer periphery of the metropolitan area. Moreover, throughout the metropolitan area, the contrast persists between the strict enforcement of planning regulations in certain areas and permissiveness in those considered to be low-income neighbourhoods, where the prevalent land use classification is termed 'housing mixed with small-scale retailing and services'. This distinction occurs both in the metropolitan municipalities and inside Mexico City proper (DF). In the latter, however, the distinction is even more marked by the exemption of a building licence for construction financed by the housing improvement programme described earlier. This exemption keeps building inspectors away from construction sites in the areas classified as 'highly or very highly marginalised' favoured by the programme, thus eliminating the already lax application of planning norms in informally developed settlements. In other words, while nothing has been done to curb the densification of existing informal settlements during the last decades throughout the metropolitan area, in Mexico City this has been positively encouraged and totally deregulated by local planning and housing policy.

The End of Agrarian Reform and the Demise of Communal Property

The role of communal property (*ejidos* and *comunidades*) in informal urbanisation in Mexico has been studied since the 1970s and there are many publications in English on the subject (Varley, 1985; Azuela 1987; Cymet, 1992). Research by these and other authors (Schteingart, 1989; Duhau, 1998; Cruz 2001, to name but a few) has contributed to understanding the wider political and cultural significance of urban informality. Among other things, these studies established that although commercial transactions of communal property were illegal, the sale of plots on *ejido* land for urban settlements was to a certain extent guaranteed by customary legal practices agreed between buyers and sellers. Before the 1970s, the urbanisation of most *ejidos* was legitimised either by the constitution of an urban zone under agrarian law, or by selling community land as if it were private property. During the following decades, the operation of the Commission for Tenure Regularisation and other federal regularising agencies provided buyers with sufficient assurance that, in the future, they would obtain property titles. Finally, amendments to Article 27 of the Constitution of 1992, officially pronouncing the end of the Agrarian Reform, has enabled the individualisation of land titles and the legal sale of community and *ejidos* (Salazar in this book).

Shortly after this constitutional reform, several published research articles predicted the immediate privatisation of *ejido* lands (Pradilla, 1992; Castañeda, 1993; Nava, 1993). This prediction was even incorporated into the 1994 National Development Programme, which assumed that 65 percent of territorial reserves for planned urban expansion would correspond to the recently liberated *ejidos*. However, this scenario just did not happen, at least not immediately. By 1996, only one-third of communities with land suitable for urban development had been procedures for legally selling a part or whole of an *ejido* (Cruz, 2001: 275–276). Several explanations for this apparent stagnation in the urbanisation of the *ejidos* were discussed, including lack of interest and lack of know-how on the part of the potential sellers, the *ejidatarios* (Jones and Ward, 1998: 86–87; Cruz, 2001: 336–339). However, as this study will show, the situation has changed since the 1990s; in Metropolitan Mexico City, *ejido* land provided a substantial proportion of land for commercially developed formal urban growth, at least until 2010, as well as continuing to be parcelled out for informal urban development.

Some Notes on Methodology

What do we mean by 'informal'?

This chapter is about measuring informal settlements, so we need some sort of working definition of them. What, then, is an 'informal' settlement' in Latin America?

'Irregular and Informal' have entered the English lexicon as the preferred adjectives to describe poor neighbourhoods in cities of the Global South. Before the 1960s, either they were indiscriminately labelled as 'slums', thus in need of clearing, or the local term was used, for example *gecekondus* (Turkey), *bidonvilles* (Algeria), *bustees* (Kolkata, Dhaka). In Latin America (see Hauser 1961), every country, every city even, had its own name, for example, *barriadas* (Peru), *favelas* (Brazil), *colonia de paracaidistas* (Mexico), *colonias proletarias* (Mexico City), *ranchos* (Venezuela), *callampas* (Chile), *fraccionamientos piratas* (Bogotá) and *comunas* (Medellín and Cali). None of these words translates as 'slum' in English, but each reflects the local context and values: whether the settlements were created by invasions or unauthorised subdivisions; if they were noted for their 'rural' features or seen as the habitat of a new urban working class. As international organisations became concerned about the rapid urbanisation of what were then called 'Third World' countries, policy-makers and academics alike began to look for generic terms that would encompass all those types of settlements whose problems clearly were not going to be solved by slum clearance. Charles Abrams' pioneering book (1964) provided a more positive view of 'squatter settlements', a term endorsed, among others, by a North American anthropologist and a British architect working in Peru during the 1960s, whose ideas were highly influential in the field. For William Manguin (1967), 'squatter settlements' were a 'solution, not a problem', while John Turner (1968a, b) proclaimed that 'squatter' or 'uncontrolled' settlements and 'self-help housing' produce 'architecture that works'. The flourishing international literature seeking generalisations based on individual studies led to the multiplication of generic terms. Dwyer (1975: 3) preferred 'spontaneous', to avoid the 'prejudicial legal implications of "squatter"'. Shlomo Angel (2000) used 'informal'. Mike Davis (2006) distinguished between 'squatters' and 'pirate urbanisation', but for him, all are 'slums'. Words such as 'marginal', 'irregular' and 'informal', conceptualised by the burgeoning corpus of Latin American urban studies from the 1970s onwards, were uncritically translated into English. Latin American scholars, such as the authors in this book, use both *irregular* and *informal*; however, *popular*, meaning 'of the people' as opposed to 'of the ruling classes', is the preferred as a non-deprecatory adjective associated with the subaltern classes' habitat (Connolly, 2017).

Of all these terms, 'informal' and 'marginal' are the only ones included in the United Nations glossary of Environment Statistics (UN, 1997) and reproduced *verbatim* in the OECD (2001) online Glossary of Statistical Terms. In these documents, 'informal settlements' have two definitions:

(i) areas where groups of housing units have been constructed on land that the occupants have no legal claim to, or occupy illegally;

(ii) unplanned settlements and areas where housing is not in compliance with current planning and building regulations (unauthorised housing).

And both sources provide a direct link to the following definition:

(a) marginal settlements are housing units that, lacking basic amenities, are not considered fit for human habitation;

(b) slums are a multidimensional concept involving aspects of poor housing, overcrowding, lack of services and insecure tenure, and that indicators relating to these can be combined in different ways to give thresholds that provide estimates of numbers of slum dwellers.

At least two definitions of 'informal' are at work here: on the one hand relating to 'legal claim to land' or property rights; and, on the other, non-compliance with planning and building regulation, implying 'sub-standard' or 'unfit' housing conditions. Both these are contingent on the respective legal and cultural norms in each context, so cross-country comparisons may be meaningless. In Latin America, the various types of the first kind of informality have received much more attention from scholars and policy-makers alike, as this book illustrates. Correspondingly, 'regularisation' generally refers to property titling, and there are heated debates about the ways, means and implications of achieving this, or even whether this is a good thing or not (Varley, 2017). There has been less work on informality regarding planning and building regulations, although the two types of illegality may or may not be mutually determinant. For instance, in the Mexican case, until 1976 the legality of a property's title deeds was completely independent of its legality *vis-à-vis* planning laws and building regulations. This changed in May 1976 when the General Law of Human Settlements stipulated that public notaries must ensure that all contracts and titles relating to property specify the land use permitted by the local development plans (LGAH 1976, Articles 44–46). However, the implementation of such a provision has been uneven and flexible, varying from region to region. Perhaps the strictest conditions exist in Mexico City (DF). Here, the regularisation of property titles has been subject to compliance with planning regulations since the 1987 Urban Development Plan defined which areas were 'urban development zones' and which were 'conservation lands' (Wigle, 2013; Connolly and Wigle, 2017).

Figure 1.   What do We Mean by 'Informal'? The Branching Tree of Irregularities in Housing

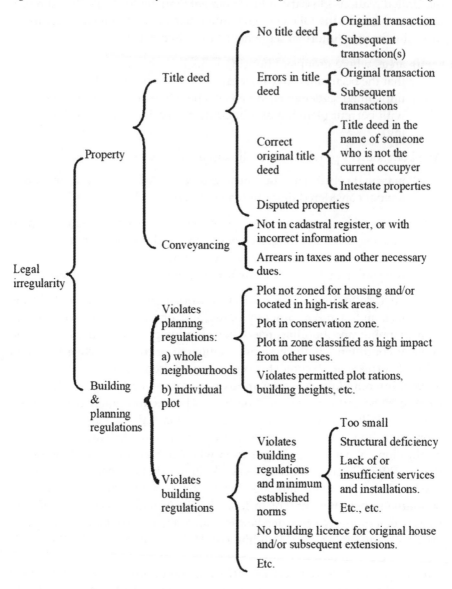

With Mexico very much in mind, Figure 1 illustrates the wide range of situations whereby an individual house, or a whole neighbourhood, might be considered 'informal'.

We can see that the possible causes for legal informality include a wide variety of situations, some of which are interconnected and concurrent while others may not be. Furthermore, the condition of 'being regular' may not be permanent; regularisation of property titles usually occurs, by processes described in this book. However, as Jiménez, Cruz and Ubaldo show, property titles become informal again as people die without leaving a will, or fail to comply with fiscal and other obligations. In fact, it is quite difficult for any property to be regular in all aspects – such as having all the documents in the name of the current owner – whatever the quality and social status of the building concerned. Consequently, a hard and fast definition of what informal settlements means in legal term is equally elusive. So how can we quantify them?

Despite the lack of precision concerning the definition of 'informal', the word is tenacious, especially in relation to land tenure, as this book testifies. Apparently, we comprehend what 'Irregular or informal' means. Elsewhere I have argued that consensus concerning the meaning of 'informal' or 'uncontrolled settlement' partly stems from the historical experience of the apartheid type of urban development formally imposed, but not always in enforced in practice, during the Latin American colonial and post-colonial period (Connolly, 2017). There is also consensus about the makeshift 'do-it-yourself', 'self-build' housing that characterises informal settlements throughout the world. Informal housing settlements violate the legal order because they change the temporal order that this legal order dictates. By occupying first and building later, informal housing transgresses the conventional order of the housing process: obtain planning permission; subdivide land; obtain building licence; put in services; build dwelling – sell or rent – occupy. By reversing this process (occupy first and all the rest later), informal housing has produced an architecture that is similar in most Latin American countries and even beyond (Ribbeck and Padilla, 2002). The fact that we can we can make cross-country comparisons is based, not so much on hard definitions, but on a shared image of what informal settlements look like and mean, in terms of day-to-day experience. From the photographs that Turner published in *Architectural Design* in 1968 to the recently much-televised *favelas* of Río, or the Caracas *barriada* on the cover of Mike Davis' book *Planet of Slums* and the 'admirable (aerial) photos of Mexico City,' published online in by Oscar Ruiz (Ruiz, 2011): all these contribute to the iconographic image of Latin American informal settlements.

I stress the importance of the urban landscape produced by the informal housing process as this provides a kind of visual synthesis of its manifold 'informalities'; more importantly, for the purposes of this chapter, it provides a first cut criterion for distinguishing informal settlements from other forms of urbanisation. In fact, almost all identification, quantification and analysis of the phenomenon in Latin America and elsewhere has been based on these characteristics. In the methodology described in the following section, this preliminary identification based on appearances may then be subject to further scrutiny, by means of case-histories, on-the-ground fieldwork and statistical analysis.

Identifying the Informal: The 'Settlement Type' Methodology

The 'settlement type' methodology refers to a technique whereby urbanised areas can be classified by their origins, using indicators such as their date of urbanisation, whether they were originally developed as 'regular' or 'informal' settlements, their density at any point in time and socio-economic status of their residents. This methodology was developed collectively over a long period by researchers working both in non-government organisations and at the Autonomous Metropolitan University at Azcapotzalco in Mexico City (Connolly, 2006b). Originally, the areas were classified on paper maps from on-the-ground knowledge of what was then a much smaller Mexico City. The appearance of neighbourhoods obviously played a fundamental role in this first round of classification. In 1990, the Mexican government started publishing census disaggregated data linked to digitised maps of the census tracts. Using this data, the same team of researchers produced a study for the Consejo Nacional de Población (CONAPO, Mexican National Population Council) aimed at generating alternative scenarios for population growth and distribution within Mexico City. The maps of the census tracts were not yet geo-referenced, so, although they were easily transposed onto existing cartography of central areas, the location of the census tracts in previously unmapped peripheral areas was only approximate, based on aerial photos and fieldwork. Notwithstanding the technical inaccuracies, this study produced the first data and cartographic representations on the distribution at a sub-municipal scale of population and housing between the different types of urban settlement (CONAPO, 1998). The main categories of urban settlement types used at this stage were: (a) historic centre; (b) *colonial popular* (low-income or informal neighbourhood), a category subdivided into four groups by centrality and density; (c) social housing; (d) 'conurbated' villages; (e) middle income residential areas; and (f) high-income residential areas. Among other things, it could confirm the long-held belief that 'over two-thirds' of Mexico City's population lived in areas that had been informally developed (Ward 1976; Connolly 1977). It also informed important studies by members of the research team on various aspects of informal urban expansion in Mexico (Duhau, 1993; Cruz, 2001; Duhau and Giglia, 2008).

By 2000 and until 2010, the census data was disaggregated by census tract defined by georeferenced cartography. Separate databases were also made available for the 1990 and 1995 census events. This enabled the construction of longitudinal data sets of census indicators from 1990 to 2010, disaggregated by census tract. With some adjustments to a minority of census tracts that have been added or changed shape or size, these indicators could then be correlated with the type and date of urbanisation, topographical features, among other variables. In this context, and following the publication of the 2000 census results, the criteria for classifying the different settlement types database were somewhat revised and the whole database was checked by field visits and statistical inference. The changes mainly concerned the central areas, and a distinction between villages that had been absorbed into the contiguously urbanised areas and outlying towns and hamlets. Table 1 shows these revised classification criteria applied for the purposes of this chapter, including the source materials and other technical considerations. After each census event of 2005 and 2010, the database was again updated and corrected using Google Earth and other satellite images, to accommodate changes in the census tract polygons. Thus, Table 1 should be read in conjunction with Figure 2, a choropleth map showing a simplified classification of census tracts by settlement type in 2010, the latest census event with data disaggregated by census tract.

Feedback on the classification of the census polygons by settlement type is constantly obtained from field studies including theses and monographs. Additional information, such as location of businesses, neighbourhood conflicts, areas affected by flooding, road and transport networks, toponyms –to name but a few – is constantly added to the database. Considering all the data from the five census events to date plus the additional information, we have a geographic information system with many hundreds of variables.

The rest of this chapter will focus primarily on one aspect of this data: the variation in the number, density and distribution of the total population and inhabited dwellings by census tract classified by settlement type, paying special attention to those that were originally developed as informal settlements. This may be considered as an update of a previous article with detailed data up till 2005 (Connolly, 2009). Additionally, given the special attention of this book on regularisation, the weight of communal property (*ejidos*) in the different type of urban development is also considered. Finally, given that the 2010 census included information on unoccupied dwellings, a brief analysis of this variable is included, enabling us to see what kind of urban habitable space is more efficiently occupied.

Results

The Role of Informal Settlements in Housing Mexico City's Population 1900 to 2010. Continuity More than Change

Figure 3 shows the enormous influence of informal urbanisation as a housing provider, despite the contextual changes described above. In 2010 it still provided shelter for more than 62 percent of all metropolitan households, three

Table 1. Methodological Definition of Formal and Informal Settlement Types

Pre-1929 Mexico City	Colonial City	Census tracts with 50 percent or more of their area included within the Perimeter 'A' of the Historic Centre, as defined by Presidential Decree published 11 April 1980.
	Inner City/pre-1929 city	Census tracts not included in the Colonial City that were urbanised between 1820 and 1929 as depicted in the 1929 cadastral map.
	Conurbated Town	Census tracts not included in the Colonial and Inner City, with 50 percent or more of their area included in polygons identified as municipal centres (*cascos urbanos*) in the 1929 Cadastral Map, subsequently absorbed by the expansion of Mexico City's central area.
Post-1929 Formal Urban Development	Social Housing Project	Census tracts with 50 percent or more of their area occupied by housing built for middle and lower income groups with the intervention of public sector finance. They include both single-family and multifamily units; identification based on aerial photographs verified by on-the-ground observation, satellite images and cross-checked by statistical analysis of census data.
	Middle Income Residential	Census tracts with 50 percent or more of their area occupied by legal settlements developed predominantly for middle-income households; identification based on aerial photographs, verified by on-the-ground observation, satellite and cross-checked by statistical analysis of census data.
	High Income Residential	Census tracts with 50 percent or more of their area occupied by legal settlements developed predominantly for high-income households, identification based on aerial photographs, verified by on-the-ground observation, satellite images and cross-checked by statistical analysis of census data.
Post-1929 Informal Urban Development	Informal Settlement or *colonia popular*	Census tracts with 50 percent or more of their area on settlements which were urbanised expressly for housing in violation with existing urban, building and / or property legislation; identification based on aerial photographs, verified by on-the-ground observation, satellite images and cross-checked by statistical analysis of census data.
	Conurbated Village	Census tracts with 50 percent or more of their area occupied by polygons identified as villages that have been absorbed by the expansion of Mexico City's central area; identification of such areas was based on on-the-ground knowledge, verified with census and other toponymical cartography.
	Non-conurbated village	Census tracts with 50 percent or more of their area occupied by polygons identified as villages not contiguous with Mexico City's central area expansion, but belonging to the municipalities included in the definition of the ZMVM; excludes positively identified formal developments and non-residential uses.
Non Residential Uses	Predominantly non-residential Non-residential	Census tracts with 50 percent of their area occupied by non-residential uses; identification based on aerial photographs, verified by on-the-ground observation, satellite images and cross-checked by census data. AGEBs with no housing at all. They may house people living in buildings not classified by the census as 'individual dwellings'; identification based on aerial photographs, verified by on-the-ground observation, satellite images and cross-checked by census data.

Source: author's elaboration.

Figure 2.   Metropolitan Mexico City 2010. Distribution of Census Tracts Classified by Informal, Formal and pre-1929 Settlement Types.

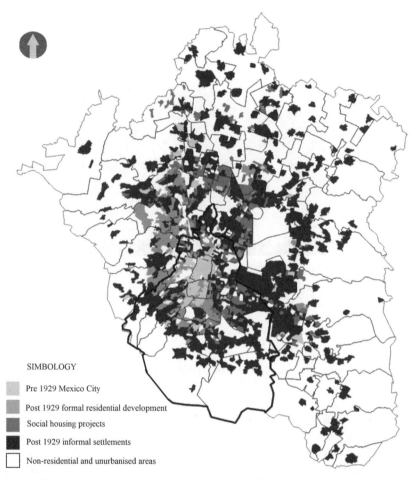

SIMBOLOGY

Pre 1929 Mexico City

Post 1929 formal residential development

Social housing projects

Post 1929 informal settlements

Non-residential and unurbanised areas

Source: Universidad Autónoma Metropolitana-Azcapotzalco, Observatorio de la Ciudad de México. Map generated by José Castro. A more detailed map in colour may be consulted at http://sociologiaurbana.azc.uam.mx/

percentage points and 1.32 million houses more than in 1990. Most of this housing (45 percent of the total increase in housing stock from 1990 to 2010) is provided by *colonias populares,* with 894 thousand additional homes over the same period, but an increasing proportion of informal housing appears in conurbated villages (11 percent) and non-conurbated villages (10 percent). As would be expected, the proportion of total dwellings in the post-1929 formal city has increased, but only slightly: from 26 percent in 1990 to 28 percent in 2010. This increase is mainly due to the massive social housing projects in the

130   *Priscilla Connolly*

Figure 3.   Metropolitan Mexico City. Distribution of Occupied Dwellings in Census Tracts Classified by Settlement Type 1990 to 2010.

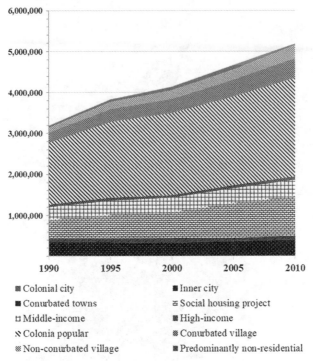

■ Colonial city   ■ Inner city
■ Conurbated towns   ⊠ Social housing project
⊡ Middle-income   ▩ High-income
⋉ Colonia popular   ▩ Conurbated village
▩ Non-conurbated village   ■ Predominantly non-residential

Source: OCIM-SIG. Universidad Autónoma Metropolitana-Azcapotzalco, Mexico City

outlying metropolitan municipalities which added 506,000 additional houses, almost doubling the total contribution of this type of housing to almost a million, or 19 percent of the total metropolitan housing stock in 2010. Clearly, the massive suburban social housing projects have mostly substituted new housing previously produced in more central formally urbanised areas. This is confirmed by the relative stagnation of housing stock in the pre-1929 city, which only shows a net gain of 70,455 houses from 1990 to 2010, despite smaller families and all the public and massive private investment in new condominiums. The colonial city registers a net loss of 3666 homes over the same period, with a total population of merely 42,300 in 2010.

The suburban housing projects also creamed off some housing demand in the informal sector, especially in the metropolitan municipalities between 2000 and 2005. Here the rate of new household production in *colonias populares* dropped to less than 20,000 per year during these years, having averaged 34,000 annually in the previous decade. In the same period, the rate of production of social housing in the metropolitan municipalities reached its highest point, averaging almost 32,000 a year. However, during the second half of the decade, when the problems of over-supply and market saturation begin to kick in, the situation was reversed. Additional houses registered in *colonias populares* within these metropolitan municipalities regained their previous levels of about 35,000 a year, more than the average yearly increase of 26,000 occupied dwellings in social housing projects.

Informal Settlement and Urban Expansion: Discontinuities in Space and Time

From the above it would appear that the relative reduction in housing production in informal settlements observed from the late 1990s until first half of the new century is only a temporary blip in the long-term trend. How much of this additional housing appears in new settlements and how much is built in existing settlements will determine urban growth and density distribution patterns. One of the essential characteristics of informal developments is the incremental type of construction of both the housing itself and the urban environment: the well-documented process of 'consolidation'. Usually there will be a steady increase in the number of homes in any one settlement until a maximum density of up to 600 persons per hectare is reached after 30 or 40 years. In fact, consolidated informal settlements generate the highest densities in the city. Thus, most new homes in these types of settlement are not located in new developments on greenfield sites but in already existing neighbourhoods. However, densification of settlements is not constant and variations over time are worth noting.

Our data show that from 1990 to 1995 only a small proportion – about 8 percent – of additional inhabited dwellings was registered on greenfield sites, identified as such by new census tracts appearing on previously undeveloped land. This is true not only in informal developments but in all types of settlement. However, this fraction increased during the second half of the decade until 2005, partly due to the massive social housing production on greenfield sites, but also because of newly-formed *colonias populares* and growth around town and villages. This happened only in the metropolitan municipalities, where as much as 55 percent of additional social housing and 22 percent of *colonias populares* appeared in new census tracts (i.e. greenfield sites) created between 2000 and 2005. In the DF, the response to government policy promoting home improvements and extensions in existing settlements, coupled with the general scarcity of land, has been a continuous densification of existing informal settlements. Of the 219,000 additional houses registered in informal settlements in the DF between 1990 and 2005, less than 1000 were built on greenfield sites and practically none appeared in the 2010 census.

The census methodology in 2010 redefined many census tracts in peripheral areas, which makes further comparisons rather difficult. However, visual assessments of Google Earth and census cartography suggest that the outward expansion reached a limit around 2005. The tendency of the city to spread further and faster towards the outermost periphery, much to the alarm of policy-makers and academic observers alike, was probably checked by market saturation and the 2008 financial crisis. In terms of cartographic representation and measurement, however, the outlying villages depict the opposite tendency. When a village reaches a population threshold of 2500 inhabitants, it is reclassified as 'urban' and assigned a census tract polygon, thus appearing on the map for the first time as 'extension of urbanised area', even though the place may have been inhabited for centuries. Because of this, the alleged recent upsurge in 'urban expansion' of Mexican cities (Eibenshutz and Benlluire, 2009; SEDATU, 2014) may be exaggerated in some contexts, and needs to be revised in the light of the reclassification of rural settlements in census methodology. In any case, after 2012, the Federal Government reversed the permissive housing policy which now directs housing finance to brownfield sites countrywide (SEDATU, 2014).

The city does not constantly expand, but grows in fits and starts, following conflicting planning and finance policies and macroeconomic climates. Neither does urban growth in whatever form stretch uniformly in time and space but is concentrated in certain localities. For example, we find new census tracts generated by social housing between 2000 and 2005 in just fourteen municipalities and of these, two-thirds of the area they occupy corresponds to a mere five (Chicoloapan, Cuautitlan, Tecámac, Cuautitlan Izcalli and Iztapaluca). Urban expansion due to new *colonias populares* is even more concentrated. In 2005, new census tracts created by this kind of settlement appear in eighteen municipalities; of these, 38 percent of their area is in Chicoloapan, with a further 17 percent in the three surrounding municipalities (Ixtapaluca, Los Reyes la Paz, and Chimalhuacán). Most of the other *colonias populares* appearing in that period are found in five other municipalities, with practically no new settlements in the rest of Metropolitan Mexico City. Between 2000 and 2005, conurbated villages generated new census tracts adding up to more than 200 hectares in only two municipalities: Tultitlan and Cuautitlan Izcalli.

There was no census count in 2015, but the detailed sample survey by municipality suggests that these trends continue. Between 2010 and 2015, 86 percent of population growth was concentrated in sixteen municipalities, each with an increase of over 20,000 inhabitants, and these are mostly the same municipalities that grew in the previous decade.

Two conclusions may be drawn from this. First, urban expansion affects only a few places at any moment in time and, second, in those places, formal and informal settlements tend to be developed side by side. Outstanding examples of this double urbanisation process is Chicoloapan, followed by

Ixtapaluca and Cuautitlan Izcalli, where the large-scale construction of social housing has been accompanied by the creation of many new informal settlements in both *colonias populares* and around villages. Clearly, the dramatic increase in the supply of formal housing for middle income and lower middle income population has not hindered the formation of informal developments: quite the opposite, they are mutually related.

The above needs to be explained in terms of the territorial origins of social agents who promote development, most importantly, the original landowners. This brings us to the question of the *ejidos*.

The Effect of Communal Property on Formal and Informal Urban Development

As might be expected, after the constitutional reform of 1992 allowing for the legal sale of *ejido* property, there was a significant increase in the contribution of *ejido* land to the total area occupied by new census tracts during the second half of the 1990s. This is true for all types of settlement, except 'middle income residential' and 'non-conurbated villages', but most significantly for new 'social housing' developments and *colonias populares*. However, it was in the following five years when *ejido* land, now certified by PROCEDE, contributed most to new urban development. Between 2000 and 2005, one-third of the total area of new census tracts generated by social housing, 1232 hectares, had been *ejidos* certified by PROCEDE (See Salazar in this volume). Another 1344 hectares of *ejido* were converted into *colonias populares*, equivalent to two-thirds of the total area of new census tracts created by this type of settlement. In total, 44 percent of Metropolitan Mexico City's expansion between 2000 and 2005 took place on *ejidos*. This estimate excludes developments in the Mexico City proper (DF) where *ejidos* have not been certified.

The boom in urbanisation of *ejidos* was concentrated in a few areas, providing greenfield sites for social housing totalling over 100 hectares in only seven municipalities (Chicoloapan, Huehetoca, Tecámac, Ixtapaluca, Acolman, Coacalco and Cuautitlán). For *colonias populares*, the concentration of the *ejido* effect is still greater, with 801 hectares in Chicoloapan providing 60 percent of the land developed this way between 2000 and 2005. An additional 30 percent of this land was contributed by three other municipalities (Los Reyes la Paz, Atenco and Iztapaluca). Likewise, significant extensions of new census tracts created around conurbated villages in certified *ejidos* only occurred in two municipalities: Tultitlán (228 hectares) and Cuautitlan Izcalli (130 hectares). The urbanisation of *ejido* land around non-conurbated villages is more dispersed, except for two municipalities where almost 100 percent of new urban census tracts occupy ex-*ejidos* (Axapusco and Chiconcuac, with 242 and 108 hectares, respectively).

Clearly, the legalisation of the sale of *ejidal* land effectively enabled its development for formal housing construction. At the same time, this option has in no way prevented even larger areas being used for various types of informal urbanisation. Thus, from 2000 to 2005 and even more so afterwards, there was a huge surge in new informal development of *ejido* lands, especially in Chicoloapan, in the hills of La Paz and Iztapaluca, as well as on the salt flats of Atenco, adjacent to Ecatepec. Given the proximity of these developments to the brand new social housing projects, questions arise about the interrelationship between legal and illegal land sales for purposes of all types of development.

Densities and Occupations Rates in Informal Settlements

In recent years, both government policy and academic commentary have built up a strong narrative that has characterised Mexican urban development as 'low density', 'fragmented' and 'sprawling'. Informal ('uncontrolled') settlements are blamed for this, along with the suburban social housing developments. While there may be some substance to this perception in some Mexican cities, in general the densities achieved by both social housing and informal settlement hardly qualify them as 'urban sprawl' (Monkkonen, 2011; Guerra, 2013). Measured in terms of total population divided by the area of all urban census tracts, including some unoccupied land and non-residential uses, the mean population density of metropolitan Mexico City is relatively high, at 85 persons per hectare both in 2000 to 2010. Over the same period, housing densities actually rose: from 19 to 23 dwellings per hectare. The only settlement types with diminished average housing density were the colonial city and all kinds of formal development. However, outside the central pre-1929 city, social housing has the highest density, with 38 dwellings per hectare in 2010, down from 42 in 2000. Average housing density in *colonias populares* was 36 dwellings per hectare, up from 31 in 2000, while maximum densities here can reach up to 200 houses per hectare.

The other public policy concern is the apparently low housing occupancy rate, thanks to which we now have data on unoccupied dwellings published as part of the census results. From this, we can say that all types of informal settlement have a much lower vacancy rate than the rest of the city. Whereas 9 percent of all houses in informal settlements were unoccupied in 2010, this percentage is 15 in the pre-1929 city and 22 in the formally developed areas. As expected, the highest vacancy rates were found in social housing (25 percent) and in the pre-1929 city (15 percent), while the lowest average is in the *colonias populares* (9 percent). If both density and occupancy rates are considered, clearly informal settlements provide more efficient residential land use.

Conclusions

The above observations represent a sample of the type of results that can be achieved by quantitative analysis based on a geographic information now available in Mexico. Many research avenues remain open, among which is more comprehensive assessment of the socio-demographic dynamics in new and existing informal settlements and the quality of housing conditions they provide. For this, it is relatively simple to identify the census data corresponding to one or more settlements as a basis for a more indepth study.

I would like to conclude with some reflections about the impact that digital spatial analysis has on the nature and dynamics of informal urbanisation. These are now firmly 'on the map', ready to be located, classified and assessed. Combining geo-demographic techniques presented here with the tracking of satellite imagery, including real-time imagery, it is easy to monitor their development in significant detail. This is precisely what the regularisation process in Mexico City now involves, together with constant field observations by official officers and inhabitants alike (Wigle, 2013). In fact, following Mexico City's example, it is likely that the violation of planning, building and environmental norms will increasingly shape the way 'informal' is perceived and defined. As the quantity and quality of data becomes available at increasingly higher resolution, we should work towards a much more sensitive approach to the complexities, variations and policy requirements of 'informal'. Hopefully we can abolish the term altogether, to replace it by meaningful categories informing planning and housing policies in the future.

References

Abrams, C. (1964) *Housing in the Modern World: Man's Struggle for Shelter in an Urbanizing World*. Faber and Faber: London.

Angel, S. (2000) *Housing Policy Matters: a Global Analysis*. Oxford University Press: Oxford.

Azuela, A. (1987) 'Low income settlements and the law in Mexico City'. *International Journal of Urban and Regional Research* **11**(4): 522–541.

Benlliure, P. (2005) 'Modificaciones al marco normativo del Distrito Federal en la edificación de vivienda 2000–2005' unpublished paper presented in *V Seminario internacional de suelo urbano*. Mexico DF, 29–30.

Castañeda, V. (1994) 'Ciudad de México: grupos de poder local, mercado ilegal de suelo periférico y expansión metropolitana'. *Revista Interamericana de Planificación* **27**: 107–108.

CONAPO (1998) *Escenarios demográficos y urbanos de la Zona Metropolitana de la Ciudad de México, 1990–2010: síntesis*. Consejo Nacional de Población: Mexico.

CONAPO (2012) *Delimitación de las zonas metropolitanas de México 2010*. Consejo Nacional de Población: Mexico DF.

CONAVI (2016) *Sistema nacional de información e indicadores de vivienda.* [WWW document]. URL http://sniiv.conavi.gob.mx/oferta/cuboVivienda.aspx [accessed 20 November 2016].

Connolly, P. (ed.) (1977) *La producción de vivienda en la Zona Metropolitana de la Ciudad de México.* Centro Operacional de Vivienda y Poblamiento AC: Mexico DF.

Connolly, P. (1988) 'Crecimiento urbano, densidad de población y mercado inmobiliario'. *Revista 'A'* **9**: 61–86.

Connolly, P. (2006a) 'Política de vivienda o .olítica de construcción?' in *La vivienda en México. construyendo análisis y propuestas.* CESOP, Cámara de Diputados, LIX Legislatura: México DF, 119–134.

Connolly, P. (2006b) *Tipos de poblamiento en la Ciudad de México.* Universidad Autónoma Metropolitana-Azcapotzalco. [WWW document]. URL http://www.ocim.azc.uam.mx/OCIM-SIG%20ABRIL/poblamiento.pdf [accessed 7 November 2016].

Connolly, P. (2009) 'Observing the Evolution of Informal Settlements: Mexico City's colonias populares 1990 to 2005'. *International Development Planning Review* **31**(1): 1–35.

Connolly, P. (2017) 'Latin American Informal Urbanism: Contexts, Concepts and Contributions with Specific Reference to Mexico' in A. Becerra and F. Hernández (eds.) *Marginal Urbanisms: Informal and Formal Development in Cities of Latin America.* Cambridge Scholars Publishing: Cambridge, 22–46.

Connolly, P. and Wigle, J. (2017) '(Re)constructing Informality and doing Regularization in the Conservation Zone of Mexico City'. *Planning Theory and Practice* **18**(2): 183–201.

Cornelius, W. (1975) *Politics and the Migrant Poor in Mexico City.* Stanford University Press: Stanford.

Cruz, M. S. (2001) *Propiedad, poblamiento y periferia rural en la Zona Metropolitana de la Ciudad de México.* RNIU/UAM-Azcapotzalco: Mexico DF.

Cymet, D. (1992) *From Ejido to Metropolis: Another Path.* Peter Lang: New York.

Davis, M. (2006) *Planet of Slums.* Verso: London and New York.

Duhau, E. (1993) 'La urbanización popular en América Latina: ¿institucionalización o pactos sociales implícitos?' in A. Azuela (coord.) *La urbanización popular y el orden jurídico en América Latina.* UNAM: México DF, 19–30.

Duhau, E. (1998) *Habitat popular y política urbana.* Miguel Ángel Porrúa/UAM-Azcapotzalco: Mexico DF.

Duhau, E. and Giglia, A. (2008) *Las reglas del desorden.* Siglo XXI: México DF.

Dwyer, D. J. (1975) *People and Housing in Third World Cites. Perspectives on the Problem of Spontaneous Settlements.* Longman: London.

Eibenshutz, R. and Benlluire, P. (2009) *Mercado formal e informal de suelo. Análisis de ocho ciudades.* Miguel Ángel Porrúa: México DF.

Esquivel, M. T. (2007) 'La actuación de los desarrolladores habitacionales privados' in S. Tamayo (ed.) *Los desafíos del Bando 2.* Gobierno del Distrito Federal: México DF, 253–290.

Fernández, A. and Meza, F. (2015) 'Informal Economies and Business Cycles in Emerging Economies: The Case of Mexico'. *Review of Economic Dynamics* **18**(2): 281–405.

Guadarrama, M. A. (2007) 'Política de gestión y dinámica del mercado del suelo' in S. Tamayo (ed.) *Los desafíos del Bando 2*. Gobierno del Distrito Federal: México DF, 291–330.

Guerra, E. (2013) *The New Suburbs: Evolving Travel Behaviour, the Built Environment, and Subway Investments in Mexico City*. Unpublished doctoral dissertation, University of California Transportation Center, UC Berkeley.

Hauser, P. M. (ed.) (1961) *Urbanization in Latin America*. International Documents Service: New York. [WWW document]. URL http://unesdoc.unesco.org/images/0005/000545/054517eo.pd [accessed 17 August 2016].

ILO/FORLAC (2014) *Informal Employment in Mexico. International Labour Organization*. [WWW document]. URL http://www.ilo.org/wcmsp5/groups/public/---americas/---olima/documents/publication/wcms_245889.pdf [accessed 18 November 2016].

INVI (2016) *Instituto de la Vivienda del Distrito Federal*. [WWW document]. URL http://www.invi.df.gob Instituto de la Vivienda del Distrito Federal.mx/portal/acciones_PMV2008.aspx [accessed 17 May 2010).

Jiménez, E. (2000) *El principio de la informalidad. Mercado del suelo para vivienda en Aguascalientes, 1975–1998*. Universidad de Guadalajara/Juan Pablos Editores: Guadalajara.

Jones, G. and Ward, P. (1998) 'Privatizing the Commons: Reforming the *Ejido* and Urban Development in Mexico'. *International Journal of Urban and Regional Research* 22(1): 76–93.

LGAH (1976) Ley General de Asentamientos Humanos. *Diario Oficial*. México DF. 26 May.

Manguin, W. (1967) 'Latin American Squatter Settlements: a Problem and a Solution'. *Latin American Research Review* 2(3): 65–98.

Monkkonen, P. (2011) 'Do Mexican Cities Sprawl? Housing-Finance Reform and Changing Patterns of Urban Growth'. *Urban Geography* 32(3): 1–20.

Moreno, A. (1979) 'La "crisis" en la ciudad' in P. González and E. Florescano (eds.). México Hoy. Siglo XXI: Mexico DF.

Nava, T. (1993) 'La contrarreforma el Artículo 27'. *Ciudades* 19: 15–23.

OECD (2001) *Glossary of Statistical Terms*. [WWW document]. URL https://stats.oecd.org/glossary/index.htm [accessed 17 August 2016].

Ortega-Alcázar, I. (2007) *Brick by Brick: an Ethnography of Self-help Housing, Family Practices and Everyday Life in a Consolidated Popular Settlement of Mexico City*. Unpublished doctoral dissertation, University of Southampton, Southampton.

Pérez, E. and Santos, C. (2013) 'Tendencias recientes en la migración interna en México'. *Papeles de Población* 76: 53–88.

Pradilla, E. (1992) 'Campo y ciudad en la nueva política agraria'. *Ciudades* 15: 9–18.

Ribbeck, E. and Padilla, S. (2002) *Die informelle Moderne: spontanes Bauen in Mexico-Stadt/Informal Modernism: Spontaneous Building in Mexico City*. Architektur und Wirtschaftsförderungs-Verlag/Universität Stuttgart: Heidelberg/Stuttgart.

Ruiz, O. (2011) *Fotos Admirables del D.F. y Área Metropolitana*. [WWW document]. URL http://es.slideshare.net/JeSvS/admirable-df-9155647 [accessed 6 November 2016].

Schteingart, M. (1989) *Los productores del espacio habitable*. El Colegio de México: México DF.

SEDATU (2014) *Programa Nacional de Desarrollo Urbano 2014–2018.* Diario Oficial 30 April 2014.

Stolarski, N. (1982) *La vivienda en el Distrito Federal. Situación actual y perspectivas.* Departamento del Distrito Federal: México DF.

STPS (2016) *Ciudad de México. Información laboral. Secretaría de Trabajo y Previsión Social.* [WWW document]. URL http://www.stps.gob.mx/gobmx/estadisticas/pdf/perfiles/perfil%20distrito%20federal.pdf [accessed 19 November 2016]

Tomas, F. (1996) 'Los asentamientos populares informales en las periferias urbanas de América Latina' in A. Azuela and F. Tomas (eds.) *El acceso de los pobres al suelo urbano.* CEMCA: Mexico DF.

Topelson, S. (2006) *El estado de la vivienda en México 2005.* CIDOC, SHF, CONAFOVI, SEDESOL: Mexico DF.

Turner, J. F. C. (1968a) 'The Squatter Settlement: an Architecture that Works'. *Architectural Design* **38**(8): 355–360.

Turner, J. F. C. (1968b) *Uncontrolled Urban Settlement: Problems and Policies.* United Nations Centre for Housing, Building and Planning: New York.

United Nations (1997) *Glossary of Environment Statistics.* United Nations Department for Economic and Social Information and Policy Analysis: New York. [WWW document]. URL http://unstats.un.org/unsd/publication/SeriesF/SeriesF_67E.pdf [accessed 17 August 2016].

Varley, A. (1985) 'Urbanisation and Agrarian Law: the Case of Mexico City'. *Bulletin of Latin American Research* **4**(1): 1–16.

Varley, A. (2017) 'Postcolonialising Informality?' *Environment and Planning D: Society and Space* **31**(1): 4–22.

Varley, A. (2017) 'Property Titles and the Urban Poor: From Informality to Displacement?'. *Planning Theory and Practice* **18**(3): 385–404.

Ward, P. (1976) *In Search of a Home: Social and Economic Characteristics of Squatter Settlements and the Role of Self Help Housing in Mexico City.* Unpublished doctoral thesis, University of Liverpool, Liverpool.

Ward, P. (2016) 'Housing Rehab for Consolidated Informal Settlements: A New Policy Agenda for the 2016 UN-Habitat III'. *Habitat International* **50**: 373–384.

Wigle, J. (2013) 'The "Graying" of "Green" Zones: Spatial Governance and Informal Settlement in Xochimilco, Mexico City'. *International Journal of Urban and Regional Research* **38**(2): 573–589.

7

Preventing 'Clouded' Titles in Previously Informal Settlements. The Administrative and Judicial Transmission of Property

EDITH R. JIMÉNEZ-HUERTA, HERIBERTO CRUZ-SOLÍS, AND CLAUDIA UBALDO-VELÁZQUEZ

University of Guadalajara, Guadalajara

Introduction

In this chapter we argue that federal mass regularisation programmes in Mexico, which have been in place for a little over four decades, are beginning to show a significant limitation. The very first owners, in whose names the deeds to the house are registered, are ageing and some have already died, most of them without having made a will. In Mexico, the purpose of a will is to guarantee the transfer of a person's property after death. In this document the owners establish to whom they wish to transfer the rights and obligations of their property. In Mexico, unlike many Latin American countries, owners have almost complete freedom to bequeath their property to whomever they wish. The Civil Codes of each state regulate succession and place only a few limitations on free succession, such as when there are minors under the age of 18 or if the owners are unable to make their will due to ill health.

Whether there is a will or not, the law protects heirs, but the problem is that people do not exercise their rights in the manner provided for in civil law. This is largely because procedures tend to be complicated, expensive or simply unknown. If the property title deeds are not legally changed to show the names of the heirs, the heirs will be living in a dwelling with its title in the name of the former owner. Here we argue that the way property is transferred after the death of the owners, ignorance, and lack of resources, can lead to a widespread return to informality. Although there already are legal and administrative alternatives for property succession, neither public policy nor the literature on residential tenure regularisation takes them into account. Hence, the benefits of regularisation can be adversely affected, beginning with the death of either spouse. The 'clean' titles obtained by the regularisation programmes will become 'clouded'; that is, there will be legal restrictions on transactions such as inheriting, selling or mortgaging the property.

In the fieldwork, it should be noted, we found that the vast majority of the owners interviewed turned out to be married men and women, married under the 'joint ownership' regime, and that they bought the property after they got married. Throughout the document we refer to the couple or one of the spouses as the owner. In Mexico under this type of marriage, upon the death of one of the spouses without a will, half of the property is intestate because each of the spouses is entitled to half. Heirs may put part of the intestate property in their name through legitimate succession, but this involves intestate proceedings. During this transition process, half of the property is not legally assigned to anyone until the trial ends. Subsequently, upon the death of the second intestate spouse if no intestate proceedings have taken place, all rights to the property would be suspended, in a new 'informal' situation. It is in this way that a new type of property informality is emerging in the settlements that were regularised more than 30 years ago. For this reason, regularisation policies are required, *a priori* and *a posteriori*, with a long-term vision that takes into account the changes occurring during the lifespan of the inhabitants of low-income settlements of informal origin. This would allow the property to remain in the hands of the persons chosen by the owners and would make it easier for the heirs to exercise their rights under the law.

At present, the idea prevails among academics and officials that the succession of property belongs solely in the legal domain governed by civil law, without taking into account the administrative realm. Here, a change of vision is fundamental because what is needed is to move from the individualistic approach of the legal domain posited by civil law to the more progressive urban law which takes into account the growing complexity of urban issues and legal problems in twenty-first-century cities (for the case of Brazil, see Fernandes 2004 and Fernandes, 2010: 43, 87). It is precisely this new vision that is highlighted in this chapter. For while the proposed succession through the 'beneficiary clause' remains a matter of civil law, the fundamental change will be to make it an administrative procedure. This is the best option to ensure the formal, cheap and expeditious transfer of ownership. Its widespread application would prevent the 'new informality' which is developing in low-income settlements. Bearing in mind that the administrative alternative of succession is absent from the discussion agenda and from public policies, the objectives of this chapter are: to point out that this 'new informality' exists; to show what it consists of; to analyse why it occurs; and, finally, to propose some alternatives to rectify the situation.

The initial version of this chapter was produced in September 2009 and published in Spanish three years later (Jiménez, Cruz and Ubaldo, 2012). The first findings of an investigation into the regularised low-income settlements that developed more than 30 years ago on *ejidos*, a type of communal land, were presented. This revised and updated version includes: recent information on succession, modifications made to the regulations, and more informed proposals made here to facilitate the transfer of property to future generations.

The information on which this work is based derives from a larger project funded by the Consejo Nacional de Ciencia y Tecnología (CONACYT, National Council for Science and Technology). Edith R. Jiménez-Huerta was head of the project, Heriberto Cruz Solís was joint head and Claudia Ubaldo Velázquez participated as a lawyer and master's research student in urban planning. A complete list of participants can be found in Jiménez, Cruz and Ubaldo, 2012. Funding for the project ended in 2012. However, the research continued until 2016 with a view to contributing to the new urban agenda of Habitat III, a document that 'lays out standards and principles for the planning, construction, development, management, and improvement of urban areas' (United Nations, 2017: iv). This was highly relevant, as the draft UN document, known as the 'zero document', did not consider the succession of housing worth including in the urban agenda for the next twenty years (United Nations, 2016a). Unfortunately, neither did the new urban agenda decided on at the conference consider the transfer of housing from one generation to the next to be a relevant issue (United Nations, 2016b). For the investigation, 243 questionnaires were completed by randomly selected owners in three consolidated and regularised low-income settlements in the city of Guadalajara in the state of Jalisco, Mexico. The three settlements, regularised by the Commission for the Regularisation of Land Tenure (CORETT) – Rancho Nuevo, Echeverría and Jalisco – were originally built on *ejido* lands. Information from some of the seven in-depth case studies, chosen from the 243 questionnaires, is also included (for a more detailed explanation of the methodology, see Ward, Jiménez and Di Virgilio, 2014). The research we conducted in Guadalajara is part of a wide-ranging project that was undertaken by members of the Latin American Housing Network in nine other countries and eleven cities in Latin America using the same research methodology and techniques (LAHN, 2009). The website contains the questionnaire databases for all the cities, in Excel, SPSS and STATA format, as well as the codes for each country, city, 'neighbourhood' and questionnaire.

In the following section we present data on the consolidated settlements (informal in origin) formed in Guadalajara between 1970 and 1985. Then the central problems of succession are discussed and the alternatives for succession that exist in Mexico are identified. In order to avoid a 'new informality', emphasis is placed on the need to generalise the use of the 'beneficiary clause' in the deeds. In this way, succession would move from the legal to the administrative sphere, the succession would become substantially easier and cheaper, and the deeds would be kept up to date and in force.

Informality and Regularisation in the Guadalajara Metropolitan Area

The regularisation programmes for informal settlements in Latin America, Africa and Asia are measures that alleviate but do not solve the problems faced by people with limited resources in accessing adequate housing. However, through them, policymakers have sought to legally recognise the housing tenure rights of the inhabitants of informal land. In Mexico, regularisation programmes that guarantee formal land tenure for low-income settlements date back half a century, to the 1970s. The most successful regularisation programme worldwide was that launched by the federal government of Mexico through CORETT (Azuela and Duhau, 1998). Unfortunately, though, it has only guaranteed full tenure for the first generation, without taking any steps to ensure an expeditious and cheap succession for the next generations. This means that in the space of one generation, clean titles will turn into 'clouded' titles.

At the beginning of the twenty-first century, the metropolis formed by Guadalajara, consisting of the central municipality and the three municipalities of the first expansion ring (Zapopan, Tlaquepaque and Tonalá), extended over 32,395 hectares. One-third of this territory was urbanised by settlements that were informal in origin (10,788 hectares) and were located on private, public and *ejido* land. Between 1970 and 1985, the period under study, the area occupied by the informal settlements was 5,733 hectares (Jiménez, Cruz and Rábago, 2004 and Jiménez, 2008). Figure 13 shows the peripheral distribution of the informal settlements in the metropolis between 1972 and 2009. The consolidated settlements of informal origin that are the object of this study were formed between 1972 and 1985. During this period, just over half the area occupied by informal settlements in the city was legalised.

In spite of the disadvantages that regularisation has brought with it (documented in Jiménez, 2000 and also Smolka, 2007: 74–78), its great advantage is that it has allowed a significant number of people to legally secure the ownership of their land and the housing they have produced themselves over the years. For those who were able to obtain property title deeds, it seemed that the regularisation was the end of a long process. To a certain extent this was the case, but not in the long run, as we shall see later.

Figure 13. Settlements that are Informal in Origin in the Guadalajara Metropolitan Area by Period of Appearance 1970–2000

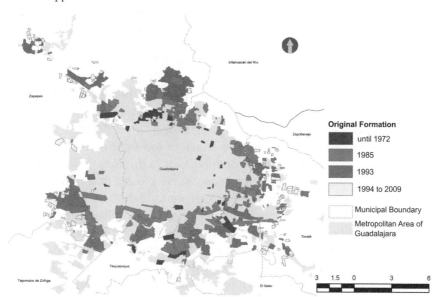

Source: based on research project data produced by Jiménez-Huerta, Edith Rosario, Cruz-Solís, Heriberto and Rábago-Anaya, Jesús (2004). The Landsat 2000 satellite image and the 2005 Municipal Geostatistical Framework of the Instituto Nacional de Estadística y Geografía (INEGI, National Institute of Statistics and Geography), were also used.

The 'New Informality' of Consolidated and Regularised Low-Income Settlements

Low-income settlements created more than three decades ago have been accumulating problems that are hidden behind an apparent integration into the urban fabric, and have therefore gone unnoticed by decision-makers and academics. For many valid reasons, attention continues to be focused on the newly created informal settlements and, since 2000, on the new subdivisions of 'social interest' housing built on a massive scale on the periphery by real estate developers and financed mainly by the Instituto del Fondo Nacional de la Vivienda para los Trabajadores, (INFONAVIT, National Fund for Workers' Housing) and to a lesser extent by private banks. The problems of consolidated settlements of informal origin are wide-ranging, from the deterioration of housing and the increase in violence to the central theme of this work, which is the 'new informality' or legal vacuum, that is emerging as a result of the ageing of the owners. Approximately two-thirds of the pioneer inhabitants who founded the informal settlements in the four central municipalities of Guadalajara were able to obtain legal security for their property through the national regularisation programme, CORETT. Unfortunately, when the owner of the regularised property dies, the surviving spouse and subsequent generations are left in a vulnerable situation, as they may lose all or part of this security if they do not exercise their rights under the law. In other words, neither individuals nor society, nor the state, are taking preventative measures to guarantee the transfer of property once one of the owners dies (see also Ward and Jiménez, 2011).

The practice of formally designating the heirs of a person's property after his death is not new; it has been known since pre-Hispanic times. It continued later with Spanish law in New Spain (García, 2015: 390) and persists to the present day. However, in Mexico a lack of foresight with regard to the bequeathing of assets has been a common feature throughout the twentieth and early twenty-first centuries. A national survey found that eight out of ten Mexicans die without making a will (Ortega and Maldonado, 2010) and the National Association of Mexican Notaries provides a similar figure, confirming that the problem of intestate property really is widespread, since almost 90 percent of those who could make a will do not have one (El Universal, 2007). In the study conducted in the Guadalajara metropolitan area, we found that 86 percent of people in consolidated low-income settlements do not make a will.

Taking these data into account, even though the legality of the title of the intestate property is not at risk, a void is created during the time between the death of the owner and the legal transfer of the property to the heirs. It is in this vacuum that family and urban conflicts arise. Even just taking into account the low-income settlements in the Guadalajara metropolitan area, these could affect up to 30 percent of the urbanised area of the city, to say nothing of irregularities in 'formal' property in Guadalajara and in other cities, which might take the figure considerably higher in some cases. Of course, the percentage of the urban area occupied by informal or once informal settlements will vary constantly, depending on the city, with more settlements still being regularised and new ones being created all the time. At any rate, if the appropriate measures are not taken, this example gives a clear idea of the great impact that the reversal of the achievements of the regularisation policies implemented more than four decades ago (1973) will have on this fundamental aspect of the material poverty of millions of Mexicans.

Problems with Succession

As mentioned at the beginning, unlike many other countries in Latin America, the law in Mexico gives people over 16 years of age full freedom to bequeath their assets and rights as they wish. The Civil Code, which governs each of the 32 states, establishes the guidelines under which owners can bequeath a home to a person they formally designate.

According to the Civil Code of the State of Jalisco (CCEJ, 1995), both spouses married under the 'joint ownership' regime – the most common form of marriage in Mexico – have full and equal rights over the property. In other words, each person can bequeath the half of the property that belongs to them to anyone they choose, whether they are family members or not. The surviving spouse owns only half of the property purchased after marriage. The best known legal procedure to ensure formal succession of a property is to make a will that states to whom the property will be left. Now, according to Article 2911 of the Civil Code, if the person who dies does not leave a will, the part of the property that belongs to him or her is intestate and that 50 percent will have to be divided among the heirs, through 'legitimate succession', in a particular order: *'in the first instance the descendants, spouse, ascendants and collateral relatives to the fourth degree, and the common-law wife or the concubine; in the absence of the foregoing, the Public Benefit'* (CCEJ, 1995).

Most of the very first owners in the three consolidated and regularised low-income settlements studied – Jalisco, Echeverría and Rancho Nuevo – obtained the deeds to their homes from CORETT in 1994, 1983, and 1982 respectively, after more than two decades of uncertainty about the ownership of their land plot. At the time of the study it was found that in 95 percent of the cases the name of the person who appears as the owner in the deeds is still the owner. In other words, the level of legal certainty that exists in these settlements is surprisingly high, and unique in the urban context. The problem is that only a small percentage of the owners in these settlements have made provisions for the formal succession of their property (only 14 percent had made a will). In the period before the study, the consequences of the lack of formal succession were not evident, since the process of ageing and death of the very first owners was just beginning. The average age of the owner in the studied cases was 58. However, there were people of up to 98 years old and one-third of the owners (37 percent) were over 65. Only 7 percent of the owners (19) had died, the majority of whom had left the property intestate, as only three of them had made a will.

It is foreseeable that over time the number of intestate properties will increase rapidly. What makes the situation serious is that owners and heirs know very little about the economic, legal and social consequences of intestate property. This study reveals some of the various consequences and problems that arise from not anticipating a formal succession of properties. Some of the most important problems are illustrated by a case that was studied in depth in the Echeverría settlement. The questionnaire (041) was applied on 29 November 2008, and six interviews were completed on different dates between 2008 and 2009, each lasting between two and a half to three and a half hours. Although the widow, three of the daughters and a nephew participated in the questionnaires and interviews, the information cited in this section was provided by the 67-year-old widow (personal communication, 29 November 2008).

People who do not provide for formal succession of their property choose one of three alternatives: (a) they do nothing; (b) they leave informal instructions to their relatives saying who gets what when they die; (c) they bequeath *inter vivos*. This popular expression is commonly used in Mexico to refer to giving one's assets away while still alive but, strictly speaking, it is wrong to say the assets are 'bequeathed' in this way because *inter vivos* refers to a gift and not a legacy. The main disadvantage of leaving informal instructions to be executed after the owner's death is that the owners only tell the family verbally who they are giving the property to, with no paperwork to prove it. In our study, 44 percent of the respondents had already made informal arrangements for succession where they specified to whom they would leave their property, or else had given some or all of their assets away while still alive.

People assume that their instructions will be respected; however, this is not always the case, as illustrated by the example cited, where the spouse died intestate and 'bequeathed *inter vivos*'. The man had 21 children: two out of wedlock, three from the first marriage that ended in divorce, nine from the second marriage where he was widowed and seven from the third, and last, marriage. The spouse in question is from the third marriage. The man now deceased refused to make a will and 'bequeathed some of his property *inter vivos*' to the children he had in his first two marriages (personal communication, 29 November 2008). Regarding the house where the widow lived, he told all the children that he had 'bequeathed' the house to her. However, after the death of the man, eleven of them legally claimed their share of the half of the property that was left intestate. The widow commented that one of the children from a previous marriage of her deceased husband had said: *'We're not going to let her get as much as a glass of water out of it'* (personal communication, 29 November 2008). What can be appreciated in this case is that the wishes that are transmitted orally, without a legal document to protect them, are not necessarily fulfilled and can generate intense family conflicts, especially in cases of very large families and of prospective heirs who are not members of the nuclear family.

A second disadvantage of the *inter vivos* method of passing on property that this case study demonstrates is that the formal transfer of ownership from the intestate party to the children, and then to the widow, was expensive, time-consuming and emotionally draining, especially for the widow, the children and the relatives living in the house in question. In order to keep her house, the widow had to initiate an intestate proceeding. In addition, she had to buy the part that eleven of the twenty children of her deceased husband legally claimed. The other nine children legally withdrew their share (and one child had already died). To do so, the widow and her daughters had to invest a great deal of time in formalities and spend substantial amounts of money. They paid MXN$165,000 (US$11,551 in 2009) to purchase the portion claimed by the children since each of the eleven children was paid MXN$15,000. In addition, a lawyer known to the family who handled the intestate proceeding was paid MXN$20,000 (US$1400). Other expenses, which have nothing to do with whether or not a will has been made, should also be included, such as those incurred by the wife in caring for her husband during the illness that led to his death, and costs associated with having the property title deeds changed to her name in due course. The latter payments included: fines for building without a building licence, municipal taxes for the 'transfer of property', fees to the Land Registry office for the 'rights' when changing owners, a charge for 'registration' of the new property title deeds in the Public Records office, and payment to the notary for the 'notarisation'. To cover these expenses, the widow had to sell part of her asset and accept the support of her three daughters who lived in the same house (one married with small children, one separated with a daughter, and one single daughter). They did not claim their share of the inheritance, but rather contributed money and carried out the formalities for the intestate proceeding. This case shows that in the worst case scenario, the surviving spouse may lose his or her property; if he or she does not have the resources, they may be obliged to sell or rent the house in order to get the money to pay their share to each of the heirs, as well as the costs of inheritance and transfer of the property.

A third disadvantage of the *inter vivos* method of passing on property is linked to the emotional realm, and the vulnerable situation that widows find themselves in when their spouse dies. Succession is usually closely linked to recent events, such as illness or an accident that caused the death of the loved one. In this case, on top of the pain caused by losing a loved one, the widow faced family conflicts with those who claimed the inheritance and wanted to force her out of the house that she literally built with her own hands. In the end, what was most painful for her was that her husband had not legally left the house to her. She said to us, in tears: 'he was very foolish about it', 'my husband didn't love me because he didn't give me anything' (personal communication, 29 November 2008). This situation shows how vulnerable the surviving spouse may be after the death of their partner, as the result of family conflicts. It also shows how this vulnerability is intensified by the lack of provision for succession. Although there are an uncommon number of heirs in this case, it is useful for illustrating that the transmission of property *inter vivos* can be expensive and emotionally draining for the surviving spouse and heirs.

Housing is very important to the living spouse because it means many things at once. It is the house that was built so the couple could have a place of their own to spend their old age in, and it is most likely to be their main asset – you can earn income from it by renting, selling or even mortgaging it if necessary. The house is also built with the idea of leaving an asset to the children. Therefore, if a person like the widow was forced to sell the house, she would lose the most important asset she had generated in her lifetime. Along with these material losses, the surviving spouse could also lose his or her independence, as they would have to live in someone else's home. It is not the same for those widowed to live with their children or relatives as it is for them to live at home. Living 'under someone's roof' they come to feel like a 'burden', as will be seen later on. In addition, changing residences also means leaving behind social networks established over decades in the settlement. Indeed, for the surviving spouses, losing their home can have major economic, social and psychological consequences (Varley and Blasco, 1999: 160). Moreover, the fact that the majority of the widowed are, and will continue to be, women should not be overlooked. In our study, three-quarters of the people who died were men. This is a general trend in Mexico, which is due to the fact that women enjoy a higher life expectancy and that women in marriages tend to be younger than the men.

Reasons for Not Making a Will

Often owners do not make legal arrangements for the succession of their property because there are misunderstandings regarding deeds and wills; the following three are the most important. The first is that the spouses assume that the owner of the entire property is the person whose name is on the title; they are unaware that it is legally owned by both of them because, as mentioned above, in most of the cases studied it was acquired by couples already married under the 'joint ownership' regime. This misunderstanding should not have any major repercussions since the deeds are registered in the Public Property Registers, where it is duly indicated who the owners are and under which regime they are married. Notaries are obliged to verify all this information, to know if an owner who wants to sell or mortgage the property needs the consent of their spouse or not. In practice, however, the situation may be different for at least two reasons. One is due to acts of corruption linked to the Public Property Registers. For example, in the process of selling property, it has been enough for the husband to declare himself single in order to avoid the provision that each spouse is entitled to half of the assets acquired during the marriage (Pérez, 2007: 413–414). Then the wife's consent would not be required for the transaction to go ahead. The other is because people act according to what they know and believe, and not necessarily according to what is legal. As Pérez (2007: 53–54) mentions, 'cultural inertia' prevails even if the law states the contrary to what is commonly assumed. This situation is important in the case of low-income settlements because there are a significant number of deeds in the name of one person, and this person is usually a man.

In the three settlements analysed, 75 percent of the deeds were in the name of just one of the spouses, with only 20 percent in the names of both; and in the remaining cases they were in the name of another person. Of the deeds that were only in the name of one spouse, the man's name prevailed (48 percent against 30 percent in the woman's name). In a study similar to this one but carried out in Mexico City in settlements older than those in Guadalajara, an even higher percentage (60 percent) of deeds were found to be in the man's name (Ward, 2008: 6).

Another problem with titling the property in the name of just one of the spouses is that couples believe that only the person whose name is on the property title deeds should make a will. In addition, some men believe that because their name appears in the deeds, they can bequeath the entire house. For example, one of the interviewees told us that her husband didn't want to leave the house to her, because he said that when he died, she was going to 'get another man in'. The same man wanted to mortgage the house and pass it on to their son who would pay the mortgage, without considering where she was going to live in the probable event that she survived him. His wife also believed that her husband was the owner (personal communication, 22 November 2008).

The second misunderstanding related to deeds and wills is that spouses assume that upon the death of one spouse, their property 'automatically' passes to the other. This is a widespread misconception, the consequences of which are significant because half of the property will in fact be intestate when one of the partners dies. While it is most likely to be the widow who will have to solve the problems arising from her late spouse's half of the intestate property, it is possible that the lack of legal certainty over half of the property would go unnoticed if all family members assumed the same thing, and if there was no need to sell the property. However, if there were heirs to claim their share, the intestate half would become a difficult emotional, economic and legal problem for the widowed spouse, as seen above. Now, even if this turns out not to be a problem for the widow, at some point the property title deeds will still have to be put in the name of the new owners, for example if the heirs decide to sell and want to get a better price for it. This situation is likely to arise, as heirs will try to sell in order to divide the inheritance.

The third and final misunderstanding most likely to prevent any formal plans of succession being made is that some owners consider that physically having property title deeds for the property is the same as owning the property. In one of the case studies, the lady said that her husband did not want to leave the house to her. She considered that the simple fact that her husband had physically given the deeds to his daughter meant the husband and daughter now owned it. That is why this woman was, in fact but not in law, in a vulnerable situation.

Correcting these misunderstandings would help people to make informed decisions about their property and its succession. Through the study we were able to detail the main reasons why most people say that no will is made; and identify which of these are also linked to misunderstandings, a lack of information, or misinformation. It is worth mentioning that several of the reasons described below coincide with the reasons given by the population at the national level (Ortega and Maldonado, 2010):

a) *Laziness and complacency.* Along with the following, this is one of the main reasons interviewees gave for not making a will; 30 percent of people had been thinking of doing it but, they say, they forgot.

b) *Family conflicts.* Another important reason why wills are not made is that when heirs are told who the property will be left to, conflicts arise between family members (15 percent). In other cases, the spouses have not been able to agree on who to leave it to.

c) *Fear.* Many people are afraid to make a will. Young people do not want to think about death, and they believe that if they do, they will die: 'I get sad, I don't want to think about it, if I do, I think I'll die' (personal communication, 4 October 2008). Older people fear that once they reveal who they are going to leave the property to, they will be 'taken out of the house … [and will become] a burden' (personal communication, 13 December 2008), or even worse: 'I'm afraid the kids will take my house and throw me out, even kill me' (personal communication, 29 November 2008). Hence, the vast majority of people choose not to say to whom they are leaving the property. Among those who do make a will, 56 percent do not tell their heirs of their decision.

d) *Lack of information.* It is not known how to bequeath one's assets. Some people are unaware that the will is the commonest legal form of securing the succession of property; many are unaware of the cost, the time it takes, where or with whom it is made. Nor do they know that the will is a private matter, so if they do not want to tell anyone, no one needs to know who they are leaving the property to, and in this way they can avoid family conflicts, at least while they are alive. This privacy also leaves them free to bequeath to the person they designate; no one should be pressured to bequeath to anyone they do not want to, otherwise the will would be invalid. Even less well-known is the 'beneficiary clause', a simpler, cheaper and more expeditious form of succession. Another example of the lack of information among the population is that young owners consider that only old people should make a will. Moreover, also unknown to most people is the fate of the property in the event that a will is not made; one man believed that if he does not make a will, 'the government takes the house' (personal communication, 6 December 2008).

e) *Indecision about who to bequeath the property to.* In some cases, the problem that owners face is that they do not know who to leave the property to, as there are many options: whether they should bequeath the property to those who have cared for the parents, to those who need it most, to men, women, the elderly, the young, etc. (see below).

In the low-income settlements, most families were nuclear families (69 percent). However, if one-third of these families are extended, succession problems can be more complex in two specific cases: on the one hand, where there is no clear distinction between a household and the house its members live in, that is, where there are more households than houses; on the other hand when, following the death of the founding couple, extended family members who are not part of the nuclear family are present in the house, and are likely to have to leave home if they were not included among the heirs. In addition to these two scenarios, there are family situations that make succession difficult. For example, there was a case where the parents did not know how to leave the home to a child who had addiction problems. They did not want to leave it in his name, because they did not want him to waste his inheritance, but they did want their son to have a place to live.

Little can be done to counteract the laziness, complacency and some of the fears the population claim to have. However, the government could contribute by better informing the population and facilitating the process of succession, in the first instance between spouses, and then between them and their children and other heirs.

Preferences for Succession

Of those interviewed, 44 percent said that they had already indicated who they wanted to keep the property. The majority wanted to leave the property to their children (65 percent), even when they had many. One-quarter said they wanted the property to go to the spouse and children (24 percent). Only a few considered that the house should be left exclusively to the spouse (4 percent). The vast majority wanted the property to go to the children (instead of going to the surviving spouse) because, as stated above, it is tacitly considered that if either spouse dies, the other spouse automatically becomes the owner of the entire property, so it would not be necessary to designate him or her. In only a few cases was leaving the property to only one, or some, of the children considered. When this happens, it is usually because there are children who do not have a close relationship with the parents, and do not 'visit' them or 'help' them. In only two cases did the owners plan to leave the home to someone other than the spouse or child: in one case to the mother and sister, and in another to the sister. These two households belonged to people who did not have children to be named as heirs. In another case, an owner was found who, instead of bequeathing it, intended to sell their home before he or his wife died, and to distribute the money from the sale among the children. This was in spite of the fact that they both still lived in the house.

As can be seen from the problems related to succession, whether testamentary or intestate, complications arise from the fact that housing in self-produced settlements and in the city in general is densely occupied. The systematic lack of formal land and accessible housing for the poor means that the parents' property is adapted to accommodate the changing needs of its occupants during their lifetime. This study shows that about one-third of the land that originally housed a family in a home had changed substantially after more than twenty years. The houses had been subdivided, new ones had been built, and there were sometimes more families than houses on the same plot. This is because it is difficult for newly married sons and daughters, or single mothers, to live independently due to a lack of economic and social resources. Therefore, it is common for them to stay with their parents, either temporarily or permanently, and they usually invest their own resources in building or adapting the property to create a place to live. If you take into account all these rights over time, rights that are socially acquired and that apply to different inhabitants of the same property, you can see how difficult it is going to be sometimes to divide the property among the heirs when the original owners die intestate. The conflicts that arise revolve around those who, for various reasons, feel entitled to inherit part of the property. Such is the case of those who contributed resources to buying, building or maintaining the property; also of those who took care of the parents, those who live in the property, and all the children of the original couple, conceived within the marriage, or outside it, even if they do not live there. Although formal succession of ownership would not resolve all the conflicts related to the transfer of ownership, it would certainly help to reduce them, facilitating the transfer from one generation to the next, while avoiding a reversal of the regularisation programmes, and leading in general to healthier residential markets.

Alternatives for the Legal Transfer of Ownership

In Mexico, a property can be legally transferred while the owner is still living, or else after his or her death. According to Articles 779 and 791 of the Civil Code, while the owner is alive the transfer can be made temporarily, through the 'family assets' regulations, or permanently, through a 'donation' (CCEJ, 1995). Article 1045 clarifies that the latter may be a 'total donation' of property and usufruct; or a 'partial donation', where the property is donated but the usufruct is retained ('lifelong usufruct') (CCEJ, 1995). The Civil Code of the State of Jalisco states that succession after death can be secured either by judicial means, through a will, or else via administrative means using the 'beneficiary clause'.

The owner's wishes to transfer his or her property after death are commonly set out in a will, which anyone can make in a notary's office. In other words, through the legal route that has been widely disseminated for the last eighteen years. At the beginning of 2000, in order to encourage the population to make a will, the Ministry of the Interior signed a general agreement with the National Association of Mexican Notaries, and also a specific one with the Associations of Notaries of each state. Through these agreements, two programmes were made available to the population, as detailed below: 'September Month of the Will' and 'Low-Cost Will'. Much less well known is the administrative succession of assets through the 'beneficiary clause'. All of these succession alternatives are regulated by the Civil Code of the State of Jalisco and there are important variations between the different states in Mexico (see Grajeda and Ward, 2012).

At the time of the research, the Civil Code of the State of Jalisco (CCEJ, 1993) already included the innovative method of succession known as the 'beneficiary clause' or 'preferential bequest'. Its novelty lies in the fact that succession could be ensured by administrative means. When the owner died, the property would be transferred to the spouse, ascendants and descendants, without the need for probate proceedings. The clause in Articles 1893 and 1894 applied only at the time of the purchase and that of the sale of homes (CCEJ, 1995). However, on 6 October 2012 important changes were made to the Civil Code: according to Decree 24, 137/LIX/12, the State Congress repealed Article 1893 and 1894 and added Article 2665-Bis in the section that deals with successions, not in the section that sets the norm for buying and selling goods, where it was before (CCEJ, 1995). These changes allowed the clause to be included not only in the cases of purchase and sale, but also in the cases of properties obtained through other means, such as exchange, inheritance, legacy, donation, gift in payment or acquisitive prescription. In addition, the regulations not only considered new properties that were purchased after 1995 (CCEJ 1995, Transitional Tenth) but also those that were built before that date. An initiative to amend Article 2665-Bis was presented in 2013. This initiative appealed to the freedom to make a will that prevails in Mexico, and proposed that the 'beneficiary clause' should, likewise, not be restricted to naming as heirs the spouse, ascendants or descendants; but that owners might decide 'voluntarily, at the time of drafting the deed or by adding an annotation at a later date' to whom to leave their property (CEJ, 2013). However, this initiative was not passed, and the restriction persists. Nevertheless, the great importance of these Articles of the Civil Code of Jalisco is that it is now possible to opt for the administrative transfer of properties. Unfortunately, this alternative method of ensuring succession is not yet widely known, even though its widespread use would have a great impact, not only on the properties we are analysing that were titled more than twenty years ago, but on the whole state and indeed the entire country.

Each alternative has advantages and disadvantages, depending on the needs or preferences of the testator, whether in life or after death. The temporary transfer of ownership during the lifetime of the owner implies the constitution of a dwelling as a 'family asset'. According to the Civil Code of the State of Jalisco (1995) the advantage of this alternative is that it is possible to designate successors, who are members of the same family, in the event of the death of the owner (section 787). The disadvantage is that the owner loses full control over his property (section 795), which means that he cannot sell as long as this option is in force (section 780). In addition, for the property to be constituted as a family asset, certain requirements must be met, and in a divorce the spouse found 'guilty' loses the right to live in the property (section 788). Moreover, under this regime, 'ownership of the property constituted [as a family asset] is not transferred to the beneficiaries. They have the right to enjoy these assets only for the purpose intended' (section 779).

In the case of a permanent transfer of ownership of the property while the donor is alive through 'donation', the donor may reserve the use and ownership of the property for himself ('lifelong usufruct'), so that he can legally enjoy the fruits of the property until his death. The 'donation' has the advantage that with the owner having decided before he or she dies who the new owner will be, conflict after their passing can be minimised. The disadvantage is that the donor ceases to be the owner and the action is permanent, unless some defect is found in the manner in which the donation was made, which provides grounds for revoking the donation (CCEJ, 1995: Chapter I).

The legal transfer of property after death through a will has the advantage today that programmes have been set up to lower the cost, and these have been widely disseminated. In addition to the right to make a will at any time that everybody has anyway, currently there are two federal programmes in force to encourage people to make a will. The federal 'Month of the Will' programme, which began in 2002, lasts indefinitely and requires the charges for making a will to be reduced by at least half during September (to MXN$1802, approx. US$93, in September 2018). In 2007, an even cheaper option (US$24, August 2016) was offered, the 'Low Cost

Will', also of indefinite duration, and this can be applied for in any month (DOF, 2007).

A very important advantage of the national 'Low Cost Will' agreement is that it refers to the 'Preferred Housing Bequest' programme and 'suggests' that states incorporate this into their legislation so that purchasers can designate their successors at the time of titling their homes. In this case, the preferred legatee may validate the succession 'in a single act of acceptance and award'. The disadvantages of the programmes are that at any time either party (notaries or government) may decide to terminate the agreement and that the conditions of both programmes vary between different states and change frequently. For example, a condition that homes do not exceed the maximum value of affordable housing or its equivalent in each state, or one that excludes owners who are over 60 or 65, are disabled or vulnerable, etc. The biggest disadvantage of the 'Low Cost Will' is that the 'preferential bequest' in Mexico is neither well disseminated nor applied.

In Jalisco, although there is the option, which other states do not provide, of transferring property after death by administrative means, this has the disadvantage that it is not widely known or disseminated among notaries and public officials in the municipalities of the state. The great advantage of transferring property using the 'beneficiary clause' (or 'preferential bequest') is that it allows heirs to be directly named in the deeds. Its low price and speed is due to the fact that there is no need for probate proceedings. According to Article 2665-Bis, following the original owner's death, it is enough for the new owner to present to the person in charge of the Public Property Registers a receipt for the payment of taxes for the transfer of ownership, a certified copy of the death certificate, and proof that the designation has not been revoked or modified (CCEJ, 1995).

Conclusions

The study identifies the problems caused by the lack of formal succession of property ownership, and points to the narrow scope of regularisation programmes in Mexico. The official objective of the regularisation was to provide legal certainty that would enhance the value of assets and ensure the transfer of ownership without conflict. Although the first goal of the programmes has for the most part been met, achieving formal succession of ownership requires additional measures to be taken in order to avoid reversing the massive success in titling that CORETT has achieved over more than four decades since its founding in 1974. Otherwise, the deeds will remain in the name of those who used to own the property and not of those who effectively own it today. This is the 'new informality' that is already brewing in Mexican cities. From the examples in Guadalajara, it can be seen that this phenomenon, currently incipient, is becoming widespread. It is therefore necessary to take both preventative and remedial measures.

Our research highlights the great significance of real estate property succession in Mexico, specifically in the now regularised settlements. It demonstrates that it is not enough just for the law to protect the rights of widowed spouses and heirs; being able to exercise these rights is also essential. A lack of economic resources, ignorance and sexist customs often prevent these rights from being exercised in everyday life. The 'beneficiary clause', an innovative alternative in Jalisco Civil Law, needs to be widely known and applied in the state. However, in order to achieve greater progress and to benefit those who have the least, this clause should be incorporated into the Civil Code of other states throughout the country.

References

Azuela, A. and Duhau, E. (1998) 'Tenure Regularization, Private Property and Public Order in Mexico' in E. Fernandes and A. Varley (eds.) *Illegal Cities, Law and Urban Change in Developing Countries*. Zed Books: London, 157–171.

CCEJ, Código Civil del Estado de Jalisco (1995) Gobierno del Estado de Jalisco: Guadalajara.

CEJ Congreso del Estado de Jalisco (2013) *Iniciativa de ley que reforma el artículo 2665-Bis del Código Civil del Estado de Jalisco*. Gobierno del Estado de Jalisco: Guadalajara.

Diario Oficial de la Federación (DOF) (2007) 'Marco de concertación entre el Gobierno Federal a través de la Secretaría de Gobernación y la Asociación del Notariado Mexicano, AC'. [WWW document]. URL http://diariooficial.segob.gob.mx/nota_detalle.php?codigo=4965757&fecha=15/03/2007 [accessed 7 July 2019].

El Universal (2007) 'Inicia Segob el martes Septiembre, Mes del Testamento', El Universal, 1 September. [WWW document]. URL http://www.eluniversal.com.mx/notas/446470.html [accessed 18 August 2018].

Fernandes, E. [2001] (2010) 'La ley y la producción de ilegalidad urbana' in M. O. Smolka and L. Mullahy (eds.) *Perspectivas urbanas. Temas críticos en políticas de suelo en América Latina*. Lincoln Institute of Land Policy: Cambridge, 6–93.

Fernandes, E. (2004) 'Del código civil al estatuto de la ciudad: algunas notas sobre la trayectoria del derecho urbanístico en Brasil'. *Boletín Mexicano de Derecho Comparado* 37(109): 41–69.

García, S. M. A. (2015) *Los que se quedan: familias y testamentos en Ocotelulco. Tlaxcala, 1572–1673*. El Colegio de Michoacán: Zamora.

Grajeda, E. and Ward, P. M. (2012) 'Inheritance and Succession in Informal Settlements of Latin American Cities: A Mexican Case Study'. *Latin American Research Review* 47 Special Issue: 139–162.

Jiménez-Huerta, E. R. (2000) *El principio de la irregularidad. Mercado de suelo para vivienda en Aguascalientes, 1975–1998*. Universidad de Guadalajara: Guadalajara; Centro de Investigaciones y Estudios Multidisciplinarios de Aguascalientes: Aguascalientes.

Jiménez-Huerta, E. R. (2008) *La renovación de asentamientos irregulares consolidados en ciudades latinoamericanas: en busca de una nueva 'generación' de políticas públicas*. Final Technical Report for CONACYT, Project number 5404: Mexico FD.

Jiménez-Huerta, E. R., Cruz-Solís, H. and Rábago-Anaya, J. (2004) *Atlas de la producción de suelo en el área metropolitana de Guadalajara*. Final Technical Report for CONACYT project number R31042 S: Mexico FD.

Jiménez-Huerta, E. R., Cruz-Solís, H. and Ubaldo Velázquez, C. (2012) 'El regreso a la irregularidad de las colonias populares. Títulos de propiedad y sucesión' in C. E. Salazar (ed.) *Irregular: suelo y mercado en América Latina*. El Colegio de México: Mexico FD, 337–377.

Latin American Housing Network (LAHN) (2009) [WWW document]. URL https://www.lahn.utexas.org/ [accessed 18 August 2018].

Ortega, M. and Maldonado, L. F. (2010) 'La cultura del testamento. Encuesta nacional en viviendas'. *Consulta Mitofsky* [WWW document.] URL http://herenciasconcausa.org/yahoo_site_admin/assets/docs/Cultura_del_Testamento_2010.21175249.pdf [accessed 7 December 2016].

Pérez, D. A. [1994] (2007) *Derecho de familia*. 2nd ed. Fondo de Cultura Económica: Mexico FD.

Smolka, M. [2001] (2007) 'Informalidad, pobreza urbana y precios de la tierra' in M. Smolka and L. Mullahy (eds.) *Perspectivas urbanas: temas críticos en políticas de suelo en América Latina*. Lincoln Institute of Land Policy: Cambridge, 71–78.

United Nations-Habitat (2016a) The Draft New Agenda: Habitat III Conference. [WWW document]. URL http://citiscope.org/sites/default/files/h3/Compilation_Habitat_III_Zero_Draft_outcome_document_asof_6_J.pdf [accessed 7 December 2016].

United Nations-Habitat (2016b) *The New Agenda: Habitat III* Conference. [WWW document]. URL https://www2.habitat3.org/bitcache/99d99fbd0824de50214e99f864459d8081a9be00?vid=591155&disposition=inline&op=view [accessed 7 December 2016].

United Nations-Habitat (2017) *New Urban Agenda*. [WWW document]. URL http://habitat3.org/wp-content/uploads/NUA-English.pdf [accessed 15 February 2019].

Varley, A. and Blasco, M. (1999) *Ageing in a Gendered World: Women's Issues and Identities*. International Research and Training Institute for the Advancement of Women (UN-INSTRAW): Santo Domingo.

Ward, P. M. (2008) 'Hacia una segunda etapa de la regularización de los títulos de propiedad en México (o visto de otra manera) "¿Ay mamá, por qué moriste sin dejar un testamento? ¡Ya tenemos que hacer la regularización de nuevo!"' in A. X. Iracheta Cenecorta and S. M. Ciriaco (eds.) *Irregularidad y suelo urbano*. El Colegio Mexiquense, AC, SEDESOL, UN-Habitat: Mexico, FD.

Ward, P. M., Jiménez-Huerta, E. R., Grajeda, E. and Ubaldo Velázquez, C. (2011) 'Self-help Housing Policies for Second Generation Inheritance and Succession of "The House that Mum & Dad Built"'. *Habitat International* **35**(3): 467–485.

Ward, P. M., Jiménez-Huerta, E. R. and Di Virgilio, M. (2014) 'Intensive Case Studies Methodology for the Analysis of Self-Help Housing Consolidation, Household Organization and Family Mobility'. *Current Urban Studies* **2**: 88–104.

Interviews

Anon., 58-year-old married woman, (2008) questionnaire, (in person), 'La renovación de asentamientos irregulares consolidados en ciudades latinoamericanas. En busca de una nueva "generación" de políticas públicas', questionnaire by Elizabeth Patricia Padilla Etienne, 22 November 2008.

Anon., 67-year-old widowed woman, (2008) questionnaire, (in person), 'La renovación de asentamientos irregulares consolidados en ciudades latinoamericanas. En busca de una nueva "generación" de políticas públicas', questionnaire by Claudia Ubaldo Velázquez and Edith Rosario Jiménez Huerta, 29 November 2008.

Anon., 64-year-old married man, (2008) questionnaire, (in person), 'La renovación de asentamientos irregulares consolidados en ciudades latinoamericanas. En busca de una nueva "generación" de políticas públicas', questionnaire by María Alejandra Núñez Villalobos, 6 December.

Anon., 65-year-old married man, (2008) questionnaire, (in person), 'La renovación de asentamientos irregulares consolidados en ciudades latinoamericanas. En busca de una nueva "generación" de políticas públicas', questionnaire by Rosa María Ortíz Aguirre, 13 December.

Anon., 36-year-old married woman, (2008) questionnaire, (in person), 'La renovación de asentamientos irregulares consolidados en ciudades latinoamericanas. En busca de una nueva "generación" de políticas públicas', questionnaire by María Alejandra Núñez Villalobos, 4 October.

Anon., 74-year-old married man, (2008) questionnaire, (in person), La renovación de asentamientos irregulares consolidados en ciudades latinoamericanas. En busca de una nueva "generación" de políticas públicas', questionnaire by Adriana Fausto Brito and Martha Eugenia Castañeda Rivera, 27 September.

8

Conclusion

CLARA SALAZAR
El Colegio de Mexico

The contributions of a wide range of authors to this book have allowed us to update analysis of debate in the region about the persistent problems linked to different forms of occupation and sale of land, and construction of built space, as well as the limited progress of land and housing policies which have been implemented to solve them. This book has provided evidence that the allocation of property rights is a long way from solving the housing problem in Latin American countries. The precarious housing situation remains because it is a functional part of the process of capitalist accumulation. Consequently, informal urbanisation is not a transitory process, nor does it function independently of the formal land market. In other words, the informal occupation of land and the self-construction of housing remain because they make it possible to keep wages low. The government policies implemented to resolve these issues are only remedial and the precarious housing situation continues, yet without generating large-scale social conflicts.

In the context of the social inequity that characterises Latin America, several states in the region have gradually given up on supporting the construction of housing for the lowest income sectors and have replaced these actions with the delivery of property title deeds. Obviously, this is a policy which reduces public spending, and has resulted in a situation that is full of tension and contradictions. This book questions the land and housing policies designed and implemented under the neoliberal principle that private property is synonymous with security and identifies private property rights as a necessary condition for the poor to generate wealth and overcome poverty. While weighing up this governmental position – one that insists that the core of the housing problem is a legal issue – other more progressive urban initiatives implemented in some of the region's countries have been presented and analysed. These initiatives seek to incorporate mechanisms for the equitable redistribution of the burdens and benefits of urbanisation into legal frameworks and public management.

This book does not deny that the definition of property rights can contribute to better planning of cities and also generate a sense of security in households. Rather, it has discussed the implications of placing property titling and construction programmes in the hands of the market. Living in decent housing is not synonymous with private property; it requires more than the provision of property title deeds to provide access to a space that guarantees protection from the elements and from eviction, and that allows for 'continuous improvement of living conditions', as agreed in the International Bill of Human Rights adopted by the United Nations in 1966. Providing decent housing requires the state to ensure that all its citizens, without exception, have access to a shelter that protects them, is equipped with the basic services necessary to satisfy their biological needs and prepare and consume food, as well as providing shelter so that the workforce can rest to recover from their daily labours, reproduce and develop their own capabilities as human beings. The population needs to inhabit this space, but not be the legal owner of it.

In fact, housing policy in several European Union countries considers the support of housing rentals with a protected price as an alternative to private property. Eurostat data shows, for example, that in the United Kingdom in 2014, 33.2 percent of the population lived in rental housing paid at market prices, but another 15.7 percent paid a protected rent. Although it is true that in the European Union only 12.7 percent of rented housing is set at a protected price, we want to show that there are other housing tenure regimes, different from private property, which other countries use to offer housing to low-income populations.

The property title programmes that are still applied in the countries of the Global South as the only way to respond to households without access to credit are a gross simplification of the housing problem. With a titling policy, national states excuse themselves from the need to create alternative policies that contribute to improving the wellbeing of society as a whole. The construction of finished housing in Latin American countries does not aim to support the lowest income segment of the population, but rather to support the market; therefore, it is aimed at people with credit capacity who can pay for housing at market prices. The population segment that cannot afford to do so is, at most, given a property title deed to a piece of land that they themselves have developed.

In this sense, the book draws on narratives that address crucial issues, in order to better understand and incorporate them into public policies designed to create viable 'decent housing' alternatives for poor households. Thus, we underline that although there are different ways for the state to offer access to housing, these are not being implemented. This creates the paradox that it is the functioning of the market, underpinned by state policies which aim to combat urban informality, that actually produces it. This combination of market operation and state policies is enacted through property title programmes that attempt to make the informal formal, by housing programmes that announce, yet fail to achieve, the expansion of lower-income housing provision, and regulations that regulate human settlements but at the same time result in disorder, uncontrolled expansion and urban segregation.

Informal Urbanisation

Here, urban informality has been analysed from its conceptual definition to methodological aspects for its empirical measurement, via the different dimensions that cause it and recognise it as a structuring element of Latin American cities. Although in public policy the phenomenon of informality has been described by international organisations as a category that denies the legal dimension, urban informality is more than that: it is a way of creating urban space. So what really defines it is not its avoidance of legal status or official planning, but rather that it constitutes the social component that official planning has not been able – or willing – to adequately meet. Informal urbanisation is the population's autonomous response to their housing needs. They have to live somewhere.

The validity of this work lies, precisely and sadly, in the permanence of these forms of popular housing. Connolly has already documented that in the case of Mexico the formation of informal settlements is a matter of continuity rather than change. Although during the first years of the new millennium in Mexico an environment of macroeconomic stability for the property sector allowed the market to significantly increase the construction of finished housing, this did not allow the incorporation of lower income sectors as buyers.

In Latin America and the Caribbean, housing policies have suffered a major setback in terms of social housing. In the context of structural reforms, which became more evident in the 1990s, states in the region moved away from supporting the construction of social housing to facilitate the success of the construction industry. In parallel, the limitations of regularisation programmes were aggravated and their actions were reduced, particularly in Mexico. This is particularly worrying in a context where the labour market has become more precarious. The Balance Preliminar de las Economías de América Latina y el Caribe (Preliminary Overview of Latin America and Caribbean Economies) (ECLAC, 2016: 53–54), indicates that unemployment has increased sharply in the region, and that between 2015 and 2016, the urban unemployment rate increased from 7.4 percent to 9.0 percent. This means that the urban unemployed increased by 4.1 million people, reaching a total of 21.3 million workers excluded from employment. Although the same report mentions that a projected recovery of 8 percent in commodity prices for 2017, and a positive impact on the terms of trade of exporting countries is expected, in social terms one cannot be very optimistic. The recovery of these prices undermines the solvency of poor households, when monetary income is related to the generalised process of deepening cuts in public spending and the impact of inflation on the slight increase in real wages in countries such as Colombia, Brazil and Mexico.

The Impossibility of Including All Land Ownership Transactions in the Formal Rules

Another of the questions that arise from reading this text is the impossibility of including all transactions related to land ownership in the formal rules, given a context in which there are no pure market forms, but rather both simple and capitalist mode of commercial construction coexist based on competitive relationships. Authors such as Abramo and Morales argue that a combination of different types of agents and rationalities participate in the construction of the Latin American urban space, who are not (as marginality theory would have it) conditioned by a lack of cultural integration which prevents transition to modernisation, but who are responding to commercial calculations. The institutionalisation of neoliberal ideas that promote the free market, and result in privatisation and the rise of private capital in the provision of housing, are reinforced by the crisis of the state as the key regulator and promoter of housing.

In this context, Latin American urbanisation is reproduced indefinitely through forms of interaction of a complementary, rather than contradictory, nature between formal and informal land markets. The consequence of this, as Abramo points out, is that it generates and reproduces two types of city construction logics that act simultaneously; one of them, compact or intensive in land use and the other, diffuse or extensive. These two logics are mutually reinforced by their own promotion mechanisms, one formal and the other informal in nature. It is therefore not possible to separate them. The author calls this phenomenon the COMP-FUSED city (compact and diffuse), which imposes itself as an unequal socio-spatial structure that, supported by state deregulation, encourages exclusion and promotes the reproduction of the informal market.

What the authors argue, then, is that there is a perverse feedback loop in the sub-markets, in which one generates demand for the other and vice versa; the result is an increase in land prices and thus the reproduction of the exclusion of low-income sectors. The first sub-market, known as the land plots, is the main contributor to urban expansion in precarious conditions and to the diffuse city model. The second refers to the consolidation of informal populated areas, in which there is gradual compaction and densification. The unequal distribution of income and the limited capacity of government policies to generate a supply of decent housing with community participation, as well as to formulate adequate regulation, produces this a type of double precariousness and its inevitable reproduction.

Property Rights and Security

Other reflections arising from the reading of this volume is the limited recognition of property rights, and especially the limits of the legal system as a way to tackle urban informality. Likewise, the inability of the government to appreciate the considerable progress achieved by the IS inhabitants in the construction of their home and their potential to meet socially established standards. This book has shown that the assumptions which underpin Hernando de Soto's neoliberal proposal, which see legal rights as a mechanism to overcome poverty and informality, and to generate economic growth, have not borne fruit as expected. They are also more limited than social practices.

The empirical information presented suggests that the legal definition of private property has not generated wider access to credit or greater household investment in housing. Equally, they show that having a property title in hand is not the *sine qua non* to achieving neighbourhood improvements. Several of the ISs referred to and analysed here are territories that lack legal security. However, the fact that these property rights have not yet been resolved has not prevented them from becoming consolidated spaces with basic services such as water, urban cleaning, electricity and paved roads. The transformations of these environments are not achieved by decree, but rather through the daily efforts of the inhabitants to build and improve their homes. They are also achieved through community work with local authorities to ensure that they deliver basic services.

The experience of community urbanisation suggests that, while government provision has established that infrastructure provision and housing improvement programmes can only be allocated after land ownership has been legally defined, this precept is far from being implemented. Clientelistic practices and the exchange of votes for the provision of services by local authorities are the price that inhabitants pay for access to these benefits prior to titling. Although clientelism is an undesirable practice that violates human dignity, in our countries it has become a real, though non-legal, mechanism that legitimises land ownership. Thus, to the extent that cooperation between *ejidatarios* (people who are rights holders in *ejidos*, or land held in common by a specific community), inhabitants (people living on *ejido* land who do not have land-title rights) and authorities has been legitimised, it has become unlikely that the threat of eviction will be used on the inhabitants, which in turn encourages them to invest in improving their homes. In this sense, security takes the form of a 'public guarantee' which, in practice, consolidates the living space and legitimises their possession of the property. It is also a type of certainty that is social in nature, very different, but valid nonetheless, from the one granted by the legal framework: that of being a property owner.

In this dynamic of 'reverse urbanisation' in Latin America, where land is first occupied, then made available for living, and then property rights are obtained, the handing over of a title acts rather like a filter in the obtaining of a grant. This is another contradiction of the policy. Titling before facilitating access to grant programmes is a restrictive, yet cohesive mechanism for improving the ordinary home. The budget allocated to housing improvement programmes is small, resulting in secondary titling for the majority of households. Although titled properties reach higher prices on the market, which could act as a stimulus for titling, we must not lose sight of the fact that the owners of an informal dwelling are not just economic subjects who self-build their house in order to turn it into a commodity. These are poor families who live in the slums because they are driven by the need for housing and who invest their social and economic resources there in order to use this asset, imbuing it with 'use-value'. The funds that constitute the inhabitant's investment in housing are not derived from the market, nor funds from the banks, nor from the state; they come from their own family resources, obtained through savings and loans from relatives.

The Paradoxes of Urban Regulation

From the official perspective, it has been argued that the lack of territorial policies and land use regulation leads to urban sprawl and the proliferation of informal settlements. At the same time, in this volume some authors have argued that excessive regulation, such as zoning that organises urban space into exclusively residential areas differentiated according to the cost of housing, commercial and industrial, has led to the expansion of urban sprawl and increased social segregation. In addition, they have pointed out that the reduction of obligations to private property, that is to say, the decline of regulation associated with insufficient public investment, has created the vicious circle of informality-regularisation-informality which puts pressure on the incomes of those excluded from the formal system, as well as increasing land prices. It cannot be said, then, that the above statements are not true, but rather contradictory, and have consequences for the establishment of an adequate housing policy.

Thus, Morales has argued that the scarcity of land arises not so much due to a lack of physical availability, but because of the limited existence of suitable urban land, and that this scarcity is strategically sustained by land retention. This in turn is promoted by the regulatory framework and by actors with different rationalities and interests creating an imbalance of rights and obligations in favour of the owners. By failing to define a system of responsibilities for proper land use, owners can retain idle land without transforming it or undertaking work, and are able to reap the benefits of public decisions and investments that improve the environment of these lands. Through this chain of inaction, the owners can appropriate the capital gains that the city is entitled to. This not only increases their profit, but also prevents the redistribution of resources that would result from investment in improvements (differential income) by the state, and increases urban segregation.

Thus, by defining specific land use in strategic locations, the regulations generate a demand that puts pressure on the available land, making it scarce and costly. Unlike the neoliberal theorists, who always hope to maximise economic efficiency, the research included here considers this increase in land and property prices to be problematic, alongside the unforeseen effects of rent speculation and intense pressure on infrastructure and public services. The increase in land prices tends to exclude those with scarce resources who, as a result, are pushed back to cheaper, unregulated land away from zones with urban services where they embark on the purchase and informal occupation of land and the self-construction of housing. As can be concluded, the creation of new settlements without sustainable urban and environmental conditions, but with the expectation of being titled, is not a scenario conducive to establishing decent housing.

Does this mean that urban regulations are inadequate to the task of combatting informality head-on and meeting the housing needs of low-income inhabitants? It would be wrong to conclude this.

The proposed urban regulation in Bogotá offers other perspectives. In this city, local authorities have made efforts to implement innovative strategies to address the shortage of urbanised land at affordable prices for Vivienda de Interés Prioritario, (VIP, Priority Housing). Maldonado notes the progress made on urban reform legislation in Colombia (Law 388 of 1997 and its regulations) allowing for intervention in the land market and production of low-priced housing. However, although offering a range of instruments used to achieve this (a land bank, the compulsory earmarking of a percentage of land for social housing; making development and construction on vacant land compulsory, the use of well-located public land, compulsory purchase of plots for small-scale projects, etc.) Maldonado reveals how difficult this is to fully implement. The gap between formal objectives and the end results of implementation emerges once private actors balk at the control of land prices, one of the undesirable effects of this strategy which damages their interests.

A lesson learned from the above is that even with changes in legislation and the creation of appropriate legal mechanisms, it is not possible to reach the lower-income sectors through public policy and the formal market. Nor is it possible to reverse the existing regimes of exclusion from access to urbanised land, services and high quality collective assets. This is because there are design flaws in the programmes that prevent them from being fully implemented. For example, the subsidy policy in Bogotá did not initially foresee the difficulties in obtaining access to cheap land for *Vivienda de Interés Social* (VIS, Social Housing), leaving its provision in the hands of the market priorities economic objectives over the social ones in terms of housing. Thus, by ensuring that the landowners maintained their profit margin, the economic benefits of the subsidies transferred to them and the builders. Something similar happened with the land bank. The availability of land responded to the expectations of the builders. For the larger builders, the most attractive option is the flexibility of the planning rules on rural land. As these are not very demanding in terms of comprehensive urban planning, builders are able to develop the whole site with relatively low investment and high profit margins. The great disadvantage of locating poor households on cheap land is that they once more concentrate such families in large, homogeneous areas, which reproduces urban segregation.

At this point, it can be concluded that for regulation to work properly, it needs to maintain the fulfilment of the social objective as a priority. In urban management, the application of land use regulations that privilege profit and the high valuation of privately owned land without any consideration for the community still prevails. Therefore, in the regulations, the state needs to include social responsibility incentives for the different agents intervening in the land market, in order to facilitate access to decent housing for the poorest families and avoid the reproduction of precarious homes.

Two other aspects relate to areas of jurisdiction. In the case of Mexico, it has been mentioned that rural and urban land ownership rights are still addressed through different jurisdictions: agrarian and civil. In the case of Colombia, the contradictions between national policies that privilege support for higher-priced housing and local attempts to democratise the city's construction and consumption have been highlighted. In both cases, the legal question emerges not as a way to address issues but as a source of dispute, where matters are resolved according to the interests and power relations of political and economic actors. The paradox occurs when these actors promote processes of land privatisation to achieve extraordinary profits, or stop initiatives to democratise the city to avoid losses in the valuation of land. In both cases, the economic objective prevails and is translated into political decisions.

Juridical-Institutional Transformation in Mexico: Unaware of the Social Reality?

It is also important to point out that the institutional legal transformation carried out in Mexico at the beginning of the 1990s which aimed to incorporate *ejido* land within the market, has ignored the fact that property relations are what determine the legitimacy of possession. The lack of knowledge of the long-established social norms concerning the transfer of land in the urban periphery had a devastating impact on the titling of property in favour of IS inhabitants.

In order to promote the liberalisation of the communal land for the market, the Mexican state recognised the *ejidatario*'s property rights over land that had already been sold to, and occupied by, poor inhabitants. The effect was to turn the *ejidatarios* into legal owners of land on which thousands of families had settled without property rights. When the state prioritised private property over social reality, it generated a whole process of institutional transformation that weakened and destroyed previous social agreements, such as the structure of IS titling.

The legal reforms transferred to private agents, functions which had been the exclusive jurisdiction of the state for three decades; after the reforms, the former could intervene in the titling. This allowed this necessary legal procedure to be transformed from a social benefit administered by the state into a commercialised service offered by non-government actors. This introduced changes in public roles and responsibilities, reduced the degree of state influence on the implementation of social redistribution procedures, and increased speculative practices on land transfer. In other words, it impacted on the informal institutions that had guaranteed reciprocal agreements in inter-temporal and inter-generational terms through which the community sectors have been provided with housing. In addition, it allowed agrarian institutions to exercise power over land management in the periphery of the city and subject to urban arrangements; this situation has made it difficult to regularise the ISs, compromising the security of its inhabitants and limiting the formalisation of their property.

The analysis warns of the fact that the process of *ejido* liberalisation, understood as the transfer of the agrarian system to the civil system in order to make land available for the market, is progressing within an institutional framework that emerged with the reforms of the 1990s which encourages exclusion and reproduces urban informality through new forms of intervention. Titling under the new rules is guaranteed under the protection of formal institutions with free market (business) 'guidelines'. The new ingredients are: (i) the designation of property title deeds to the settlers is no longer done by the authority but by the owner (*ejidatario*) of the property; there are no rules for this and civilians can make executive decisions according to their own criteria and interests; and (ii) the administrative procedures required for the title can be managed by private companies. The primacy of private property has reached its peak; the legal owners of the land (*ejidatarios*) can even, by means of a 'mandate agreement', demand that the former authority (CORETT) specify the titling, that is, to legitimise its sale outside the regulatory norm.

All of the above occurs within a framework in which the recognition of property rights promised to the poor has not been resolved. The backlog in titling increases because the ongoing informal access to land is added to that which has yet to be formalised. Moreover, over time, effective titling creates a new irregularity because it is limited to the first generation of owners. Jimenez et al. have pointed out the need to qualify the positive effects of legal formalisation of the property, since these do not consider possible new irregularities that emerge in relation to succession. Although the land has been regularised, people do not undertake legal procedures available in civil law to ensure succession, a matter that falls not just within the legal domain, but also to the administration and is highly subjective. In practice, normative behaviour prevails over legal behaviour, which in the family domain leaves property rights undefined for the next generation, resulting in family conflicts.

This also leads us to reflect on the rights and obligations involved in private property. The formalisation of property rights is unthinkable without direct taxation of property, so taxes on property, inheritance and related financial transactions must be rethought in a paradigm of differentiated taxation based on property values, in order to achieve more effective actions and a progressive redistributive impact.

Alternatives to Land Access and Housing beyond Titling

When analysing the coverage of the regularisation processes, which, although it benefits those granted titles, is mitigated by delay and decreasing formalisation of ownership, we cannot help but wonder why these programmes remain in force in the official discourse, and what the alternatives might be.

A matter of concern in this regard is that the inhabitants do not appear as partners in public policies, that is to say, they are the object, not the subjects, of such policies. Through the official discourse, the expectation that a property title deed is a priority has been sown in the social conscience, and to the extent that it is transmitted as the only way to create a family asset, households incorporate it into their way of life without question. This reduces the pressure of the population on the demand for decent housing. For a population that earns the least and lacks information on the exercising of their rights, alternatives to a paradigm as simple and relatively achievable as receiving a property title deed to land that is already owned may be meaningless. This may be convenient for the state, but it is inconvenient for human development. For this reason, it is necessary to move towards alternative land and housing policies that offer options beyond titling, and surpass the allocation of sporadic benefits, which end up falling into the pockets of agents other than those they are intended. Effective poverty eradication requires, in addition to legal security, investment and public policies associated with other areas such as education, income generation and infrastructure provision. Overcoming the simplistic vision of titling implies democratising access to land by recognising the existence of diverse forms of home tenure and construction. Separation in the allocation of property rights (possession, use, exploitation, exclusion and disposal) and differentiation of housing components (land and construction) can also be useful tools when granting rights and obligations.

For the new sites, it is thus necessary to promote policies that link access to land and the provision of services and urban infrastructure, and housing, as well as the application of appropriate fiscal measures. The policy of creating territorial reserves (preventive) is presented as a viable alternative, as is the revision of the official story of land shortage in the city. However, its implementation has incurred significant impediments, as shown in the case of Colombia, making it clear that if we want to move the issue of land management forward, the private sector is not more efficient than the public sector, and its interests may actually impede progress in social redistribution.

One aspect that is central to this book's desire to promote alternative proposals is undoubtedly the strengthening of a legal framework, creating incentives that aim to set out the roles and responsibilities, both of state agencies and other agents involved in the land market. This includes both the simple owners who retain the land and those who invest in the construction of the built space. The mechanisms of control, regulation and sanction over the behaviour and actions of agents operating in the market are fundamental to press for changes in their practices and behaviour.

The experience of the policies analysed here highlights the need to encourage processes that guarantee access to urbanised land at low prices in order to offer it to sectors with limited resources, and to generate integrated housing for the construction of cities through collective efforts. The implementation of policies based on socially progressive legal frameworks is difficult to achieve, but it allows for a gradual halt in the tendency to only employ mechanisms which promote the success of a market that does not guarantee social redistribution. The analysis shows that the promises of current neoliberal policies have not been fulfilled. This is what has happened with the adoption of legal rules on property, promoted by multilateral organisations in the countries of the Global South. Its ineffectiveness as an instrument for overcoming poverty or consolidating decent housing makes its application and even its political recognition untenable upon closer examination. For this reason, we consider it imperative to make the results known and examine the mechanisms that allow the market to function. Only in this way is it possible to dismantle the obscure and ambiguous arguments on which a public policy is based that replaces precarious homes with more precarious homes while merely embellishing them with property title deeds.

References

Economic Commission for Latin America and the Caribbean (ECLAC) (2016) *Preliminary Overview of the Economies of Latin America and the Caribbean*, 2016. Santiago. [WWW document]. URL http://repositorio.cepal.org/bitstream/handle/11362/40826/62/S1601332_en.pdf [accessed 5 February 2019].
Eurostat (2014) *Statistics Explained*. [WWW document]. URL https://ec.europa.eu/eurostat/statistics-explained/index.php?title=File:Housing_cost_overburden_rate_by_tenure_status,_2014_(%25_of_population)_YB16.png [accessed 5 February 2019].

Index